THE LAW *of* CHRIST

COVENANT OF GRACE

THE COMMANDMENTS OF GOD

AND PROPHECIES OF THE HOLY TRUTH

FOR THE THIRD MILLENNIUM

CE

TSIDKENU MEKODDISHKEM

WESTBOW PRESS®
A DIVISION OF THOMAS NELSON & ZONDERVAN

WestBow Press books may be ordered through booksellers or by contacting:

WestBow Press
A Division of Thomas Nelson & Zondervan
1663 Liberty Drive
Bloomington, IN 47403
www.westbowpress.com
844-714-3454

Cover Graphics/Art Credit: Tsidkenu Mekoddishkem

ISBN: 978-1-6642-9193-5 (sc)
ISBN: 978-1-6642-9195-9 (e)

Library of Congress Control Number: 2023902635

Print information available on the last page.

WestBow Press rev. date: 04/22/2023

TABLE OF CONTENTS

INTRODUCTION

The name of Jesus Christ is known by the Word of God. The Word of God forms the New Testament, providing the New Covenant. In these scriptures, the LORD says to keep the commandments to the best of our ability in faith and good conscience.

Search the scriptures; for in them you think you have eternal life: and these are they which testify of me. (Jn. 5:39)

Most theological scholars agree that Jesus Christ the Son of God was crucified between years 33 and 35 AD.

The Son of Man must be delivered into the hands of sinful men, and be crucified, and the third day rise again. (Lk. 24:7)

Be not ignorant of this one thing, that one day is with the Lord as a thousand years, and a thousand years as one day. (2 Pet. 3:8)

Blessed and holy is he that has part in the first resurrection: on such the second death has no power, but they shall be priests of God and of Christ, and shall reign with them a thousand years. (Rev. 20:6)

(2 Pet. 1:20, 21, 19; 2 Cor. 11:4, 6; Rom. 7:12, 22; 8:1; 10:4; 1 Cor. 9:21; 1 Tim. 1:8; Heb. 7:22, 14; Rom. 3:31)

Knowing this first, that no prophecy of the scripture is of any private interpretation. For the prophecy came in old time not by the will of man: but holy men of God spoke as they were moved by the Holy Spirit. We have also a more certain word of prophecy; to which you do well that you take heed, as to a light that shines in a dark place, until the day dawn, and the day star arises in your hearts. For if he that returns preaches another Jesus, whom we have not preached, or if you receive another spirit, which you have not received, or another covenant, which you have not accepted, you might well bear with him.

We have been thoroughly made manifest among you in all things. Wherefore the law is holy, and the commandments holy, and fair, and good. For I delight in the law of God after the inward man. There is therefore now no condemnation to those who are in Christ Jesus, who walk not after the flesh, but after the Spirit. For Christ is the end of the law, for righteousness to everyone who believes. To those not having the law I became like one not having the law; although I am not being without God's law, but am under Christ's law, so to attain those not having the law. But we know that the law is good, if one uses it lawfully; by so much more Jesus has become a certainty of a better covenant. For it is evident that our Lord arose from Judah, of which tribe Moses spoke nothing concerning priesthood. Do we then make void the law through faith? Not to be, rather, we establish the law.

(Jas. 1:1; Ps. 78:2-4; Lk. 8:10; Rev. 5:1; Isa. 29:11; Ezk. 20:49; Jn. 16:32, 25; 6:29; Dan. 12:7-9; Rev. 22:10)

To the twelve tribes which are scattered abroad, greetings. I will utter dark sayings of old which we have heard and known, and our fathers have told us. We will not hide them from our children, showing to the generation to come the praises of the LORD, and his strength, and his wonderful works that he has done. As he said, "To you it is given to know the mysteries of the kingdom of God: but to others in metaphors; that seeing they might not see and hearing they might not understand." I saw in the right hand of him that sat on the throne a book written within and on the backside, sealed with seven seals. For the vision of all has become to you as the words of a book that is sealed, which men deliver to one that is learned, saying, "Read this please:" and he says, "I cannot; for it is sealed." Then I said, "Ah Lord GOD! They are saying of me, 'Is he not speaking metaphors?'"

Behold, the hour is coming, yea, is now here, that you are scattered, every man to his own, and shall leave me alone: and yet I am not alone, because the LORD is with me. Though I have been speaking metaphorically, a time is coming when I will no longer speak to you in figurative language, but I will tell you plainly about the LORD. The work of God is this: to believe in the one he has sent. When he shall have accomplished to scatter the power of the holy people, all these things shall be finished. I heard, but I understood not: then I said, "O my Lord, what shall be the end of these things?" He said, "Go your way: for the words are closed up and sealed until the time of the end." "Seal not the sayings of the prophecy of this book: for the time is here."

PREFACE

(Gal. 6:2; Rom. 6:14; Eph. 2:15; 1 Jn. 3:5; Gal. 3:13; Rom. 8:2; 1 Jn. 2:8; Heb. 10:26, 27; 1 Thess. 4:8; Ps. 103:18, 19; Rev. 21:5; 19:10; Ps. 111:9; Heb. 10:16; Jn. 15:17)

Serve each other's burdens, and so fulfill the law of Christ.

Sin shall not have dominion over you, for you are not under law but under grace.

But by abolishing in his flesh the enmity, the law of statutes in ordinances, he was manifested to take away our sins; and in him is no sin.

Christ redeemed us from the curse of the law by becoming a curse for us; for the law of the Spirit of life in Christ Jesus has made us free from the law of sin and death.

Now, the new injunction I write to you; this is true in him and in you, because the darkness is passing away, and the true light is now shining.

If you sin willfully after you have received the knowledge of the truth, there remains no more sacrifice for your sins, but a certain fearful anticipation of judgment and fiery indignation which shall devour the opposition.

Therefore, he who rejects this does not reject man, but God, who has also given to us his Holy Spirit.

To such as keep his covenant, and to those who remember his commandments to do them; the LORD has established his throne in heaven, and his kingdom rules over all.

He that sat upon the throne said, “Behold, I make all things new.”

Also, he said, “Write: for these words are true and faithful.” Worship God, for the testimony of Jesus is the spirit of prophecy.

He sent redemption to his people; he commanded his covenant forever.

Holy and revered is his name.

This is the covenant that I will make with them after those days. These things I command you, that you love each other.

SECTION 1

COVENANT OF COMMANDMENTS

(Deuteronomy 4:2, 13)

2 You shall not add to the word which I command you, nor take anything out of it, that you keep the commandments of the LORD your God which I command you. 13 So he declared to you his covenant which he commanded you to perform, that is, the Ten Commandments.

(Matthew 22:37-39)

37 "You shall love the Lord your God with all your heart, with all your soul, and with all your mind." 38 This is the first and greatest commandment. 39 The second is like it: "You shall love your neighbor as yourself."

(Mark 12:29-31)

29 Primarily it is, "Hear, O Israel; 'The Lord our God is one species: 30 and you shall love the Lord your God with all your heart, and with all your soul, and with all your mind, and with all your strength.'" 31

Secondly this: "You shall love your neighbor as yourself." There is no other commandment greater than these.

(Genesis 1:1-3, 6, 9, 11, 14, 15, 20, 24, 26-29)

1 In the beginning, God created all physics and all chemistry;
(the true laws that cannot be broken, without exception). 2 Then,
the universe was formless and void, darkness was throughout
infinity, and the Spirit of God resonated on the surface of the
energy. (YHWH created evolution.) 3 God said, Let there be light:
and there was light. 6 God said, Let there be a firmament in the
midst of the energy, and let it divide the energy from the matter. 9
God said, Let the energy under the heaven be gathered together
to one place and let the solid mass appear, and it was so. 11
God said, Let the earth bring forth plants, the vegetation yielding
seed, and the fruit tree yielding fruit after its kind, whose seed
is in itself, upon the earth: and it was so. 14 God said, Let there
be lights in the firmament of the heaven to divide the day from
the night; and let them be for signs, and for seasons, and for
days, and years; 15 and let them be for lights in the firmament
of the heaven to give light upon the earth: and it was so. 20 God
said, Let the waters bring forth abundantly the moving creature
that has life (Protozoa). 24 God said, Let the earth bring forth
the breathing creature after its phyla. 26 God said, Let us make
man in our image, after our likeness: and let them have dominion
over the fish of the sea, and over the fowl of the air, and over the
cattle, and over all the earth, and over every creeping thing that
creeps upon the earth. 27 So God created man in his own image,
in the image of God he created him; male and female he created
them. 28 Then God blessed them, and God said to them, "Be
fruitful and multiply; fill the earth and subdue it; have dominion
over the fish of the sea, over the birds of the air, and over every
living thing that moves on the earth." 29 God said, "Behold, I have
given you every herb that yields seed which is on the face of all
the earth, and every tree whose fruit yields seed; to you it shall
be for sustenance." (Heterotrophs)

(Genesis 2:7, 16, 17, 24)

7 The LORD God formed man of the dust of the ground and breathed into his nostrils the breath of life; and man became a living being. (God created man via the evolutionary process, as Eukaryotes.) 16 The LORD God commanded the man, saying, "Of every tree of the garden you may freely eat (mitosis); 17 but of the tree of the knowledge of good and evil you shall not eat (meiosis), for in the day that you eat of it you shall surely die." 24 Therefore a man shall leave his father and mother and be joined to his wife, and they shall become one flesh.

(Genesis 5:2)

2 He created them male or female and blessed them and called them Mankind (Hominidae) in the day they were created.

(Genesis 6:3, 7, 19, 20)

3 The LORD said, "My Spirit shall not strive with man forever, for he is indeed flesh; yet his days shall be one hundred and twenty years." 7 So the LORD said, "I will destroy man whom I have created from the face of the earth, both man and beast, creeping thing and birds of the air, for I am sorry that I have made them." 19 Of every living thing of all flesh you shall bring two of every sort into the ark, to keep them alive with you; they shall be male or female. 20 Of the birds after their kind, of animals after their kind, and of every creeping thing of the earth after its kind, two of every kind will come to you to keep them alive.

(Genesis 7:3)

3 Males and females, to keep the species alive on the face of all the earth.

(Genesis 8:22)

22 While the earth remains, seedtime and harvest, cold and heat, winter and summer, and day and night shall not cease.

(Genesis 9:7, 12-17)

7 As for you, be fruitful and multiply; bring forth abundantly in
the earth and multiply in it. 12 God said, "This is the sign of the
covenant I am making between me and you and every living
creature with you, a covenant for all generations to come: 13 I have
set my rainbow in the clouds, and it will be the sign of the covenant
between me and the earth. 14 Whenever I bring clouds over the
earth and the rainbow appears in the clouds, 15 I will remember
my covenant between me and you and all living creatures of every
kind. Never again will the waters become a flood to destroy all life.
16 Whenever the rainbow appears in the clouds, I will see it and
remember the everlasting covenant between God and all living
creatures of every kind on the earth. 17 So God said to Noah,
"This is the sign of the covenant I have established between me
and all life on the earth."

(Genesis 11:1)

1 The whole earth was of one language, and of one speech.

(Genesis 17:10)

10 This is my covenant, which you shall keep, between me and you and your seed after you; every male child among you should be circumcised.

(Exodus 8:20)

20 Thus says the LORD, "Let my people go, that they may serve me."

(Exodus 13:7)

7 Unleavened breads shall be eaten seven days. No leavened bread shall be seen among you, nor shall leaven be seen among you in all your quarters. (Natural, organic, and whole grain standards apply.)

(Exodus 19:12)

12 You shall set limits for the people all around, saying, take heed to yourselves that you do not go to the mountain or touch its base: whoever touches the mountain shall surely be put to death.

(Exodus 20:3, 4, 7-10, 12-17, 23, 24)

3 You shall have no other gods before me. 4 You shall not make for yourself a carved image, or any likeness in heaven above, or that is in the earth beneath, or that is in the water under the earth.
7 You shall not take the name of the LORD your God in vain, for the LORD will not hold him guiltless who takes his name in vain. 8
Remember the sabbath day, to keep it holy. 9 Six days you shall labor and do all your work, 10 but the seventh day is the sabbath of the LORD your God. In it you may do no work. 12 Honor your father and your mother, that your days may be long upon the land which the LORD your God is giving you. 13 You shall not murder.
14 You shall not commit adultery. 15 You shall not steal. 16 You shall not bear false witness against your neighbor. 17 You shall not covet your neighbor's house; you shall not covet your neighbor's wife, nor his male servant, nor his female servant, nor anything that is your neighbor's. 23 You shall not make anything to be with me: gods of silver or gods of gold you shall not make for yourselves.
24 An altar of earth you shall make for me.

(Exodus 21:14, 16)

14 But if a man schemes and kills another man deliberately, take him away from my altar and put him to death. 16 Anyone who

abducts another and either ransoms him or he is found in his possession, shall surely be put to death.

(Exodus 22:19, 21, 22, 28)

19 Whoever lays with an animal shall surely be put to death. 21 You shall neither mistreat a stranger nor oppress him, for you were strangers in the land. 22 You shall not afflict any widow or fatherless child. 28 You shall not revile God, nor curse a ruler of your people.

(Exodus 23:1-3, 6-9, 12)

1 You shall not circulate a false report. Do not put your hand with the wicked to be an unrighteous witness. 2 You shall not follow a crowd to do evil; nor shall you testify in a dispute so as to turn aside after many to corrupt. 3 You shall not show partiality to a poor man in his dispute. 6 You shall not corrupt the judgment of your poor in his dispute. 7 Keep yourself far from a false matter; do not kill the innocent and righteous. For I will not justify the wicked. 8 You shall take no bribe, for a bribe blinds the discerning and perverts the words of the righteous. 9 Also you shall not oppress a stranger, for you know the heart of a stranger. 12 Six days you shall do your work, and on the seventh day you may rest.

(Exodus 31:15)

15 Work shall be done for six days, but the seventh is the sabbath of rest, holy to the LORD.

(Exodus 34:17)

17 You shall make no molded gods for yourselves.

(Leviticus 3:17)

17 This shall be a perpetual enactment throughout your generations in all your dwellings: you shall eat neither animal fat nor blood.

(Leviticus 13:40, 41)

40 As for the man whose hair has fallen from his head, he is bald, but he is clean. 41 He whose hair has fallen from his forehead, he is bald on the forehead, but he is clean.

(Leviticus 18:6, 18-20, 22-24)

6 None of you shall approach to any that is near of kin to him, to uncover their nakedness: I am the LORD. 18 You shall not marry a woman in addition to her sister as a rival while she is alive, to uncover her nakedness 19 Also you shall not approach a woman to uncover her nakedness during her menstrual impurity. 20 You shall not have intercourse with your neighbor's wife and be defiled with her. 22 You shall not lie with a male as with a woman. It is an abomination. 23 Nor shall you mate with any animal, to defile yourself with it. Nor shall any woman go before an animal to mate with it. It is perversion. 24 Do not defile yourselves with any of these things; for by all these the nations are defiled, which I am casting out before you.

(Leviticus 19:4, 9-18, 26-30, 32-36)

4 Do not turn to idols, nor make for yourselves molded gods: I am the LORD your God. 9 When you reap the harvest of your land, you shall not wholly reap the corners of your field, nor shall you gather the gleanings of your harvest. 10 You shall not glean your vineyard, nor shall you gather every grape of your vineyard; you shall leave them for the poor and the stranger: I am the LORD your God. 11 You shall not steal, nor deal falsely, nor lie to one another. 12 You shall not swear by my name falsely, nor shall you profane the name of your God: I am the LORD. 13 You shall not cheat your neighbor, nor rob him. The wages of him who is hired shall not remain with

you all night until morning. 14 You shall not curse the deaf, nor put an obstacle before the blind, but shall fear your God: I am the LORD. 15 You shall do no injustice in judgment. You shall not be partial to the poor, nor honor the person of the mighty. 16 You shall not go about as a talebearer among your people; nor shall you take a stand against the life of your neighbor: I am the LORD. 17 You shall not hate your brother in your heart. You shall surely rebuke your neighbor, but not bear sin because of him. 18 You shall not take vengeance, nor hold any grudge against the children of your people, but you shall love your neighbor as yourself: I am the LORD. 26 You shall not eat the blood: neither shall you use superstitions. 27 Do not cut the hair at the sides of your head or trim the edges of your beard. 28 Do not cut your bodies for the dead or take the mark on yourselves. I am the LORD. 29 Do not degrade your daughter by making her a prostitute. 30 Observe my sabbaths and have reverence for my sanctuary. I am the LORD. 32 Show respect for the elderly and revere your God. I am the LORD. 33 When an alien lives with you in your land, do not mistreat him. 34 The alien living with you must be treated as one of your native-born. Love him as yourself. 35 Do not use dishonest standards when measuring length, weight or quantity. 36 Use honest scales and honest weights.

(Leviticus 20:11-16)

11 The man who lays with his father's wife or has uncovered his father's nakedness; both of them shall surely be put to death. Their blood shall be upon them. 12 If a man lies with his daughter-in-law, both of them shall surely be put to death. They have committed perversion. Their blood shall be upon them. 13 If a man lies with a male as he lies with a woman, both of them have committed an abomination. They shall surely be put to death. Their blood shall be upon them. 14 If a man marries a woman and her mother, it is wickedness. They shall be burned with fire, both he and they, that there may be no wickedness among you. 15 If a man mates with an animal, he shall surely be put to death, and you shall kill the animal. 16 If a woman approaches any animal and mates with it, you shall kill the woman and the animal. They shall surely be put to death. Their blood is upon them.

(Leviticus 21:5, 7, 10, 13-15)

5 Priests should not shave their heads or shave off the edges of their beards or cut their bodies. 7 They must not marry women defiled by promiscuity or divorced from their husbands, because priests are holy to their God. 10 The high priest, the one among his brothers who has been ordained to wear the priestly garments, must not let his hair become unkempt or tear his clothes. 13 The woman he marries must be a virgin. 14 He must not marry a widow, a divorced woman, or a woman defiled by prostitution, but only a virgin from his own people (pornography is prostitution), 15 so he will not defile his offspring among his people. I am the LORD, who makes him holy.

(Leviticus 22:9, 20)

9 The priests are to keep my requirements so that they do not become guilty and die for treating them with contempt. I am the LORD, who makes them holy. 20 Whatever has a defect, you shall not offer, for it will not be accepted for you.

(Leviticus 25:23, 24)

23 The land must not be sold permanently, because the land is mine and you are as aliens and tenants. 24 Throughout the country that you hold as a possession, you must provide for the redemption of the land.

(Leviticus 26:1, 2)

1 You shall make no idols nor graven image, neither set you up a standing image, or image of stone in your land, to bow down before it: for I am Yahweh of Elohim. 2 Observe my sabbaths and have reverence for my sanctuary. I am the Lord.

(Leviticus 27:29, 30)

29 No career criminal, which shall be convicted by man, shall be redeemed; but shall surely be put to death. 30 All the tithe of the land, whether of the seed of the land, or of the fruit of the tree, is the LORD's: it is holy to the LORD.

(Numbers 1:2, 3)

2 Take a census of all the congregations by their families, according to the number of names individually, 3 from twenty years old and above, all who are able to go to war. You shall number them by their armies.

(Numbers 5:3)

3 You shall put out both male and female; you shall put them outside the camp, that they may not defile their camps in the midst of which I dwell (quarantine).

(Numbers 6:2, 5)

2 If a man or woman wants to make a special vow, a vow of separation to the LORD, 5 during the entire period of his vow of separation no razor may be used on his head. He must be holy until the period of his separation to the LORD is over; he must let the hair of his head grow long.

(Numbers 10:9)

9 When you go to war in your land against the enemy who oppresses you, then you shall sound an alarm, and you will be remembered before the LORD your God, and you will be saved from your enemies.

(Numbers 15:27, 29-31)

27 If a person sins unintentionally, it shall be forgiven him. 29 You
shall have one law for him who sins unintentionally, for him who
is native-born and for the stranger who sojourns among them.
30 But the person who does anything presumptuously, whether
he is native-born or a stranger, that one brings reproach on
the LORD, and he shall be cut off from among his people. 31
Because he has despised the word of the LORD and has broken
his commandments, that person shall be completely cut off; his
guilt shall be upon him.

(Numbers 30:2)

2 If a man vows a vow to the LORD or swears an oath to bind himself by some agreement, he shall not break his word; he shall do according to all that proceeds out of his mouth.

(Numbers 31:18)

18 But keep alive for yourselves all the young girls who have not known a male intimately.

(Numbers 35:31)

31 Moreover you shall take no ransom for the life of a murderer who is guilty of death, but he shall surely be put to death.

(Deuteronomy 1:17)

17 You shall not show partiality in judgment; you shall hear the small as well as the great; you shall not be afraid in any man's presence, for the judgment is God's. The case that is too hard for you, bring to me, and I will hear it.

(Deuteronomy 4:15-18)

15 Take careful heed to yourselves, for you saw no form when the LORD spoke to you at Horeb out of the midst of the fire, 16 lest you act corruptly and make for yourselves a carved image in the form of any figure: the likeness of male or female, 17 the likeness of any beast that is on the earth or the likeness of any winged bird that flies in the air, 18 the likeness of anything that creeps on the ground or the likeness of any fish that is in the water beneath the earth.

(Deuteronomy 5:32, 33)

32 Therefore you shall be careful to do as the LORD your God has commanded you; you shall not turn aside to the right hand or to the left. 33 You shall walk in **all** the ways which the LORD your God has commanded you, that you may live and that it may be well with you, and that you may prolong your days in the land which you shall possess.

(Deuteronomy 6:5, 13, 14, 16, 18)

5 You shall love the LORD your God with all your heart, with all your soul, and with all your strength. 13 You shall fear the LORD your God and serve him and shall take oaths in his name. 14 You shall not go after other gods, the gods of the peoples who are around you. 16 You shall not test the LORD your God. 18 You shall do what is right and good in the sight of the LORD.

(Deuteronomy 7:5, 26)

5 But thus you shall deal with them: you shall destroy their altars, and break down their sacred pillars, and cut down their wooden images, and burn their carved images with fire. 26 Nor shall you bring an abomination into your house, lest you be doomed to destruction like it. You shall utterly detest it and utterly abhor it, for it is an accursed thing.

(Deuteronomy 8:20)

20 As the nations which the LORD destroys before you, so you shall perish, because you would not be obedient to the voice of the LORD your God.

(Deuteronomy 10:14)

14 Indeed, heaven and the highest heavens belong to the LORD your God, also the earth with all that is in it.

(Deuteronomy 11:1, 19, 26-28)

1 Therefore, you shall love the LORD your God, and keep his
charge, his judgments, and his commandments always. 19 You
shall teach them to your children, speaking of them when you sit
in your house, when you walk by the way, when you lie down, and
when you rise up. 26 Behold, I set before you today a blessing and
a curse: 27 the blessing, if you obey the commandments of the
LORD your God which I command you today; 28 and the curse, if
you do not obey the commandments of the LORD your God, but
turn aside from the way which I command you today, to go after
other gods which you have not known.

(Deuteronomy 12:8, 9)

8 You shall not at all do as we are doing here today; every man
doing whatever is right in his own eyes: 9 for as yet you have not
come into the rest and the inheritance which the LORD your God
is giving you.

(Deuteronomy 14:3)

3 You shall not eat any detestable thing.

(Deuteronomy 15:4-14)

4 However, there shall be no poor among you, since the LORD will surely bless you in the land which the LORD your God is giving you as an inheritance to possess, 5 if only you listen obediently to the voice of the LORD your God, to observe carefully all this commandment which I am commanding you today. 6 For the LORD your God shall bless you as he has promised you, and you will rule over all nations, but they will not rule over you. 7 If there is a poor man with you, one of your brothers, in any of your gates in your land which the LORD your God is giving you, you shall not harden your heart, nor close your hand from your poor brother; 8 but you shall freely open your hand to him, and shall generously give him sufficient for his need in whatever he lacks. 9 Beware that there be not a thought in your wicked heart, saying, The seventh year, the year of release, is at hand, and your eye be evil against your poor brother, and you give him nothing, and he cries out to the LORD against you, and it becomes sin among you. 10 You shall surely give to him. 11 Therefore I command you, saying, "You shall open your hand wide to your poor and your needy, in your land." 12 If he serves you six years, then in the seventh year you shall let him go free from you. 13 When you send him away free from you, you shall not let him go away empty-handed. 14 You shall supply him liberally.

(Deuteronomy 16:9, 15, 17)

9 You shall count seven weeks for yourself; begin to count the seven weeks from the time you begin to put the sickle to the grain. 15 Seven days you shall keep a sacred feast to the LORD your God in the place which the LORD chooses, because the LORD your God will bless you in all your produce and in all the work of your hands, so that you surely rejoice. 17 Everyone shall give proportionately, according to the blessing of the LORD your God which he has given you.

(Deuteronomy 17:2, 4-7)

2 If a man or woman living among you in one of the towns the LORD gives you is found doing evil in the eyes of the LORD your God in violation of his covenant, 4 and this has been brought to your attention, then you must investigate it thoroughly. If it is true and it has been proved that this detestable thing has been done, 5 take the man or woman who has done this evil deed to your city gate and put that person to death. 6 On the testimony of two or three witnesses a person shall be put to death, but no one shall be put to death on the testimony of only one witness. 7 The hands of the witnesses must be the first in putting him to death, and then the hands of all the people. You must purge the evil from among you.

(Deuteronomy 18:13, 15, 22)

13 You shall be holy before the LORD your God. 15 The LORD your God will raise up for you a prophet like me from your midst, from your brethren: him you shall hear. 22 When a prophet speaks in the name of the LORD, if the thing does not happen or come to pass, that is the thing which the LORD has not spoken; the prophet has spoken it presumptuously; you shall not be afraid of him.

(Deuteronomy 20:10-12)

10 When you go near a city to fight against it, then proclaim an offer of peace to it. 11 Then it shall be that if they accept your offer of peace, and open to you, all the people who are found in it shall be placed under tribute to you and serve you. 12 Now if the city will not make peace with you, but makes war against you, then you shall besiege it.

(Deuteronomy 22:25, 26)

25 But if a man finds a betrothed young woman in the countryside, and the man forces her and lies with her, then only the man who lay with her shall die. 26 But you shall do nothing to the young woman; there is in the young woman no sin deserving of death,

for just as when a man rises against his neighbor and kills him, even so is this matter.

(Deuteronomy 24:5, 16)

5 When a man has taken a new wife, he shall not go out to war or be charged with any obligation; he shall be free at home one year and bring happiness to his wife whom he has taken. 16 Parents shall not be put to death for their children, nor shall the children be put to death for their parents; a person shall be put to death only for his own sin.

(Joshua 1:9)

9 Be strong and courageous. Do not be fearful; do not be discouraged, for the LORD your God will be with you wherever you go.

(Joshua 4:2)

2 Take for yourselves twelve men from the people, one man from every tribe.

(Joshua 6:19)

19 But all the silver, and gold, and vessels of brass and iron, are consecrated to the LORD: they shall come into the treasury of the LORD.

(Joshua 7:13, 15)

13 Get up, sanctify the people and say, "Sanctify yourselves for tomorrow," because thus says the LORD God: "There is an accursed thing in your midst; you cannot stand before your enemies until you take away the accursed thing from among you." 15 Then it shall be that he who is taken with the accursed thing

shall be burned with fire, he and all that he has, because he has transgressed the covenant of the LORD, and because he has done a disgraceful thing.

(Judges 13:4, 5)

4 Now therefore beware, I pray for you, and drink no wine nor hard liquor, and eat not any unclean thing: 5 for, lo, you will conceive and bear a child.

(Psalms 82:3, 4)

3 Defend the poor and fatherless; do justice to the afflicted and needy. 4 Deliver the poor and needy; free them from the hand of the wicked.

(Proverbs 31:8, 9)

8 Speak up for those who cannot speak for themselves, for the rights of all who are destitute. 9 Speak up and judge fairly; defend the rights of the poor and needy.

(Amos 2:4, 6)

4 Thus says the LORD; "For three transgressions of Judah, and for four, I will not turn back; because they have despised the law of the LORD, and have not kept his commandments, and their lies caused them to error, after which their fathers have walked. 6 Thus says the LORD; "For three transgressions of Israel, and for four, I will not turn back.

(Hosea 9:16, 17)

16 The fruitful are smitten, their root is dried up, they shall bear no fruit: yea, though they conceive, yet will I slay the beloved of

their womb; 17 my God will cast them away, because they did not hearken to him.

(Hosea 11:9)

9 I am the Almighty, and not a mortal; the Holy One in your midst.

(Isaiah 7:20)

20 In that day the Lord will shave with a razor.

(Jeremiah 18:7-10)

7 When I shall speak concerning a nation, and concerning a kingdom, to take away and to tear down, and to destroy it; 8 if that nation, against whom I have pronounced, turn from their evil, I will repent of the evil that I thought to do to them. 9 Then when I shall speak concerning a nation, and concerning a kingdom, to build and to plant it; 10 if it does evil in my sight, that it obeys not my voice, then I will repent of the good, wherewith I said I would benefit them.

(Ezekiel 4:9)

9 Also take for yourself wheat, barley, beans, lentils, millet, and spelt; prepare them in one container, and make bread of them for yourself.

(Ezekiel 33:9, 12, 14, 16)

9 Nevertheless, if you warn the wicked of his way to turn from it; if he does not turn from his way, he shall die in his iniquity; but you have delivered your soul. 12 The righteousness of the righteous shall not deliver him in the day of his transgression: as for the wickedness of the wicked, he shall not fall thereby in the day that

he turns from his wickedness; neither shall the righteous be able to live for his righteousness in the day that he sins. 14 Again, when I say to the wicked, "You shall surely die;" if he turns from his sin and does that which is lawful and right; 16 none of his sins that he committed shall be remembered of him: he does that which is lawful and right; he shall surely live.

(Malachi 3:10)

10 Bring all the tithes into the storehouse, that there may be food in my house, and prove me now herewith, says the LORD of hosts,

(Matthew 4:4, 7, 10, 17)

4 It is written, "Man shall not live by bread alone, but by every word that proceeds from the mouth of God." 7 Again it is written, "You shalt not test the Lord your God." 10 You shall worship the Lord your God, and him only you shall serve. 17 Repent, for the kingdom of heaven is near.

(Matthew 5:3-12, 16, 22, 32, 34, 37, 42, 44, 48)

3 Blessed are the poor in spirit: for theirs is the kingdom of heaven. 4 Blessed are they that mourn: for they shall be comforted. 5 Blessed are the meek: for they shall inherit the earth. 6 Blessed are they which do hunger and thirst after righteousness: for they shall be filled. 7 Blessed are the merciful: for they shall obtain mercy. 8 Blessed are the pure in heart: for they shall see God. 9 Blessed are the peacemakers: for they shall be called the children of God. 10 Blessed are they which are persecuted for righteousness' sake: for theirs is the kingdom of heaven. 11 Blessed are you, when man shall revile you, and persecute you, and shall say all manner of evil against you falsely, for my sake. 12 Rejoice and be exceedingly glad: for great is your reward in heaven: for so they persecuted the prophets which were before you. 16 Let your light so shine before man, that they may see your good works and glorify your LORD in heaven. 22 Whosoever is angry with his

brother without a cause shall be in danger of the judgment: and whosoever shall say to his brother "You're worthless," shall be in danger of the council: but whosoever shall say "You fool," shall be in danger of hell fire. 32 But I tell you that anyone who divorces his wife, except for fornication, causes her to become an adulteress, and anyone who marries the divorced woman commits adultery.
34 Do not declare at all: either by heaven, or by the earth; for it is God's throne. 37 Simply let your "Yes" be "Yes," and your "No," "No," anything beyond these is evil. 42 Give to him who asks you, and from him who wants to borrow from you do not turn away.
44 Love your enemies, bless those who curse you, do good to those who hate you, and pray for those who spitefully use you and persecute you. 48 Be perfect, therefore, as your heavenly LORD is perfect.

(Matthew 6:1, 4, 6-21, 31, 33, 34)

1 Beware of practicing your charity before man for recognition by them; otherwise, you have no reward with your LORD who is in heaven. 4 Your charity should be in secret; and your LORD who sees in secret will reward you openly. 6 But, when you pray, go into your room, and when you shut your door, pray to your LORD who is in the secret place; and your LORD who sees in secret will reward you openly. 7 When you pray, do not use vain repetitions as the heathen; for they think that they will be heard for their many words. 8 Therefore do not be like them. For your LORD knows the things you have need of before you ask him. 9
In this manner, therefore, pray: "Our Father in heaven, hallowed be your name. 10 Your kingdom come. Your will be done, on earth as it is in heaven." 11 "Give us this day our daily bread, 12 and forgive us our debts, as we forgive our debtors." 13 "Lead us not into temptation but deliver us from evil. For yours is the kingdom and the power and the glory forever"; amen. 14 For if you forgive man their trespasses, your heavenly LORD will also forgive you.
15 But if you do not forgive man their trespasses, neither will your LORD forgive your trespasses. 16 Moreover, when you fast, do not be like the hypocrites, with a sad countenance. 17 But, when you fast, anoint your head and wash your face, 18 so that you do not appear to man to be fasting, but to your LORD who is in

the secret place; and your LORD who sees in secret will reward you openly. 19 Do not reserve for yourselves treasures on earth, where moth and rust destroy and where thieves break in and steal. 20 But reserve for yourselves treasures in heaven, where neither moth nor rust destroys and where thieves do not break in and steal. 21 Where your treasure is, there your heart will be also. 31 Therefore do not worry, saying, "What shall we eat?" or "What shall we drink?" or "What shall we wear?" 33 But seek first the kingdom of God and his righteousness, and all these things shall be added to you. 34 Therefore do not be concerned about tomorrow; but tomorrow, then be concerned about it. Sufficient for the day is the evil thereof.

(Matthew 7:1, 2, 5-8, 12-15)

1 Do not judge, that you are not judged. 2 For in the same way you judge others, you will be judged, and with the measure you use, it will be measured to you. 5 First take the plank out of your own eye, and then you will see clearly to remove the speck from your brother's eye. 6 Do not give dogs what is sacred; do not throw your pearls to swine. If you do, they may trample them under their feet, and then turn and tear you to pieces. 7 Ask and it will be given to you; seek and you will find; knock and it will be opened to you. 8 For everyone who asks receives; he who seeks finds; and to him who knocks, it will be opened. 12 So in everything, do to others what you would have them do to you, for this sums up the law and the prophets. 13 Enter through the narrow gate. For wide is the gate and broad is the way that leads to destruction, and many enter through it. 14 But small is the gate and narrow the way that leads to life, and only a few find it. 15 Watch out for false prophets. They come to you in sheep's clothing, but inwardly they are ravening wolves.

(Matthew 8:22)

22 Follow me, and let the dead bury their own dead.

(Matthew 9:37, 38)

37 The harvest is plentiful, but the workers are few. 38 Ask the Lord of the harvest, therefore, to send out workers into his harvest field.

(Matthew 10:7, 8, 12, 13, 16, 23, 28, 42)

7 As you go, teach this message: "The kingdom of heaven is near." 8 Heal the sick, raise the dead, cleanse the diseased, force out demons. Freely you have received, freely give. 12 When you come into a house, greet it. 13 If the house is worthy, let your peace come upon it: but if it is not worthy, let your peace return to you. 16 Be therefore wise as serpents, and harmless as doves. 23 When you are persecuted in one place, flee to another. 28 Do not fear those who kill the body but cannot kill the soul; but rather fear him who is able to destroy both soul and body in hell. 42 If anyone gives even a cup of cold water to one of these least ones, because he is my disciple, I tell you the truth, he will certainly not lose his reward.

(Matthew 11:28-30)

28 Come to me, all you who are weary and burdened, and I will give you rest. 29 Take my yoke upon you and learn from me, for I am gentle and humble in heart, and you will find rest for your souls. 30 For my yoke is easy and my burden is light.

(Matthew 12:8, 25, 31, 32, 36, 37)

8 The Son of Man is Lord of the sabbath. 25 Jesus knew their thoughts and said to them, "Every kingdom divided against itself will be ruined, and every city or household divided against itself will not stand." 31 So I tell you, every sin and blasphemy will be forgiven to man, but the blasphemy of the Spirit will not be forgiven to man. 32 Anyone who speaks a word against the Son of Man will be forgiven, but anyone who speaks against the Spirit will not be forgiven, either in this age or in that to come. 36 Every careless word that man shall speak, they shall render account of it in the

day of judgment: 37 for by your words you shall be justified, and by your words you shall be condemned.

(Matthew 13:12, 49, 50)

12 For whoever has, to him shall be given, and he shall have an abundance; but whoever does not have, even what he has shall be taken away from him. 49 So it will be at the end of the age; the angels shall come forth, and take out the wicked from among the righteous, 50 and will cast them into the furnace of fire; there shall be weeping and gnashing of teeth.

(Matthew 15:11, 18-20)

11 Not what enters into the mouth defiles the man, but what proceeds out of the mouth, that defiles the man. 18 But those things which proceed out of the mouth come from the heart, and they defile a man. 19 For out of the heart proceed evil thoughts, murders, adulteries, fornications, thefts, false witness, blasphemies. 20 These are the things which defile a man, but to eat with unwashed hands does not defile a man.

(Matthew 16:19, 24, 25)

19 I will give you the keys of the kingdom of heaven, and whatever you bind on earth will be bound in heaven, and whatever you release on earth will be released in heaven. 24 If anyone desires to come after me, let him deny himself, and take up his cross, and follow me. 25 For whoever desires to save his life will lose it, but whoever loses his life for my sake will find it.

(Matthew 18:7, 15-17, 20, 34, 35)

7 Woe to the world because of offenses! For offenses shall occur, but woe to the one by whom the offense occurs. 15 Moreover if your brother sins against you, go and tell him his fault between you

and him alone. If he hears you, you have gained your brother. 16 But if he will not hear, take with you one or two more, that by the mouth of two or three witnesses every word may be established. 17 If he refuses to hear them, tell it to the ministry. But if he refuses even to hear the ministry, let him be to you like a heathen and a tax collector. 20 For where two or three are gathered together in my name, I am there in the midst of them. 34 As his master was angry and delivered him to the torturers until he should pay all that was due to him: 35 so my heavenly Father also will do to you if each of you, from his heart, does not forgive his brother his trespasses.

(Matthew 19:6, 9, 21)

6 So then, they are no longer two but one flesh. Therefore, what God has joined together, let not man separate. 9 Whoever divorces his wife, except for sexual immorality, and marries another, commits adultery; and whoever marries her who is divorced commits adultery. 21 If you want to be perfect, go, sell what you have and give to the poor, and you will have treasure in heaven; and come, follow me.

(Matthew 20:25-28)

25 You know that the rulers of the seculars assert authority over them, and those who are great control privileges over them. 26 Yet it shall not be so among you; but whoever desires to become great among you, let him be your servant. 27 Whoever desires to be first among you, let him be your servant: 28 just as the Son of Man did not come to be served, but to serve, and to give his life a ransom for many.

(Matthew 22:14, 21, 30)

14 For many are called, but few are chosen. 21 Render therefore to Caesar the things that are Caesar's, and to God the things that are God's. 30 For in the resurrection they neither marry nor are given in marriage but are like angels of God in heaven.

(Matthew 23:8-12)

8 But do not be called *Rabbi*; for one is your teacher, and you are all brothers. 9 Do not call anyone on earth your father; for one is your Father, he who is in heaven. 10 Do not be called leaders; for one is your leader, that is, Christ. 11 But the greatest among you shall be your servant. 12 Whoever exalts himself shall be humbled; and whoever humbles himself shall be exalted.

(Matthew 24:42, 44)

42 Watch therefore, for you do not know what hour your Lord is coming. 44 Therefore you also be ready, for the Son of Man is coming at an hour you do not expect.

(Matthew 25:1, 29, 30, 40, 45)

1 At that time the kingdom of heaven will be like ten virgins who took their lamps and went out to meet the bridegroom. 29 For everyone who has will be given more, and he will have an abundance. Whoever does not have, even what he has will be taken from him. 30 Send that worthless servant outside, into the darkness, where there will be weeping and gnashing of teeth. 40 Then the king will answer and say to them, "Assuredly, I say to you, inasmuch as you did it to one of the least of these my brethren, you did it to me." 45 Then he will answer them, saying, "Assuredly, I say to you, inasmuch as you did not do it to one of the least of these, you did not do it to me."

(Matthew 28:18-20)

18 All authority in heaven and on earth has been given to me. 19 Therefore go and make disciples of all nations, indoctrinating them (baptism) in the name of the LORD and of the Son and of the Holy Spirit, 20 teaching them to obey everything I have commanded you. Surely, I am with you always, even to the end of the age.

(Mark 1:15)

15 The time has come; the kingdom of God is near. Repent and believe the covenant.

(Mark 2:27, 28)

27 The sabbath was made for man, and not man for the sabbath.
28 Therefore the Son of Man is Lord of the sabbath also.

(Mark 3:4, 28, 29)

4 It is lawful to do good on the sabbath days, or to do evil; to save life, or to kill. 28 I tell you the truth, all the sins and blasphemies of man will be forgiven them. 29 But whoever blasphemes against the Holy Spirit will never be forgiven; he is guilty of an eternal sin.

(Mark 4:9, 24, 25)

9 He who has ears to hear, let him hear. 24 Take heed what you hear. With the same measure you use, it will be measured to you; and to you that hear, more will be given. 25 For whoever has, to him more will be given; but whoever does not have, even what he has will be taken away from him.

(Mark 8:34, 35)

34 Whoever desires to come after me, let him deny himself, and take up his cross, and follow me. 35 For whoever desires to save his life will lose it, but whoever loses his life for my sake and the covenant's shall save it.

(Mark 9:35, 40, 43, 45, 47)

35 If anyone desires to be first, he shall be last of all and servant of all. 40 He who is not against us is on our side. 43 If your hand is

gangrenous, cut it off. It is better for you to enter into life maimed, rather than having two hands, to go to hell, into the fire that shall never be quenched. 45 If your foot has frostbite, cut it off. It is better for you to enter life lame, rather than having two feet, to be cast into hell, into the fire that shall never be quenched. 47 If your eye is severely infected, pluck it out. It is better for you to enter the kingdom of God with one eye, rather than having two eyes, to be cast into hell fire.

(Mark 10:9, 11, 12, 21, 42-45)

9 Therefore what God has joined together, let not man separate. 11 Whoever divorces his wife and marries another commits adultery against her. 12 If a woman divorces her husband and marries another, she commits adultery. 21 One thing you lack: go and sell all you possess, and give to the poor, and you shall have treasure in heaven; and come, follow me. 42 You know that those who are recognized as rulers by the seculars control it over them; and their rich men exercise authority over them. 43 But it is not so among you, but whoever wishes to become great among you shall be your servant; 44 and whoever wishes to be first among you shall be servant of all. 45 For even the Son of Man did not come to be served, but to serve, and to give his life a ransom for many.

(Mark 11:24-26)

24 Therefore I say to you, "Whatever things you ask when you pray, believe that you receive them, and you will have them." 25 "Whenever you stand praying, if you have anything against anyone, forgive him, that the LORD in heaven may also forgive you your trespasses." 26 "But if you do not forgive, neither will the LORD in heaven forgive your trespasses."

(Mark 12:25, 30, 31)

25 For when they rise from the dead, they neither marry nor are given in marriage, but are like angels in heaven. 30 You shall love

the Lord your God with all your heart, with all your soul, with all your mind, and with all your strength. 31 You shall love your neighbor as yourself. No other commandment is greater than these.

(Mark 13:11, 37)

11 But when they arrest you and deliver you up, do not worry in advance, or premeditate what you will speak. But whatever is given you in that hour, speak that; for it is not you that speak, but the Holy Spirit. 37 Be vigilant.

(Mark 16:15, 16)

15 Go into all the world and preach the covenant for every creature. 16 He who believes and is indoctrinated will be saved; but he who does not believe will be condemned.

(Luke 4:8, 12)

8 Worship the Lord your God and serve him only. 12 You shall not test the Lord your God.

(Luke 6:27-31, 35-38)

27 Love your enemies, do good to those who hate you, 28 bless those who curse you, and pray for those who spitefully use you. 29 To him who strikes you on one cheek, offer the other also; and from him who takes away your blanket, do not withhold your coat either. 30 Give to everyone who asks of you; and from him who takes away your goods do not ask them back. 31 As you want man to do to you, do also to them likewise. 35 But love your enemies, do good, and lend, hoping for nothing in return; and your reward will be great, and you will be sons of the Most High. For he is kind to the unthankful and evil. 36 Be merciful, as your LORD also is merciful. 37 Judge not, and you shall not be judged. Condemn not, and you shall not be condemned. Forgive, and you will be forgiven. 38 Give,

and it will be given to you: good measure, pressed down, shaken together, and running over; it will be put into your arms. For with the same measure that you use, it will be measured back to you.

(Luke 9:23, 24)

23 If anyone desires to come after me, let him deny himself, and take up his cross daily, and follow me. 24 For whoever desires to save his life will lose it, but whoever loses his life for my sake will save it.

(Luke 10:16)

16 He who hears you hears me, he who rejects you rejects me, and he who rejects me rejects him who sent me.

(Luke 11:9, 10, 28)

9 Ask, and it will be given to you; seek, and you will find; knock, and it will be opened to you. 10 For everyone who asks receives, and he who seeks finds, and to him who knocks it will be opened. 28 More than that, blessed are those who hear the word of God and keep it.

(Luke 12:4, 5, 15, 21-23, 29-31, 33, 34, 40)

4 Do not be afraid of those who kill the body, and after that have no more that they can do. 5 But I will show you whom you should fear: fear him who, after he has killed, has power to cast into hell; yes, I say to you, fear him. 15 Take heed and beware of covetousness, for one's life does not consist in the abundance of the things he possesses. 21 This is how it will be with anyone who acquires treasure for himself but is not rich toward God. 22 Do not worry about your life, what you will eat; or about your body, what you will wear. 23 Life is more than food, and the body more than clothes. 29 Do not seek what you should eat or what you should drink,

nor have an anxious mind. 30 For all these things the nations of the world seek after, and your LORD knows that you need these things. 31 Rather seek the kingdom of God, and all these things shall be added to you. 33 Sell what you have and give charity; provide yourselves bags which do not grow old, a treasure in the heavens that does not fail, where no thief approaches nor moth destroys. 34 For where your treasure is, there your heart will be also. 40 Therefore you also be ready, for the Son of Man is coming at an hour you do not anticipate.

(Luke 13:24)

24 Strive to enter through the narrow gate, for many, I say to you, will seek to enter and will not be able.

(Luke 16:13)

13 No servant can serve two masters; for either he will hate the one and love the other, or else he will be loyal to the one and despise the other. You cannot serve God and riches.

(Luke 17:3)

3 Take heed to yourselves. If your brother sins against you, rebuke him; and if he repents, forgive him.

(Luke 19:27)

27 But those enemies of mine who do not want me to reign over them, bring them here and kill them in front of me.

(John 2:16)

16 Make not the LORD's house a house of merchandise.

(John 3:16, 17)

16 God so loved the earth, that he gave his only begotten Son, that
whosoever believes in him should not perish, but have everlasting
life. 17 For God sent his Son to the earth not to condemn the earth;
but that the earth through him might be saved.

(John 4:24)

24 God is a Spirit: and they that worship him must reverence him in spirit and in truth.

(John 5:39)

39 Search the scriptures; for in them you think you have eternal life: and these are they which testify of me.

(John 7:24)

24 Judge not according to appearance, but judge with righteous judgment.

(John 11:25, 26)

25 I am the resurrection and the life. He who believes in me,
though he may die, he shall live. 26 Whoever lives and believes
in me shall never die.

(John 12:25, 26, 48)

25 He who loves his life loses it; and he who hates his life in this
world shall keep it to life eternal. 26 If anyone serves me, let him
follow me; and where I am, there shall my servant also be; if
anyone serves me, the LORD will honor him. 48 He who rejects
me, and does not receive my words, has that which judges him:
the word that I have spoken will judge him in the last day.

(John 13:15, 16, 20, 34)

15 For I have given you an example, that you should do as I have done to you. 16 A servant is not greater than his master; nor is he who is sent greater than he who sent him. 20 He who receives whomever I send receives me; and he who receives me receives him who sent me. 34 A new commandment I give to you, that you love one another; as I have loved you, that you also love one another.

(John 14:6, 21, 27, 28)

6 I am the way, the truth, and the life. No one comes to the LORD except through me. 21 He who has my commandments and keeps them, it is he who loves me. He who loves me will be loved by the LORD, and I will love him and manifest myself to him. 27 Peace I leave with you; my peace I give you. I give to you not as the world gives. Do not let your hearts be troubled and do not be afraid. 28 If you loved me, you would rejoice that I am going to the LORD, for the LORD is greater than I.

(John 15:12-14, 16, 17, 22, 23, 27)

12 This is my commandment, that you love one another as I have loved you. 13 Greater love has no one than this, than to lay down one's life for his friends. 14 You are my friends if you do whatever I command you. 16 You did not choose me, but I chose you and appointed you that you should go and bear fruit, and that your fruit should remain, that whatever you ask the LORD in my name he may give you. 17 These things I command you, that you love one another. 22 If I had not come and spoken to them, they would have no sin, but now they have no excuse for their sin. 23 He who hates me hates the LORD also. 27 You also must testify, for you have been with me from the beginning.

(John 20:22, 23)

22 Receive the Holy Spirit. 23 If you forgive the sins of any, they are forgiven to them; if you retain the sins of any, they are retained.

(Acts 1:7)

7 It is not for you to know times or seasons which the LORD has placed in his own authority.

(Acts 2:44, 45)

44 All that believed were together and had all things common; 45 and sold their possessions and goods, and divided them among all, as anyone had need.

(Acts 18:9)

9 Do not be afraid, but speak, and do not keep silent.

(Acts 20:35)

35 You must support the weak; and remember the words of the Lord Jesus, that he said, "It is more blessed to give than to receive."

(Romans 3:20, 31)

20 Therefore by the deeds of the law there shall no flesh be justified in his sight: for by the law is the knowledge of sin. 31 Do we then make void the law through faith? Certainly not: yea, we establish the law.

(Romans 4:4, 5)

4 Now when a man works, his wages are not credited to him as a gift, but as an obligation. 5 However, to the man who does not work but trusts God who justifies the unrighteous, his faith is credited as righteousness.

(Romans 7:2, 3)

2 The married woman is bound by law to her husband while he is living; but if her husband dies, she is released from the law concerning the husband. 3 So then, if she marries another man while her husband is still alive, she is called an adulteress. But if her husband dies, she is released from that law and is not an adulteress, even though she marries another man.

(Romans 12:9-21)

9 Love must be sincere. Hate what is evil; adhere to what is good. 10 Be devoted to one another in brotherly love. Honor each other above yourselves. 11 Never be lacking in zeal, but keep your spiritual fervor, serving the Lord. 12 Be joyful in hope, patient in affliction, faithful in prayer. 13 Share with God's people who are in need. Practice hospitality. 14 Bless those who persecute you; bless and do not curse. 15 Rejoice with those who rejoice; mourn with those who mourn. 16 Live in harmony with one another. Do not be proud but associate with people of low status. Do not be conceited. 17 Do not repay anyone evil for evil. Be considerate and honest in the presence of all people. 18 If it is possible, to the best of your ability, live at peace with everyone. 19 Do not take revenge, but give place for wrath, for it is written: "Vengeance is mine; I will repay," says the Lord. 20 On the contrary: if your enemy is hungry, feed him; if he is thirsty, give him drink. 21 Do not be overcome by evil but overcome evil with good.

(Romans 13:7-10, 12-14)

7 Render to all their due: if you owe taxes, pay taxes; if revenue, then revenue; if respect, then respect; if honor, then honor. 8 Owe no one anything except to love one another, for he who loves another has fulfilled the law. 9 For this, "You shall not commit adultery, you shall not murder, you shall not steal, you shall not covet," and if there is any other commandment, it is summed up in this saying, "You shall love your neighbor as yourself." 10 Love does no harm to its neighbor. Therefore, love is the fulfillment of

the law. 12 Set aside the deeds of darkness and put on the armor of light. 13 Let us walk properly, as in the day, not in revelry and drunkenness, not in lewdness and lust, not in strife and envy. 14 Rather, clothe yourselves with the Lord Jesus Christ, and do not contemplate how to gratify the lusts of the flesh.

(1 Corinthians 7:8-11, 14, 15, 27, 28, 38, 39)

8 But I say to the unmarried and to the widows: "It is good for them if they remain even as I am; 9 but if they cannot exercise self-restraint, let them marry." For it is better to marry than to burn with passion. 10 Now to the married I command, yet not I but the Lord: "A wife is not to depart from her husband." 11 But even if she does depart, let her remain unmarried or be reconciled to her husband: and a husband is not to divorce his wife. 14 The unbelieving husband is sanctified by the wife, and the unbelieving wife is sanctified by the husband; otherwise, your children would be unclean, but now they are holy. 15 But if the unbeliever departs, let him depart; a brother or a sister is not under bondage in such cases. But God has called us to peace. 27 Are you bound to a wife? Do not seek to be released. Are you released from a wife? Do not seek a wife. 28 But even if you do marry, you have not sinned; and if a virgin marries, she has not sinned. 38 He that gives his own daughter in marriage does well; and he that gives her not in marriage shall do better. 39 A woman is bound to her husband as long as he lives. But if her husband dies, she is free to marry anyone she wishes, but he must belong to the Lord.

(1 Corinthians 9:14)

14 Even so the Lord has commanded that those who teach the covenant should live from the covenant.

(1 Corinthians 10:14, 32)

14 Therefore, my beloved, flee from idolatry. 32 Give no offense, either to the Jews or to the Greeks or to the congregation of God.

(1 Corinthians 13:4-7)

4 Love is patient, love is kind. Love does not envy, it does not boast, it is not conceited. 5 It is not rude, it is not self-seeking, it is not easily provoked, it keeps no record of wrongs. 6 It does not delight in iniquity but rejoices with the truth. 7 It always endures, always faithful, always confident, always submissive.

(1 Corinthians 14:26, 29, 31-34, 40)

26 Let all things be done for edification. 29 Two or three prophets should speak, and the others should weigh carefully what is said. 31 You may all prophesy in turn, that everyone may be instructed and encouraged. 32 The spirits of prophets are subject to the control of prophets. 33 For God is not a God of disorder but of peace, as in all the congregations of the saints. 34 Women should remain silent in the congregation. They are not allowed to preach, but must be in submission, as also says the law. 40 Let all things be done decently and in order.

(2 Corinthians 7:1)

1 Let us cleanse ourselves from all filthiness of the flesh and spirit, perfecting holiness in the fear of God.

(2 Corinthians 8:14)

14 At the present time your surplus will supply what they need, so that in turn their surplus will supply what you need. Then there will be equality.

(2 Corinthians 13:5)

5 Test yourselves, whether you are in the faith; prove your own selves. Know you not your own selves, how that Jesus Christ is in you, unless you are reprobates?

(Galatians 3:22, 28)

22 But the scripture has confined all under sin, that the promise by faith in Jesus Christ might be given to those who believe. 28 There is neither Jew nor Greek, there is neither slave nor free, there is neither male nor female; for you are all one in Christ Jesus.

(Galatians 5:1, 6)

1 It is for freedom that Christ has set us free. Stand firm, then, and do not let yourselves be burdened again by a yoke of bondage. 6 For in Christ Jesus neither circumcision nor uncircumcision means anything, but faith working through love.

(Galatians 6:10, 15)

10 So then, while we have opportunity, let us do good to all people, and especially to those who are of the household of faith. 15 For neither is circumcision anything, nor uncircumcision, but a new creation.

(Ephesians 4:25-27)

25 Therefore, laying aside falsehood, speak truth, everyone with his neighbor. 26 Be angry, and do not sin. 27 Do not give an opportunity to the accuser.

(Ephesians 5:21, 22, 24-26, 33)

21 Submit to one another out of reverence for Christ. 22 Wives, submit to your husbands as to the Lord. 24 Now as the congregation submits to Christ, so also wives should submit to their husbands in everything. 25 Husbands, love your wives, just as Christ loved the theocracy and gave himself up for her 26 to make her holy, cleansing her by the washing with water through the word. 33 However, each one of you also must love his wife as he loves himself, and the wife must respect her husband.

(Ephesians 6:1, 4, 5, 7, 9, 18)

1 Children, obey your parents in the Lord, for this is right. 4
Dads, do not exasperate your children; instead, bring them up
in the training and instruction of the Lord. 5 Servants, obey your
corporeal masters with respect and fear, and with sincerity of
heart, just as you would obey Christ. 7 Serve wholeheartedly,
as if you were serving the Lord, not man. 9 Masters, treat your
servants in the same way. Do not threaten them, since you know
him, who is both their master and yours is in heaven, and there is
no favoritism with him. 18 Pray in the Spirit on all occasions with
all kinds of prayers and requests. With this in mind, be alert and
always keep praying for all the faithful.

(Philippians 2:3, 4)

3 Do nothing out of selfish ambition or vain conceit, but in humility
consider others better than yourselves. 4 Each of you should look
not only to your own interests, but also to the interests of others.

(Philippians 3:2)

2 Beware of dogs, beware of evil workers, beware of the concision.

(Colossians 2:8-10, 14, 22, 23)

8 See to it that no one takes you captive through philosophy and
empty delusions, according to the tradition of man, according to
the elementary principles of the world, rather than according to
Christ. 9 For in him all the fulness of the deity dwells in bodily form,
10 and in him you have been made complete, for he is the head
over all rule and authority. 14 Having canceled out the certificate
of debt consisting of decrees against us, which were hostile to
us; he has taken it out of the way, having nailed it to the cross. 22
These are all destined to perish with use, because they are based
on human commands and teachings. 23 Such regulations indeed
have an appearance of wisdom, with their self-imposed worship,

their false humility and their harsh treatment of the body, but they lack any value in restraining sensual indulgence.

(Colossians 3:11-15, 18-25)

11 Here there is no Greek or Jew, circumcised or uncircumcised, barbarian, or primitive, slave or free, but Christ is all and is in all. 12 Therefore, as God's chosen people, holy and dearly loved, clothe yourselves with compassion, kindness, humility, gentleness and patience. 13 Tolerate each other and forgive whatever grievances you may have against one another. Forgive as the Lord forgave you. 14 Over all these virtues put on love, which binds them all together in perfect unity. 15 Let the peace of Christ rule in your hearts, since as members of one body you were called to peace. Always be thankful. 18 Wives, submit to your husbands, as is appropriate in the Lord. 19 Husbands, love your wives and do not be harsh with them. 20 Children, obey your parents in everything, for this pleases the Lord. 21 Dads, do not embitter your children, or they will become discouraged. 22 Servants, obey your corporeal masters in everything; and do it, not only when their eye is on you and to win their favor, but with sincerity of heart and reverence for the Lord. 23 Whatever you do, work at it with all your heart, as working for the Lord, not for man, 24 since you know that you will receive an inheritance from the Lord as a reward. It is the Lord Christ you are serving. 25 Anyone who does wrong will be repaid for his wrong, and there is no partiality.

(Colossians 4:1, 2)

1 Masters, provide your servants with what is right and fair. 2 Devote yourselves to prayer, being watchful and thankful.

(1Thessalonians 5:11-22)

11 Therefore encourage one another and build each other up, just as in fact you are doing. 12 Now we ask you, brothers, to respect those who work hard among you, who are over you in the Lord,

and who admonish you. 13 Hold them in the highest regard in love because of their work. Live in peace with each other. 14 We urge you, brothers, warn those who are idle, encourage the timid, help the weak, be patient with everyone. 15 Make sure that nobody pays back wrong for wrong, but always try to be kind to each other, and to everyone else. 16 Be joyful always; 17 pray continually; 18 give thanks in all circumstances, for this is God's will for you in Christ Jesus. 19 Do not put out the Spirit's fire; 20 do not treat prophecies with contempt. 21 Test everything. Hold on to the good. 22 Avoid all appearance of evil.

(2 Thessalonians 3:10, 14, 15)

10 If anyone will not work, neither should he eat. 14 If anyone is disobedient to our word in this epistle, note that person and do not keep company with him, that he must be converted. 15 Yet do not count him as an enemy, but admonish him as a brother.

(Titus 3:1, 2, 9, 10)

1 Remind them to be subject to rulers and authorities, to obey, to be prepared for every good work, 2 to speak evil of no one, to be peaceable, meek, showing all humility to all people. 9 But avoid foolish disputes, genealogies, contentions, and strivings about the law. 10 Remove a disruptive person after the first and second admonition.

(1 Timothy 2:9-12, 15)

9 The women adorn themselves in modest apparel, with propriety and moderation, not with braided hair or gold or pearls or costly clothing, 10 but, which is proper for women professing godliness, with good works. 11 Let a woman learn in silence with all submission. 12 Do not permit a woman to preach or to assert authority over a man, but to be in silence. 15 Nevertheless she will be saved in childbearing if they continue in faith, love, and holiness, with mental discipline.

(1 Timothy 3:2-4, 12)

2 The overseer therefore must be without reproach, the husband of one wife, temperate, sober, orderly, hospitable, able to teach, 3 not addicted to wine or hostile, but gentle, uncontentious, not greedy; 4 one who manages his own household well, keeping his children under control with all dignity. 12 Let the attendant be the husband of one wife, ruling their children and their own house properly.

(1 Timothy 4:7, 12, 14-16)

7 But reject the profane, and old fables, and assert yourself toward godliness. 12 Let no one despise your youth, but be an example to the believers in word, in conduct, in love, in spirit, in faith, in purity. 14 Do not neglect the gift that is in you, which was given to you by prophecy with the imposition by the hands of the eldership. 15 Meditate on these things; give yourself entirely to them, that your progress may be evident to all. 16 Take heed to yourself and to the doctrine. Continue in it, for in doing this you will save both yourself and those who hear you.

(1 Timothy 5:1-8, 19-23)

1 Do not harshly rebuke an older man, but appeal to him as a father, to the younger men as brothers, 2 the older women as mothers, to the younger women as sisters, in all purity. 3 Honor widows who are widows indeed; 4 but if any widow has children or grandchildren, let them first learn to practice reverence in regard to their own family and provide for their parents; for this is appropriate in the sight of God. 5 Now she who is a widow indeed, and who has been left alone has fixed her hope on God. 6 But she who gives herself to wanton pleasure is dead even while she lives. 7 Prescribe these things as well, so that they may be above reproach. 8 But if anyone does not provide for his own, and especially for those of his household, he has denied the faith, and is worse than an unbeliever. 19 Do not receive an accusation against an elder except from two or three witnesses. 20 Those who are sinning rebuke in the presence of all, that the others also

may fear. 21 Observe these things without prejudice, doing nothing with partiality. 22 Do not lay hands on anyone hastily, neither share in other people's sins; keep yourself pure. 23 No longer drink only water but use a little wine for your stomach's sake and your frequent ailments.

(1 Timothy 6:1, 2, 8, 12, 17, 18)

1 Let as many bondservants as are under sentencing consider their own masters worthy of all honor, so that the name of God and his doctrine may not be blasphemed. 2 Those who have believing masters, let them not despise them because they are brethren, but rather serve them because those who are benefited are believers and beloved. Teach and invoke these things. 8 But having food and clothing, with these be content. 12 Fight the good fight of faith, take hold on eternal life. 17 Instruct those who are wealthy in this present world not to be conceited or trust in the uncertainty of riches, but on God, who abundantly supplies us with all things to enjoy. 18 Do good, to be abundant in good works, to be generous and ready to share.

(2 Timothy 1:14)

14 That virtue which was committed to you, keep by the Holy Spirit who dwells in us.

(2 Timothy 2:3, 6, 22-25)

3 Endure hardship as a good soldier of Jesus Christ. 6 The farm worker ought to be the first to receive a share of the crops. 22 Now flee from youthful lusts, and pursue righteousness, faith, love, and peace with those who call on the Lord from a pure heart. 23 But refuse foolish and ignorant speculations, knowing that they produce conflict. 24 The Lord's bondservant must not be quarrelsome, but be kind to all, able to teach, patient when wronged, 25 with gentleness correcting those who are in opposition, that perhaps God may grant them repentance to acknowledge the truth.

(2 Timothy 4:2)

2 Proclaim the word. Be ready in season and out of season. Convince, rebuke, implore, with all persistence and doctrine.

(Hebrews 12:14)

14 Follow peace with all people, and holiness, without which no one shall see the Lord.

(Hebrews 13:1-5, 7-9, 16, 17)

1 Let brotherly love continue. 2 Do not forget hospitality for
strangers, for by so doing some have unknowingly entertained
angels. 3 Remember the prisoners as if chained with those who
suffer adversity. 4 Marriage is honorable among all, and the bed
undefiled; but fornicators and adulterers God will judge. 5 Let your
conduct be without covetousness; be content with such things as
you have. 7 Remember those who rule over you, who have spoken
the word of God to you, whose faith to follow. 8 Jesus Christ is the
same yesterday, and today, and forever. 9 Do not be involved with
deviant and strange doctrines. 16 But do not forget to do good and
to share, for with such sacrifices God is well pleased. 17 Obey
those who rule over you and be submissive. Let them do so with
joy and not with grief.

(James 1:4, 5, 16, 19, 21, 22)

4 But let patience have its perfect work, that you may be perfect
and complete, lacking nothing. 5 If any of you lacks wisdom, let
him ask of God, who gives to all generously and without reproach,
and it will be given to him. 16 Do not be deceived. 19 Let every
man be quick to hear, slow to speak, slow to anger. 21 Therefore
putting aside all filthiness and excesses of wickedness, in humility
receive the word implanted, which is able to save your souls. 22
But prove yourselves doers of the word, and not merely hearers
who deceive themselves.

(James 2:1, 12, 13, 26)

1 Hold the faith of our Lord Jesus Christ, as glory, with no partiality.
12 So speak and so do as those who will be judged by the law of
freedom. 13 For judgment is without mercy to anyone who has
shown no mercy. Mercy triumphs over judgment. 26 For as the
body without the spirit is dead, so faith without works is dead also.

(James 4:7-11)

7 Therefore submit to God. Resist the enemy and he will flee from
you. 8 Draw near to God and he will draw near to you. Cleanse
your hands and purify your hearts. 9 Lament, mourn and weep. Let
your laughter be turned to mourning and your joy to heaviness. 10
Humble yourselves in the sight of the Lord, and he will lift you up.
11 Do not speak evil of one another, brethren.

(1 Peter 2:1, 11, 13, 14, 16-18)

1 Therefore, lay aside all malice, all guile, hypocrisy, envy, and all
evil speaking. 11 Abstain from fleshly lusts which conflict against
the soul. 13 Therefore submit yourselves to every ordinance of
man for the Lord's sake, whether to the king as supreme, 14 or to
governors, as to those who are sent by him for the punishment of
evildoers, or for the praise of those who do good. 16 Be as free,
and not using your freedom for a cloak of wickedness, but as
servants of God. 17 Honor all mankind. Love the brotherhood. Fear
God. Honor the king. 18 Convicts, be submissive to your masters
with all fear, not only to the good and gentle, but also to the harsh.

(1 Peter 3:1-4, 7-9, 14-16)

1 Wives, likewise, be submissive to your own husbands, so that
even if some do not obey the word, they, without a word, may
be won by the conduct of their wives, 2 when they observe your
chaste conduct accompanied by fear. 3 Do not let your adornment
be merely outward, arranging the hair, wearing gold, or putting on
fine apparel. 4 Rather let it be the hidden person of the heart, with

the incorruptible beauty of a gentle and quiet spirit. 7 Husbands, in the same way be considerate as you live with your wives and treat them with respect as the weaker vessel and as heirs with you of the gracious gift of life, so that nothing will hinder your prayers. 8 Finally, all of you, live in harmony with one another; be sympathetic, love as brothers, be compassionate and humble. 9 Do not repay evil with evil or insult with insult, but with blessing, because to this you were called, so that you may inherit a blessing. 14 But even if you should suffer for the sake of righteousness, you are blessed. So do not fear their intimidation, and do not be troubled, 15 but sanctify Christ as Lord in your hearts, always ready to make a defense to everyone who asks you to give account for the hope that is in you, yet with gentleness and reverence; 16 and keep a good conscience so that in the thing in which you are slandered, those who revile your good behavior in Christ, may be shamed down.

(1 Peter 4:7-10)

7 Be mentally disciplined and sober for prayer. 8 Above all, love each other deeply, because love covers a multitude of sins. 9 Offer hospitality to one another without complaining. 10 Each one should use whatever blessing he has received to serve others, faithfully administering God's grace in its various forms.

(1 Peter 5:2, 3, 5-7)

2 Be authoritative in God's congregation that is under your care, serving as overseers: not because you must, but because you are willing, as God wants you to be, not greedy for money, but eager to serve, 3 not domineering over those entrusted to you, but being examples to the congregation. 5 You younger men, likewise, be subject to your elders; and all of you, clothe yourselves with humility toward one another, for God opposes the proud, but gives grace to the humble. 6 Humble yourselves, therefore, under the mighty hand of God, that he may exalt you at the proper time. 7 Cast all your concerns upon him because he cares for you.

(2 Peter 1:5-7)

5 Also beside this, giving all diligence, add to your faith virtue;
and to virtue knowledge; 6 and to knowledge temperance; and
to temperance patience; and to patience godliness; 7 and to
godliness brotherly kindness; and to brotherly kindness charity.

(1 John 1:9)

9 If we confess our sins, he is faithful and just to forgive us our sins,
and to cleanse us from all unrighteousness.

(1 John 2:15, 23)

15 Love not the world, neither the things that are in the world. If
anyone loves the world, the love of the LORD is not in him. 23
Whoever denies the Son does not have the LORD either; he who
acknowledges the Son has the LORD also.

(1 John 3:18, 23)

18 Let us love, not in word or in tongue, but in deed and in truth. 23
This is his commandment: that we should believe on the name of his
Son Jesus Christ and love one another, as he gave us commandment.

(1 John 4:1, 7, 21)

1 Believe not every spirit, but prove the spirits, whether they are of
God, because many false prophets have gone out into the world. 7
Let us love one another, for love is of God; and everyone who loves
is born of God and knows God. 21 This commandment we have
from him, that one who loves God should love his brother also.

(1 John 5:21)

21 Dear children, guard yourselves against idols.

(2 John 1:6)

6 This is love, that we walk according to his commandments. This is the commandment, just as you have heard from the beginning, that you should walk in it.

(3 John 1:14)

14 Greet your friends by name.

(Revelation 7:3)

3 Do not harm the earth or the sea or the trees.

(Revelation 9:4)

4 Harm not the grass of the earth, or any green thing, or any tree.

(Revelation 22:17-19)

17 Let him who thirsts return. Whoever desires, let him take the water of life freely. 18 If anyone adds to these things, God will add to him the plagues that are written in this book; 19 and if anyone takes away from the words of the book of this prophecy, God shall take away his part from the Book of Life, from the holy city, and from the things which are written in this book.

(Matt. 19:17; 5:19; Jn. 4:23, 24; 14:15, 21; 15:10; 1 Jn. 5:3; 2:2, 3; 3:22)

If you enter into life, keep the commandments. Whosoever therefore shall break one of these least commandments, and shall teach man so, he shall be called the least in the kingdom of heaven: but whosoever shall do and teach them, the same shall be called great in the kingdom of heaven. But the hour is coming, and now is, when true worshipers will reverence the LORD in spirit and truth, for the LORD is seeking such to revere him. God is a Spirit, and those who revere him must reverence in spirit and truth. If you love me, keep my commandments. He that has my commandments, and keeps them, he it is that loves me: and he that loves me shall be loved by the LORD, and I will love him, and will manifest myself to him. If you keep my commandments, you shall abide in my love; even as I have kept the LORD's commandments and abide in his love. This is the love of God, that we keep his commandments: and his commandments are not grievous. He is the propitiation for our sins: and not for ours only, but also for the sins of the entire world. Hereby we do know that we know him, if we keep his commandments. Whatsoever we ask, we receive of him, because we keep his commandments and do those things that are appropriate in his sight.

Section 1 Index

Deut. 4:2, 13; **Mt.** 22:37-39; **Mk.** 12:29-31; **Gen.** 1:1-3, 6, 9, 11, 14, 15, 20, 24, 26-29; 2:7, 16, 17, 24; 5:2; 6:3, 7, 19, 20; 7:3; 8:22; 9:7, 12-17; 11:1; 17:10; **Exod.** 8:20; 13:7; 19:12; 20:3, 4, 7-10, 12-17, 23, 24; 21:14, 16; 22:19, 21, 22, 28; 23:1-3, 6-9, 12; 31:15; 34:17; **Lev.** 3:17; 13:40, 41; 18:6, 18-20, 22-24; 19:4, 9-18, 26-30, 32-36; 20:11-16; 21:5, 7, 10, 13-15; 22:9, 20; 25:23, 24; 26:1, 2; 27:29, 30; **Num.** 1:2, 3; 5:3; 6:2, 5; 10:9; 15:27,29-31; 30:2; 31:18; 35:31; **Deut.** 1:17; 4:15-18; 5:32, 33; 6:5, 13, 14, 16, 18; 7:5, 26; 8:20; 10:14; 11:1, 19, 26-28; 12:8, 9; 14:3; 15:4-14; 16:9, 15, 17; 17:2, 4-7; 18:13, 15, 22; 20:10-12; 22:25, 26; 24:5, 16; **Josh.** 1:9; 4:2; 6:19; 7:13, 15; **Judg.** 13:4, 5; **Ps.** 82:3, 4; **Prov.** 31:8, 9; **Am.** 2:4, 6; **Hos.** 9:16, 17; 11:9; **Isa.** 7:20; **Jer.** 18:7-10; **Ezk.** 4:9; 33:9, 12, 14, 16; **Mal.** 3:10; **Mt.** 4:4, 7, 10, 17; 5:3-12, 16, 22, 32, 34, 37, 42, 44, 48; 6:1, 4, 6-21, 31, 33, 34; 7:1, 2, 5-8, 12-15; 8:22; 9:37, 38; 10:7, 8, 12, 13, 16, 23, 28, 42; 11:28-30; 12:8, 25, 31, 32, 36, 37; 13:12, 49, 50; 15:11, 18-20; 16:19, 24, 25; 18:7, 15-17, 20, 34, 35; 19:6, 9, 21; 20:25-28; 22:14, 21, 30; 23:8-12; 24:42, 44; 25:1, 29, 30, 40, 45; 28:18-20; **Mk.** 1:15; 2:27, 28; 3:4, 28, 29; 4:9, 24, 25; 8:34, 35; 9:35, 40, 43, 45, 47; 10:9, 11, 12, 21, 42-45; 11:24-26; 12:25, 30, 31; 13:11, 37; 16:15, 16; **Lk.** 4:8, 12; 6:27-31, 35-38; 9:23, 24; 10:16; 11:9, 10, 28; 12:4, 5, 15, 21-23, 29-31, 33, 34, 40; 13:24; 16:13; 17:3; 19:27; **Jn.** 2:16; 3:16, 17; 4:24; 5:39; 7:24; 11:25, 26; 12:25, 26, 48; 13:15, 16,

20, 34; 14:6, 21, 27, 28; 15:12-14, 16, 17, 22, 23, 27; 20:22, 23; **Ac.** 1:7; 2:44, 45; 18:9; 20:35; **Rom.** 3:20, 31; 4:4, 5; 7:2, 3; 12:9-21; 13:7-10, 12-14; **1 Cor.** 7:8-11, 14, 15, 27, 28, 38, 39; 9:14; 10:14, 32; 13:4-7; 14:26, 29, 31-34, 40; **2 Cor.** 7:1; 8:14; 13:5; **Gal.** 3:22, 28; 5:1, 6; 6:10, 15; **Eph.** 4:25-27; 5:21, 22, 24-26, 33; 6:1, 4, 5, 7, 9, 18; **Phil.** 2:3, 4; 3:2; **Col.** 2:8-10, 14, 22, 23; 3:11-15, 18-25; 4:1, 2; **1 Thess.** 5:11-22; **2 Thess.** 3:10, 14, 15; **Ti.** 3:1, 2, 9, 10; **1 Tim.** 2:9-12, 15; 3:2-4, 12; 4:7, 12, 14-16; 5:1-8, 19-23; 6:1, 2, 8, 12, 17, 18; **2 Tim.** 1:14; 2:3, 6, 22-25; 4:2; **Heb.** 12:14; 13:1-5, 7-9, 16, 17; **Jas.** 1:4, 5, 16, 19, 21, 22; 2:1, 12, 13, 26; 4:7-11; **1 Pet.** 2:1, 11, 13, 14,16-18; 3:1-4, 7-9, 14-16; 4:7-10; 5:2, 3, 5-7; **2 Pet.** 1:5-7; **1 Jn.** 1:9; 2:15, 23; 3:18, 23; 4:1, 7, 21; 5:21; **2 Jn.** 1:6; **3 Jn.** 1:14; **Rev.** 7:3; 9:4; 22:17-19.

(Mt. 19:17; 5:19; Jn. 4:23, 24; 14:15, 21; 15:10; 1 Jn. 5:3; 2:2, 3; 3:22).

SECTION 2

PROPHECIES OF THE HOLY TRUTH FOR THE THIRD MILLENNIUM COMMON ERA

1. Parakletos

(Jn. 14:15-17, 26; 16:13, 14; 4:37, 36; 16:8-11; Lk. 16:15; Jn. 5:41, 44-47; Exod. 23:20, 21)

If you love me, then keep my commandments. I will pray to the LORD, and he shall send you another *counselor*, that he may abide with you forever; even the Spirit of Truth whom the world cannot receive, because it sees him not, neither knows him: but you know him, for he dwells with you and shall be among you. But the *reaper*, which is the Holy Spirit, whom the LORD will send in my name, he shall teach you all things, and bring all things to your remembrance whatsoever I have said to you. Although when he, the Spirit of Truth, is here, he will guide you into all truth: for he shall not speak of himself; but whatsoever he will hear, that shall he speak: and he will show you things to come. He will glorify me: for he shall receive of mine and shall show it to you. For in this the saying is true: "One sows, and another reaps." He who reaps receives wages, and gathers fruit for eternal life, that both he who sows and he who reaps may rejoice together. When he is here, he will reprove the world of sin, of righteousness, and of judgment. Of sin, because they believe not on me; of righteousness, because I go to the LORD and you see me no more; of judgment, because the rulers of this world are judged. He said to them, "You are those who justify yourselves before man, but God knows your hearts. For what is highly esteemed among man is an abomination in the sight of God."

I receive not honor from man. How can you believe, which receive honor one of another, and seek not the honor that comes from God only? Do not think that I will accuse you to the LORD: there is one that accuses you, even Moses, in whom you trust. If you believed Moses, you would have believed me: for he wrote of me. But if you believe not his writings, how shall you believe my words?

Behold, I send a prophet before you to keep you in the way and to bring you into the place that I prepared. Beware of him and obey his voice; do not provoke him, for he will not pardon your transgressions; for my name is in him.

2. The End Times

(Mk. 16:6; Mt. 24:26; Jn. 5:36; Rev. 10:11; 2 Cor. 6:9; 1 Cor. 4:13, 9; Jn. 4:38; 7:16; Mt. 10:40; Ecc. 4:1; Jas. 5:4; 1 Cor. 6:7; 2 Pet. 3:11, 10)

Be not alarmed, you are looking for Jesus the Nazarene, who was crucified. He has risen, he is not here. Therefore, if they shall say to you, "Behold, he is in the desert"; go not forth: "behold, in the secret chambers"; believe not. The works that the LORD has given me to finish, the same works I do, provide witness of me, that the LORD sent me. Then I was told, "You must prophesy again before many peoples, nations, languages and kings."

As unknown, yet well known; as dying, and behold, we live; as disciplined, and not killed: being defamed, we entreat; we have been made as the filth of the world, the offscouring of all things until now. Thus, we are made a spectacle to the world, to angels, and to man. He sent me to reap that for which I have not labored: others labored, and I entered into their labors. My doctrine is not mine, but his that sent me. He who receives me receives him who sent me.

So, I returned and considered all the oppressions that are done under the sun: and behold the tears of the oppressed, and they had no *advocate*; and on the side of their oppressors was power; but they had no *advocate*.

Behold, the compensation of the laborers who have reaped down your fields, which is withheld by fraud, is disputed: and the complaints of those who have reaped entered into the ears of the Lord of forces. Therefore, it is utterly a fault among you. Therefore, since all these things will be dissolved, what manner of persons ought you be in holy conduct and godliness, in which the heavens will pass away with a great noise, and the elements will melt with intense heat; both the earth and the works that are in it will be burned away.

3. Third Woe

(Rev. 11:14; Jer. 25:11; Mt. 24:21; Rev. 2:22; 9:20, 21; Jn. 18:21; Isa. 2:9; Jer. 25:12, 13; Mk. 13:7, 8; Mt. 24:29; Jer. 29:10)

The second woe has passed: the third woe is coming soon. This whole land shall be a desolation, and an astonishment; and these nations shall serve the king of Babylon seventy years. For then there will be great distress, unequaled from the beginning of the world until now, and never to be equaled again. Indeed, I will cast them into a sickbed, and those who commit adultery with them into great tribulation, unless they repent of their deeds. But the remainder of mankind, who were not killed by these plagues, did not repent of the works of their hands, that they should not worship evil spirits, and idols of gold, silver, brass, stone, and wood, which can neither see nor hear nor walk. Nor did they repent of their murders or their politics, or their sexual immorality or their thefts. Behold, they know what I said. The average man bows down, and each man humbles himself: therefore, forgive them not.

Thus, it shall come to pass, when seventy years are accomplished, that I will punish the king of Babylon, and that nation, says the LORD, for their iniquity, and will make it perpetual desolation. I will bring upon that land all my words which I have pronounced against it, even all that is written in this book, prophesied against all the nations. But when you hear of wars and rumors of wars, do not be troubled; for such things must occur, but the end is not yet. For nation will rise against nation, and kingdom against kingdom. There will be earthquakes in various places, and there will be famines and disasters. These are the beginnings of sorrows.

But immediately after the tribulation of those days the sun will be darkened, and the moon will not give its light, the stars will fall from heaven, and the powers of the heavens will be shaken. For thus says the LORD, that "after seventy years are accomplished at Babylon I will visit you, and perform my good word toward you, in causing you to return to this place."

4. The Sanctification

(Rev. 10:1, 2; Mt. 16:19; Rev. 16:17; 10:7; Mt. 24:37, 38, 39; Ezk. 1:28; Gen. 9:12-16; Mal. 3:6; Heb. 13:8)

I saw another mighty angel descending from heaven, clothed with a dark cloud. A rainbow was on his head, his face was like the sun and his feet like pillars of fire. He had a little book open in his hand. I will give you the keys of the kingdom of heaven. The seventh angel poured out his crucible into the air; and there came a great voice out of the temple of heaven, from the throne, saying "It is done." But in the days of the voice of the seventh angel, when he shall begin to sound, the mystery of God should be finished, as he declared to his servants the prophets.

But as in the days of Noah, so also will be the coming of the Son of Man. For as in the days before the flood, they were eating and drinking, marrying and giving in marriage, until the day Noah entered the ark, and they knew not, until the flood came and took them all away: so also will the coming of the Son of Man be. The appearance of the brilliant light all around him was like that of a rainbow in a cloud on a rainy day. This was the appearance of the similitude of the glory of the LORD. And God said: "This is the sign of the covenant that I make between me and you, and every living creature with you, for perpetual generations: I set my rainbow in the cloud, and it shall be the sign of the covenant between me and the earth. It shall be, when I bring a cloud over the earth, that the rainbow shall be seen in the cloud; and I will remember my covenant between me and you and every living creature of all flesh; the waters shall never again become a flood to destroy all flesh. The rainbow shall be in the cloud, and I will look upon it to remember the everlasting covenant between God and every living creature of all flesh that is on the earth." For I am the LORD, I do not change. Therefore you are not consumed, O sons of Jacob. Jesus Christ is the same yesterday, and today, and through the ages.

5. Everlasting Power

(2 Pet. 3:8; Hos. 6:2; Lk. 18:33; Mk. 8:31; Mt. 16:3; Heb. 10:30; Lk. 22:29, 30; Rev. 20:6; 7:4; Isa. 24:7, 21; Ecc. 9:11; Lk. 22:25, 26; 2 Cor. 12:9; Ps. 138:6; Heb. 13:5; Rom. 8:28; Ps. 100:5)

One day is with the Lord as a thousand years, and a thousand years as one day. After two days will he revive us: in the third day he will raise us up, and we shall live in his sight. The third day he shall rise again. Then he began to teach them, that the Son of Man must suffer many things and be rejected by the elders, and by the chief priests, and scribes, and within three days rise again. You know how to discern the appearance of the sky, but not the signs of the times? Then again, the Lord shall judge his people.

I appoint to you a kingdom, as the LORD has appointed to me; that you may eat and drink at my table in my kingdom and sit on thrones judging the twelve tribes of Israel. Blessed and holy is he that has part in the first resurrection, on such the second death has no power, but they shall be priests of God and of Christ, and shall reign with him a thousand years; therefore, I heard the number of them which were sealed: and there were sealed one hundred and forty-four thousand of all the tribes of the children of Israel.

The new wine mourns, the vine languishes, all the cheerful hearts do sigh. So, it will happen in that day, that the LORD will punish the host of heaven, on high, and the kings of the earth, on earth. I returned and saw under the sun that the race is not to the swift, nor the battle to the strong, nor bread to the wise, nor riches to men of understanding, nor favor to men of skill; but time and randomness happen to them all. The executives of the seculars exercise lordship over them, and those who assert authority over them are called "*capitalists*." But it must not be that way among you, on the contrary, he who is strongest among you, let him be as the weaker and he who governs as he who serves. My grace is sufficient for you: for my power is made perfect in weakness.

Though the LORD is on high, yet he regards the lowly; but the proud he knows from afar. For he himself has said, "I will never leave you nor forsake you." We know that all things work together for good to them that love God, to them who are the called according to his purpose. For the LORD is good; his mercy is everlasting; and his truth endures to all generations.

6. Universality

(Eph. 3:9; 4:6; Phil. 3:21; 1 Cor. 8:6; Col. 1:15-18; 1 Pet. 2:5; Heb. 9:14, 15; Mk. 14:24; Isa. 65:8; 48:9; Rom. 6:16)

Thus, to bring to light what is the administration of the mystery which for ages has been hidden in God, who created all things; one God and Father of all, who is above all, and through all, and in all. Who will transform the body of our humble status into conformity with the body of his excellence, by the assertion of the power that he has, even to subject all things to himself. But to us there is but one God, the LORD, of whom are all things, and we in him; and one Lord Jesus Christ, by whom are all things, and we by him. He is the image of the invisible God, the firstborn over all creation. For by him all things were created in heaven and on earth, visible and invisible, whether thrones or dominions or principalities or powers. All things were created through him and for him. He is before all things, and in him all things consist. He is the head of the body, the theocracy, which is the beginning, the firstborn from the dead, that in all things he may have the preeminence.

You also, as living stones, are being built up as a spiritual dwelling of a holy priesthood, to offer up spiritual sacrifices acceptable to God through Jesus Christ. Now much more shall the blood of Christ, who through the eternal spirit offered himself without fault to God, cleanse your conscience from dead works to serve the living God.

For this cause, he is the mediator of a new covenant, that death having taken place for the redemption of the transgressions that were under the first covenant, they that have been called may receive the promise of the eternal inheritance. As he said to them, "This is my blood of the new covenant, which is shed for many." Thus says the LORD, "As the new wine is found in the cluster, and one says, 'Destroy it not; for a blessing is in it': so will I do for my servants' sakes, that I may not destroy them all." "For my name's sake I will defer my anger, and for my praise I will restrain it from you, so that I do not cut you off."

Do you not know that to whom you submit yourselves servants to obey, his servants you are to whom you obey, whether of sin to death, or of obedience to justification?

7. Seven Woes

(Lk. 6:24, 25; Isa 5:8; Hab. 2:9; Isa. 3:11; 5:21; Jas. 3:16; Ac. 8:20; Lk. 16:11, 14; 20:14; Mic. 2:2; 3:11; Mt. 8:20; 1 Cor. 11:22; Jer. 5:27-29; Mic. 6:12; Rev. 2:9; Jas. 5:1; Rev. 18:17; Jas. 1:9, 10; Prov. 13:10-13; Mt. 23:12; Ezk. 28:4; Isa. 14:15; Jn. 8:24; Heb. 11:6; Lk. 19:14; 18:32, 33)

Woe to you rich, for you already received your comfort. Woe to you who are full now, for you will go hungry. Woe to you who laugh now, for you will mourn and weep. Woe to you who add house to house and join field to field until no space is left and you live alone in the land. Woe to him that covets an evil covetousness to his house, that he may set his nest on high, that he may be delivered from the power of evil. Woe to the wicked! It shall be ill with him, for the reward of his hands shall be given him. Woe to those who are wise in their own eyes, and prudent in their own sight! For where envying and strife is, there is confusion and every evil work. May your money perish with you, because you thought you could buy the gift of God with money! Therefore, if you have not been faithful in the unrighteous wealth, who will trust you with the true riches?

The Pharisees also, who were covetous, heard these things: and they derided him. They reasoned among themselves, saying, "This is the heir. Come, let us kill him, that the inheritance may be ours." They covet fields and take them by force, also houses, and seize them. So they oppress a man and his house, a man and his inheritance. Their heads judge for a bribe, their priests teach for pay, and their prophets divine for money; but the son of man has no place to lay his head. Do you not have houses to eat and drink in? Or do you disrespect the ministry of God and discredit those who have none? What shall I say to you? Shall I praise you in this? I praise you not.

As a cage is full of birds, so their houses are full of deceit. Therefore, they have become great and acquire wealth, but the right of the needy they do not defend. "Shall I not punish them for these things?" says the LORD. "Shall I not avenge myself on such a nation as this?" For their rich men are full of violence, their inhabitants have spoken lies. I know your deeds and crises and your indebtedness, yet you are rich! Go to now, you wealthy, weep and howl for your miseries that shall come upon you. In one hour, such great wealth has been brought to ruin! Let the brother of low degree rejoice in that he is exalted; but the rich, in that he is made low: because as the flower of the grass he shall pass away.

By pride comes nothing but strife, but with the well-advised is wisdom. Wealth gained by dishonesty will be diminished, but he who gathers by labor will increase. Hope deferred makes the heart sick, but when the desire comes, it is a tree of life. He who despises the word will be destroyed, but he who fears the commandments will be rewarded. Whosoever shall exalt himself shall be abased; but he that humbles himself shall be exalted.

With your wisdom and your understanding, you have gained riches for yourself, and gathered gold and silver into your treasuries. But you are brought down to the grave, to the depths of the pit. I said therefore to you, that you shall die in your sins; for unless you believe that Jesus is messiah, you shall die in your sins. But without faith it is impossible to please him, for he who comes to God must believe that he is. But his citizens hated him, and sent a delegation after him, saying, "We will not have this man to reign over us." He was handed over to the seculars: they mocked him, insulted him, spit on him, flogged him and killed him. On the third day he was risen again.

8. Throne of Seven Spirits

(Rev. 21:2; Heb. 8:13; Isa. 55:1; 23:18; Deut. 28:1; Rev. 1:10, 11; Am. 5:8; Rev. 1:20; 4:5)

I saw the holy city, *New Jerusalem*, coming down out of heaven from God. In that he says a *New Covenant*, he has made the first obsolete. Now what is becoming obsolete and outdated is ready to vanish away. Everyone who thirsts returns to the waters; and those who have no money, come to buy and eat. Enter, buy wine and milk without money and without price. Her merchandise and her hire shall be holiness to the LORD: it shall not be treasured nor laid up; for her merchandise shall be to them that dwell before the LORD, to eat sufficiently, and for durable clothing.

Now it shall come to pass, if you diligently obey the voice of the LORD your God, to observe carefully all his commandments which I command you today, that the LORD your God will set you high above all nations of the earth. I was in the Spirit on the Lord's day, and heard behind me a great voice, as of a trumpet, saying: "I am the Alaph and the Taw, the First and the Last." "What you see, write in a book and send it to seven denominations." He made the seven stars and Orion; he turns the shadow of death into morning and makes the day dark as night; he calls for the waters of the sea and pours them out on the face of the earth; the LORD is his name.

The mystery of the seven stars that you saw in my right hand and of the seven golden lampstands is this: "The seven stars are the angels of the seven denominations, and the seven lampstands are the seven denominations." Out of the throne proceeded lightning, thundering and voices: there were seven lamps of fire burning before the throne, which are the seven spirits of God.

9. The Theocracy

(1 Cor. 15: 24, 26, 54, 27, 28; Heb. 1:2, 3; Isa. 52:13; Mt. 28:18; Eph. 1:19-23; 3:6; 2:16-18)

Then comes the end, when he delivers the kingdom to God the LORD, when he shall nullify all rule and all authority and power. The last enemy that will be destroyed is death. So, when this corruptible has developed incorruption, and this mortal has developed immortality, then shall be brought to pass the saying that is written: "Death is consumed in victory."

But when he says all things are put under him, it is evident that he who put all things under him is excepted. Now when all things are made subject to him, then the Son himself will also be subject to him who put all things under him, that God may be all in all. In these last days he spoke to us by his Son, whom he appointed heir of all things, and through whom he made eternity. The Son is the radiance of God's glory and the exact representation of his being, sustaining all things by the power of his word. After he provided purification for sins, he sat down at the right hand of the Majesty in heaven.

Behold, my servant will act wisely; he will be raised and lifted up, and highly exalted. All power is given to me in heaven and earth. That is the exceeding greatness of his power toward us who believe, according to the working of his mighty power which he worked in Christ when he raised him from the dead and seated him at his right hand in the heavenly places, far above all principality and power, and force and dominion, and every name that is named, not only in this age but also in that which is to come. He put all things under his feet, and gave him to be head over all things to the theocracy, which is his body, the fullness of him who fills all in all; that the seculars should be fellow heirs, of the same body, and partakers of his promise in Christ through the covenant, and that he might reconcile them both to God in one body through the cross, thereby putting to death the animosity. He came and preached peace to you who were afar off and to those who were near. For through him we both have access by one Spirit to the LORD.

10. The Ethereal

(Jer. 33:25, 26; 2 Cor. 10:18; Rom. 2:29; Heb. 13:6; Jn. 10:17; Mk. 12:27; 1 Thess. 4:17; Deut. 4:11; Mt. 21:43; Lk. 13:19; Jn. 12:24; Ecc. 11:4; Lk. 17:20, 21)

Thus says the LORD: "If my covenant is not with day and night, and if I have not appointed the ordinances of heaven and earth, then I will cast away the descendants of Jacob and David my servant, so that I will not take any of his descendants to be rulers over the descendants of Abraham, Isaac, and Jacob. But I will restore their fortunes and will have mercy on them." For not he who commends himself is approved, but whom the Lord commends; whose praise is not of man, but of God.

The Lord is the comforter, and I shall not fear what man will do to me. For this reason, the LORD loves me, because I lay down my life that I might take it again. He is not the God of the dead, but the God of the living. You are therefore seriously mistaken. Then we which are alive and remain shall be caught up together with them in the *troposphere*, to meet the Lord under the *ionosphere*: and so shall we ever be with the Lord.

They came near and stood below the mountain; and the mountain burned with fire into the midst of heaven, with darkness, clouds, and thick darkness. Therefore, I say to you, "The kingdom of God shall be taken from you and given to a nation bringing forth the fruits thereof."

It is like a mustard seed, which a man took, threw into his garden, and it grew and became a great tree; and the fowls of the air perched in the branches of it. Unless a kernel of grain falls into the ground and dies, it remains alone; but if it dies, it produces many seeds. But he that observes the wind shall not sow; and he that regards the clouds shall not reap. The kingdom of God comes not with observation: for, behold, the kingdom of God is within you.

11. The Natural World

(Lk. 6:22; Ps. 49:6, 7, 11-13; Prov. 14:20; Jn. 15:18; Jas. 4:4, 11; 2:6; Prov. 18:23; 22:16; 23:4; 28:6, 11; Isa. 47:10)

Blessed are you, when men shall hate you, and when they shall separate you from their company, and shall reproach you, and cast out your name as evil, for the Son of Man's sake. They trust in their wealth and boast themselves in the multitude of their riches. None of them can by any means redeem his brother, nor give to God a ransom for him. Yet their inward thought is that their houses are forever, and their dwelling places to all generations; they call their lands after their own names. Nevertheless, man in honor remains not: he is like beasts that perish. This their way is their folly: yet their posterity approves their sayings.

The poor man is hated even by his own neighbor, but the rich man has many friends. If the world hates you, you know that it hated me before it hated you. Whoever therefore will be a friend of the world is an enemy of God. He who slanders a brother or judges a brother, speaks evil of the law and judges the law. But if you judge the law, you are not a doer of the law but a judge. But you have insulted the poor. Is it not the rich who are exploiting you? Are they not the ones who are dragging you through court? A poor man pleads for mercy, but a rich man answers harshly. He who oppresses the poor for profit, and gives to the rich, is surely deficient.

Labor not to be rich: cease from your own wisdom. Better is the poor who walks in his integrity than one corrupt in his ways, though he is rich. The rich man is wise in his own eyes, yet the poor who has understanding searches him out. You trusted in your wickedness: you have said, "No one sees me." Your wisdom and your knowledge, it corrupted you that you have said in your heart, "I am, and no one else beside me."

12. Arbitrary Valuation

(Mt. 22:15, 16, 20, 21; Ezk. 14:3; Jer. 51:11; Isa. 13:17; Hag. 2:8; Ezk. 20:3; Heb. 9:8, 10; 2 Thess. 2:10)

Then went the Pharisees and took counsel how they might entangle him in his talk. So, they sent to him their disciples with the Herodians. He said to them, "Whose image and inscription is this?" They said to him "Caesar's," and he said to them, "Render therefore to Caesar the things that are Caesar's, and to God the things that are God's."

Son of Man, these men have taken their idols into their heart, and put the stumbling block of their iniquity before their face: should I be inquired of at all by them? Behold, I will stir up the Medes against them, they will not regard silver; and as for gold, they will not delight in it.

The LORD has raised up the spirit of the kings of the Medes for his purpose against Babylon to destroy it, because it is the vengeance of the LORD, the vengeance for his temple. "The silver is mine and the gold is mine" declares the LORD Almighty. Son of Man, speak to the elders of Israel, and say to them, "Thus says the Lord GOD: 'Have you come to inquire of me?' 'As I live,' says the Lord GOD, 'I will not be inquired of by you.'"

The Holy Spirit indicating this, that the way into the holiest of all was not yet made manifest while the first tabernacle was still standing: concerned only with foods and drinks, various washings, and fleshly ordinances imposed until the time of reformation; with all unrighteous deception among those who perish, because they did not receive the love of the truth, that they might be saved.

13. Iniquity of Oppression

(3 Jn. 1:9; Prov. 1:30; Jer. 25:4; Mt. 8:12; 25:42, 43; 10:33; Lk. 14:24; Heb. 13:10, 14; 1 Pet. 2:4; Isa. 28:13, 10; Prov. 17:11; Hos. 8:4, 3; 6:6, 7; Jer. 3:10, 11; Hos. 6:11; Rom. 3:5, 6; Jn. 1:9, 10; 8:45; Exod. 20:7; Mk. 7:7; Mt. 10:24; 7:21; Lk. 6:46; Mt. 22:18; Lk. 6:8; Ps. 78:7; Mt. 12:25; Jn. 2:24, 25; 1 Cor. 3:20; Jn. 15:24, 25; Isa. 53:9; 1 Pet. 2:22; Mt. 13:34; Ps. 69:4; Jb. 41:11; Ti. 1:15)

I wrote to the congregations, but *Asmodeus*, who loves to have preeminence among them, does not accept us. They would none of my counsel: they despised all my reproof. The LORD has sent to you all his servants the prophets, rising early and sending them, but you have not listened nor inclined your ear to hear. But the sons of the kingdom will be cast out into outer darkness. There will be weeping and gnashing of teeth. For I was hungry, and you gave me no meat: I was thirsty, and you gave me no drink: I was a stranger, and you took me not in. But whoever denies me before man, him I will also deny before the LORD who is in heaven. For I say to you that none of those men who were invited shall taste my supper. We have an altar from which they have no right to eat what is served in the tabernacle. For here we do not have an enduring city, but we are looking for the city that is to come; approaching him as to a living stone disallowed indeed by man but chosen by God and precious.

But the word of the LORD was to them, precept upon precept, line upon line, here a little, there a little, that they might go and fall backward, and be broken, snared and taken. For precept must be upon precept, line upon line, here a little, there a little. But Israel has rejected the good; the enemy will pursue them.

A rebellion seeks only evil: therefore, a cruel messenger shall be sent against it. They have set up kings, but not by me; they have appointed princes, but I was not aware. With their silver and gold, they have made idols for themselves, that they must be cut off. For I desired mercy, and not sacrifice; and the knowledge of God more than burnt offerings. But they as man have transgressed the covenant: there they dealt treacherously against me. Yet for all this her treacherous sister Judah has not turned to me with her whole heart, but feignedly, says the LORD.

Thus, the LORD said to me, "The backsliding Israel has justified herself more than treacherous Judah." Also, Judah, a harvest is in place for you, when I return the captivity of my people. But if our unrighteousness commends the righteousness of God, then how should God judge the world? Yet because I tell the truth, you do not believe me.

There was the true light which, coming into the world, enlightens every man. He was in the world, and the world was made through him, but the world did not know him. You shall not take the name of the LORD your God in vain, for the LORD will not hold him guiltless who takes his name in vain. But in vain they do worship me, teaching as doctrines the precepts of men. A disciple is not above his teacher, nor a servant above his master. Not everyone who says to me, "Lord, Lord," will enter the kingdom of heaven; but he who does the will of the LORD who is in heaven. Why do you call me, "Lord, Lord," and do not what I say? But Jesus perceived their wickedness, and Jesus knew their thoughts. That they might set their hope in God, and not forget the works of God, but keep his commandments. But he knew their thoughts. Jesus did not entrust himself to them, because he knew all men, and had no need that anyone should testify of man, for he knew what was in man. The Lord knows the thoughts of the wise, that they are vain.

If I had not done among them the works which no one else did, they would have no sin; but now they have seen and also hated both me and the LORD. But that the word might be fulfilled which is written in their law, "They hated me without a cause." Yet he made his grave with the wicked and with the wealthy in his death; because he had done no violence, neither was any deceit in his mouth, who did not sin.

All things Jesus spoke to the multitude in parables; and without a parable he spoke not to them. But they that hate me without a cause are more than the hairs of my head: they that would cut me off, being my enemies wrongfully, are mighty: and that which I took not away I have to restore. Who prevented me, that I should repay him? Whatsoever is under the whole heaven is mine. To the pure all things are pure: but to them that are defiled and unbelieving nothing is pure; but both their mind and conscience are defiled.

14. Love of the World

(Rom. 3:29, 27, 28; 2 Cor. 10:11, 12; Mt. 11:19; Rom. 3:14-18; Isa. 29:9; Mk. 7:20-23; Jn. 14:28; 5:37; Isa. 55:9; Jn. 3:12; Mt. 23:23; Jn. 10:37-39; Lk. 11:53, 54; Jer. 23:36; Isa. 1:15; 3:8, 9; 5:20; Mk. 4:22)

Is God the God of believers only? Is he not the God of seculars too? Yes, of seculars also. On what principle? On that of observing the law? No, but on that of faith. For we maintain that a person is justified by faith apart from observing the law. Let such a person consider this, that what we are in word by letters when we are absent, such we will also be in deed when we are present. For we dare not class ourselves or compare ourselves with those who commend themselves.

The Son of Man came eating and drinking, and they say, "Here is a glutton and a drunkard, a friend of tax collectors and sinners. But wisdom is proved right by its actions." Whose mouths are full of cursing and bitterness, their feet are swift to shed blood: destruction and misery are in their ways; the way of peace they have not known. There is no fear of God before their eyes.

Pause and wonder; cry out, and cry: they are drunken, but not with wine; they stagger, but not with strong drink. What comes out of a man, that defiles a man. For from within, out of the heart of man, proceeds evil thoughts, adulteries, fornications, murders, thefts, covetousness, wickedness, deceit, lewdness, an evil eye, blasphemy, pride, foolishness. All these evil things come from within and defile a man.

If you loved me, you would rejoice, because I go to the LORD: for the LORD is greater than I. You neither heard his voice at any time, nor have seen his shape. As the heavens are higher than the earth, so his ways are higher than your ways, and his thoughts than your thoughts. If I told you earthly things and you do not believe, how shall you believe if I tell you heavenly things?

Woe to you, scribes and Pharisees, hypocrites; for you tithe mint and anise and cumin but have omitted the weightier matters of the law; justice, mercy, and faith: these you ought to have done, and not to leave the other undone. If I do not the works of the LORD, do not believe me; but if I do, though you do not believe me, believe the works, that you may know and believe that the LORD is in me, and I in him.

Therefore, they sought again to seize him, but he escaped out of their hands. The scribes and the Pharisees began to urge him vehemently, and to provoke him to speak of many things: laying wait for him, and seeking to catch something out of his mouth, that they might accuse him.

The burden of the LORD shall you mention no more: for every man's word shall be his burden; for you have perverted the words of the living God, of the LORD of hosts our God. Even though you make many prayers, I will not hear. Your hands are full of blood. For Jerusalem is ruined, and Judah is fallen: the showing of their countenance is a witness against them. They declare their sin as Sodom (666), they hide it not. Woe to their soul, for they have brought evil upon themselves. Woe to those who call evil "good," and good "evil"; who put darkness for light, and light for darkness. For there is nothing hidden, which shall not be manifested; neither was it kept secret, but that it shall shine forth.

15. Consequence of Inequity

(Mt. 6:24, 33; Jn. 10:1; Mt. 27:20; Lk. 23:18, 19; Mk. 15:15; 14:21; Jn. 8:44, 46; Gen. 6:5, 6; Jn. 10:10; Ps. 52:7; 1 Sam. 16:7; 1 Pet 4:15; Zec. 5:3; Rom. 2:16; Ps. 109:22; Mt. 19:23; 11:12; Jn. 10:36; Ps. 82:6, 7; Ezk. 28:9; Rom. 14:10; Zec. 7:9, 10; Lk. 17:3, 4; Mt. 18:21, 22; 10:34; Ezk. 38:21; Mic. 7:6; Ezk. 38:22, 23; Mal. 2:17; Am. 3:6; 5:9, 10; Isa 59:4; Ezk. 13:6; Mt. 23:5; 6:5; Gal. 1:10-12.; Jb. 28:12, 13, 17; Prov. 16:16; Isa. 13:12, 6; Hos. 4:1; Zeph. 1:2-6; Mt. 24:20, 21; Mk. 13:20)

No one can serve two masters; for either he will hate the one and love the other, or he will hold to one and despise the other. You cannot serve both God and riches. But seek first the kingdom of God and his righteousness, and all those things shall be added to you.

I tell you the truth, the man who does not enter the congregation by the gate, but climbs in by some other way, is a thief and a robber. But the chief priests and elders persuaded the multitude that they should ask for Barabbas and destroy Jesus. So, they cried out all at once, saying, "Away with this man, and release to us Barabbas"; who for certain sedition committed in the city, and for murder, was sent to prison. Wanting to satisfy the crowd, Pilate released Barabbas to them; he had Jesus flogged and remanded him over to be crucified. The Son of Man will go just as it is written about him. But woe to the man who betrayed the Son of Man! It would be better for him if he had not been born.

GOD saw that the wickedness of man was great in the earth, and that every contrived purpose of his heart was only evil continually; and the LORD regretted that he made man on the earth, and it grieved him to his heart. You are of your flesh the devils, and the lusts of your flesh you will do. Which of you convicted me of sin? The thief comes only to steal, and kill, and destroy; but I came that they might have life and might have it more abundantly. Lo, this is the man that made not God his strength; but trusted in the abundance of his riches and strengthened himself in his wickedness. Do not consider his appearance or his stature, for I have rejected him.

If you suffer, it should not be as a murderer or thief or any other type of criminal, or even as an *interloper.* This is the curse that goes out over the face of the whole earth: every felon shall be executed, according to this; and, every perjurer shall be executed, according to this. In that day God shall judge the secrets of man by Jesus Christ in accordance with the scriptures. But I am poor and needy, my heart is broken within me.

Assuredly, I say to you that it is impassable for a rich man to enter the kingdom of heaven. But from the days of John the Baptist until now the kingdom of heaven suffers violence, and the violent take it by force. Do you say of him, whom the LORD sanctified and sent into the world, "You are blaspheming," because I said, "I am the Son of God"? "I said 'You are gods,' you are all sons of the Most High." But you will die like mere men; you will fall like all the other rulers. Will you then say, "I am a god," in the presence of him who kills you? You will be a man, not a god, in the hands of him who slays you. But why do you judge your brother? Or why do you show contempt for your brother? For we shall all stand before the judgment seat of Christ.

Thus speaks the LORD of hosts, saying, "Execute true judgment, and show mercy and compassion every man to his brother: oppress not the widow, nor the fatherless, the stranger, nor the poor; and let none of you imagine evil against his brother in your heart." So, watch yourselves. If your brother sins, rebuke him, and if he repents, forgive him. If he sins against you seven times in a day, and seven times returns to you and says, "I repent," forgive him. Lord, how often shall my brother sin against me, and I forgive him? Up to seven times? Jesus said, "I do not say to you, up to seven times, but up to seventy times seven."

Do not think that I came to bring peace on the earth; I did not come to bring peace, but a sword. "Thus, I will call for a sword against Gog throughout all the mountains," says the Lord GOD. Every man's sword will be against his brother. The son falls away from his dad, the daughter rises up against her mother, the daughter in law against her mother-in-law: a man's enemies are they of his own household. I will bring him to judgment with pestilence and bloodshed; I will rain down on him, on his troops, and on the many peoples who are with him, flooding rain, great hailstones, fire, and brimstone. “Thus, I will magnify myself and sanctify myself, and I will be known in the eyes of many nations. Then they shall know that I am the LORD.” [Gog is the North Atlantic Treaty Organization 30 Member states as of March 2022: Albania, Belgium, Bulgaria, Canada, Croatia, Czechia, Denmark, Estonia, France, Germany, Greece, Hungary, Iceland, Italy, Latvia, Lithuania, Luxembourg, Montenegro, Netherlands, North Macedonia, Norway, Poland, Portugal, Romania, Slovakia, Slovenia, Spain, Turkey, the United Kingdom, and the United States.]

You have wearied the LORD with your words. “How have we wearied him?” you ask. By saying, that all who do evil are good in the eyes of the LORD, and he is pleased with them, or where is the God of justice? When the alarm sounds in a city, do not the people tremble? When disaster comes to a city, has not the LORD caused it? He flashes destruction on the stronghold and brings the fortified city to ruin. You hate the one who reproves in the court and despise him who tells the truth. No one calls for justice, nor does any plead for truth. They trust in empty words and speak lies; they conceive evil and bring forth iniquity. They have envisioned futility and false divination, saying, “Thus says the LORD!” But the LORD has not sent them; yet they hope that their word may be confirmed. All their works they do to be seen by man. But when you pray, you shall not be like the hypocrites. For they love to pray standing in public and on the corners of the streets, that they may be seen by man. Assuredly, I say to you, they have their reward. For if I yet pleased man, I should not be the servant of Christ. But I certify to you, that the covenant that is disclosed by me is not after man; I neither received it of man, neither was I taught it, but by the revelation of Jesus Christ.

But where shall wisdom be found? Where is the place of understanding? Man knows not the price thereof; neither is it found in the land of the living. The gold and the crystal cannot equal it: and the exchange of it shall not be for jewels of fine gold. How much better is it to get wisdom than gold, and to get understanding to be chosen rather than silver. I will make a man more precious than pure gold, even a man than the golden wedge of Ophir. Howl ye, for the day of the LORD is approaching; it shall come as a destruction from the Almighty.

Hear the word of the LORD, you children of Israel: for the LORD has a controversy with the inhabitants of the land, because there is no truth, nor mercy, nor knowledge of God in the land. "I will utterly consume everything from the surface of the land," says the LORD; "I will consume man and beast; I will consume the birds of the heavens, the fish of the sea, and the stumbling blocks with the wicked. I will cut off man from the surface of the earth," says the LORD. "I will stretch out my hand against Judah, and against all the inhabitants of Jerusalem; those who worship the host of heaven on the housetops; those who worship and swear by the Lord, but who also swear by their king; those who have turned back from the LORD, and have not sought the LORD, nor inquired of him." And pray that your flight may not be in winter or on the sabbath. For then there will be great tribulation, such as has not been from the beginning of the world until now, and never shall be. And except that the LORD had shortened those days, no flesh would be saved: but for the sake of the chosen, whom he selected, he shortened those days.

16. Failure of Leadership

(Am. 5:11, 12; Isa. 14:20; Am. 8:4-6; Prov. 22:22, 23; Ecc. 5:13; Ps. 49:17; Mt. 5:26; Jas. 4:12, 16; Obad. 1:11; Isa. 14:26, 22; 48:1; Hos. 10:15; Am. 7:12, 13; Rev. 12:7-9; Jn. 12:49; Jer. 10:22; 9:11; Jn. 14:1-3; 1 Cor. 15:50; Heb. 12:20; 2:9; Jn. 3:33; 1 Cor. 6:3; Heb. 1:6; Ps. 104:4, 5; Ps. 71:10, 11; 2 Chr. 34:25; Rom. 6:15; 2 Pet. 2:4)

Forasmuch therefore as your treading is upon the poor, and you take from him burdens of grain: you have built houses of hewn stone, but you shall not dwell in them; you have planted pleasant vineyards, but you shall not drink the wine of them. For I know your manifold transgressions and your mighty sins: they afflict the just, they take a bribe, and they turn aside the poor in the gate from their right. You will not join them in burial, for you have destroyed your land and killed your people. The offspring of the wicked will never be mentioned again.

Hear this, you that consume the needy, and make the poor of the land fail; making the measure decrease and the price increase, falsifying the scales by deceit; buying the poor with silver and the needy for a pair of sandals, selling even the sweepings with the wheat. Do not take from the poor because he is poor, nor oppress the afflicted at the gate; for the LORD will plead their cause and plunder the souls of those who plundered them.

I have seen a grievous evil under the sun: wealth hoarded to the harm of its owner, for when he dies, he shall carry nothing away: his glory shall not descend after him. Truly I say to you, "You shall not depart from here, until you have repaid every last token." There is one lawgiver, who is able to save and to destroy. Who are you to judge another? But as it is, you boast in your arrogance; all such boasting is evil. On the day you stood aloof while strangers carried off his wealth and foreigners entered his gates and cast lots for Jerusalem, you were like one of them. This is the plan determined for the entire world; this is the hand stretched out over all nations. "I will rise up against them," declares the LORD Almighty. "I will cut off from Babylon her name and survivors, her offspring and descendants," declares the LORD.

Hear this, O house of Jacob, which are called by the name of Israel, and are come forth out of the waters of Judah, which swear by the name of the LORD and make mention of the God of Israel, but not in truth, nor in righteousness. Thus, it will be done to you, O Bethel, because of your great wickedness. When day dawns, the king of Israel will be utterly cut off. Then the prince said to the dragon, "Get out, you seer! Go back to the land of Judah. Earn your bread there and do your prophesying there. Don't prophesy anymore here, because this is the king's sanctuary and the temple of the kingdom."

Thus, there was war in heaven, Mikael and his angels waging war with the dragon, and the dragon and his *apostles* waged war and prevailed not; neither was their place found anymore in the heavens: he was sent out into the earth, and his *disciples* were sent out with him. I have not spoken of myself; but the LORD who sent me, he gave me instruction, what I should say, and what I should speak.

Behold, the noise of the report has come, and a great commotion out of the north country, to make the cities of Judah desolate, and a den of dragons. And I will make Jerusalem heaps and a den of dragons; and I will make the cities of Judah desolate, without an inhabitant. You believe in God, believe also in me. I go to prepare a place for you, that where I am, there you may be also. Flesh and blood cannot inherit the kingdom of God. If even an animal touches the mountain, it must be killed.

But we do see him who has been made slightly lower than the angels, because of the suffering of death crowned with glory and honor, that by the grace of God he might taste death for everyone. He who has received his witness has set his seal to this, that God is true. Do you not know that we shall judge angels? How much more, things that pertain to this life? Again, when God brings his firstborn into the world, he says, "Let all God's angels worship him." Who makes his angels spirits; his ministers a flaming fire: who laid the foundations of the earth, that it should not be removed forever! My enemies speak against me; and they that lay wait for my soul take counsel together, saying, "God has forsaken him: persecute and take him; for there is none to deliver him."

Because they have forsaken me, and have burned incense to lower gods, that they might provoke me to anger with all the works of their hands; therefore, my wrath shall be poured out upon this place, and shall not be quenched. What then? Should we sin because we are not under law but under grace? Certainly not. For God spared not the angels that sinned, but cast them down to hell, and delivered them into chains of darkness, to be reserved until judgment.

17. The Serpent Dragon

(Num. 21:8, 9; Jn. 3:14, 15; 6:40; 12:32; 8:28; Rev. 20:1-3)

Thus, the LORD said to Moses, "Take a living serpent, and set it on a pole; and it shall be that everyone who is bitten, when he looks at it, shall live." So, Moses set a live snake in bronze and put it up on a pole. Then when anyone was bitten by a snake and looked at the bronzed snake, he lived. As Moses lifted up the serpent in the wilderness, even so must the Son of Man be lifted up, that whoever believes in him should not perish but have eternal life. This is the will of him who sent me, that everyone who sees the Son and believes in him may have everlasting life; and I will raise him up at the last day. And I, if I am lifted up from the earth, will draw all peoples to myself. When you have lifted up the Son of Man, then shall you know that I am, and I do nothing of myself, but as the LORD taught me, I speak these things.

Then I saw an angel coming down from heaven, having a key to the infinite void and a great chain in his hand. He laid hold on the dragon, that serpent of old, and bound him for a thousand years; and he cast him into the bottomless pit, and closed him down, and set a seal on him, so that he should deceive the nations no more until the thousand years were finished.

18. Curse of the Occupiers

(Rev. 2:12, 13; Ac. 26:18; Rev. 2:24; Hos. 2:11; Ezk. 14:6; Jer. 10:15; Lk. 21:6; 2 Pet. 3:8; Lk. 12:56; Obad. 1:21; Mt. 12:25; Lk. 21:20; Ezk. 13:15, 16; 2 Chr. 15:6; Deut. 4:26, 27)

These things say he which has the sharp sword with two edges; "I know your works, and where you dwell, even where the adversary's seat is: and you hold fast my name and have not denied my faith"; to open their eyes, and to turn them from darkness to light, and from the power of conflict to God, that they may receive forgiveness of sins, and inheritance among them which are sanctified by faith that is in me.

But to you I say, and to as many as have not this doctrine, and which have not known the depths of opposition as they speak; "I will put upon you no other burden." I will also put an end to all their mirth, their feasts, their new moons, their sabbaths, and all their festal assemblies. Therefore, say to the house of Israel, "Thus says the Lord GOD; 'Repent, and turn yourselves away from your idols; and turn away your faces from all your abominations.'" They are vanity, and the work of errors: in the time of their visitation, they shall perish.

These things you see: the days will come in which no stone shall remain upon another that will not be thrown down. Beloved, do not forget this one thing, that with the Lord one day is as a thousand years, and a thousand years as one day. You can discern the face of the sky and of the earth, but how is it you do not discern this time? The saviors shall come up on mount Zion to judge mount Seir, and the kingdom shall be the LORD's.

Every kingdom divided against itself is brought to desolation, and every city or house divided against itself will not stand. But when you see Jerusalem surrounded by armies, then know that its desolation is near. Thus, will I accomplish my wrath on the wall and on those who have patched it with untampered mortar; and I will say to you, "The wall is no more, nor those who patched it, that is, the prophets of Israel who prophesy concerning Jerusalem and who see visions of peace for her when there is no peace," says the Lord GOD.

Nation is destroyed of nation, and city of city: for God did vex them with all adversity. I call heaven and earth to witness against you this day, that you shall soon utterly perish from off the land into where you go over Jordan to possess it; you shall not prolong your days upon it but shall utterly be destroyed. Then the LORD shall scatter you among the nations, and you shall be left few in number among the heathen, there where the LORD shall lead you.

19. Neutrality

(Josh. 3:11; Am. 1:13, 15; Zec. 11:3; Isa. 1:17; Lk. 13:29; Zec. 8:16, 17; Mal. 1:14)

Behold, the ark of the covenant of the LORD of all the earth is crossing over before you into the Jordan. Thus says the LORD: "For three transgressions of the people of Ammon, and for four, I will not turn away, because they ripped up the woman with child in testimony, that they might expand their territory." "Their king shall go into captivity, he and his princes together," says the LORD. A voice is howling from the shepherds; for their glory is spoiled: a voice of the roaring of young lions; for the pride of Jordan is spoiled.

Learn to do well; seek judgment, relieve the oppressed, judge the fatherless, plead for the widow. They will come from the east and the west, from the north and the south, and recline in the kingdom of God. These are the things that you shall do: speak everyone the truth to his neighbor; execute the judgment of truth and peace in your gates. Let none of you imagine evil in your hearts against his neighbor; and love no false oath: for all these are things that I hate, says the LORD. "But cursed is the deceiver, which has in his flock a male, and vows, but sacrifices corruption to the LORD: for I am a great King, and my name is dreadful among the heathen," says the LORD of hosts.

20. The Birthright

(Mic. 5:2; Mt. 1:17; Isa. 62:5; 7:14, 16; Rev. 12:4, 2; Mt. 2:16, 13, 14; Rev. 12:6; Lam. 1:15; Jer. 31:21, 4; Rev. 12:14; Jer. 31:13; 1 Cor. 7:34; Am. 5:2; Jl. 1:8; Isa. 45:5-7; 48:11; Rom. 9:33)

But you, Bethlehem the fruitful, though you are small among the thousands of Judah, yet out of you, **one** shall come forth to me to be ruler in Israel, whose origin proceeds from before the everlasting. So, all the generations from Abraham to David are fourteen generations, from David until the captivity in Babylon are fourteen generations, and from the captivity in Babylon until the messiah are fourteen generations. For as a young man marries a virgin, so shall your sons marry you; and as the bridegroom rejoices over the bride, so shall your God rejoice over you.

Therefore, the LORD himself will give you a sign: the virgin will be with child and will give birth to a son, and before the child shall know to refuse the evil and choose the good, the land that you dread will be forsaken by both her kings. Then the dragon stood before the woman who was ready to give birth, to devour her child as soon as it was born. Then being with child, she cried out in labor and in pain to give birth.

When Herod realized that he had been outwitted by the Magi, he was furious, and he gave orders to kill all the males in Bethlehem and its vicinity who were two years old and under, in accordance with the time he had learned from the Magi. His tail drew a third of the stars of heaven and threw them to the earth. When they had gone, a messenger of the Lord appeared to Joseph in a dream. "Get up," he said, "Take the child and his mother and escape to Egypt. Stay there until I tell you, for Herod is going to search for the child to kill him." So, he got up, took the child and his mother during the night and left for Egypt. Then the woman fled into the wilderness, where she had a place prepared by God, that they should feed her there one thousand two hundred and sixty days. The LORD has rejected all my mighty men in my midst; he has called an assembly against me to crush my young men; the LORD trampled as in a winepress the virgin daughter of Judah.

Set up signposts, make landmarks; set your heart toward the highway, the way in which you went. Turn back, O virgin of Israel, turn back to these your cities. Again I will build you, and you shall be rebuilt, O virgin of Israel! You shall again be adorned with your tambourines and shall go forth in the dances of those who rejoice. The woman was given two wings of a great eagle, that she might fly into the wilderness to her place, where she is nourished for a time and times and half a time, from the presence of the serpent. Then shall the virgin rejoice in the dance, both young and old together: for I will turn their mourning into joy, and will comfort them, and make them rejoice from their sorrow.

There is a difference between a wife and a virgin. The unmarried woman cares about the things of the Lord, that she may be holy both in body and in spirit. But she who is married cares about the things of the world, how she may please her husband. The virgin of Israel is fallen; she shall no more rise: she is forsaken upon her land; there is none to raise her up. Mourn like a virgin in sackcloth grieving for the husband of her youth. I am the LORD, and there is none else, there is no God beside me: I strengthened you, though you have not known me: that they may know from the rising of the sun, and from the west, that there is none beside me. I am the LORD, and there is none else. I form the light, and create darkness: I make peace, and create evil; I the LORD do all these things. For my own sake, I do this. How could I let myself be defamed? I will not yield my glory to another. As it is written, "Behold, I lay in Zion a stone of stumbling and a rock of offense, and he who believes in him cannot be disproved."

21. The Firstborn

(Hos. 9:1; Mic. 7:8; Jn. 2:18, 19; 5:16; 7:15; 5:17; 7:13; Mk. 7:4; 1 Tim. 4:3; Mt. 12:12; 23:8; Mk. 7:8; Jn. 5:18; 7:1; Mt. 23:34-37; 23:31, 32; 21:12; Ezk. 15:6-8; 5:9; Isa. 14:29,31; 2 Cor. 6:16; 7:9, 10; Jer. 32:40, 42; Lev. 26:14-18; Lk. 10:20)

Do not rejoice, O Israel, with joy like other peoples. Rejoice not against me, O my enemy: when I fall, I shall arise; when I sit in darkness, the LORD shall be a light to me. The Jews therefore answered and said to him, "What sign do you show to us, seeing that you do these things?" Jesus answered and said to them, "Destroy this temple, and in three days I will raise it up." For this reason, the Jews persecuted Jesus, because he had done these things on the sabbath. The Jews marveled, saying, "How does this man know writings, having never learned?" But Jesus answered them, "My Father has been working until now, and I have been working."

However, no one spoke openly of him for fear of the Jews. At the marketplace, they do not eat unless they cleanse themselves; and there are many other things which they have received in order to observe, such as the washing of cups and pitchers and copper pots: and to abstain from foods, [and drugs] which God created to be received with thanksgiving for them which believe and know the truth. How much then is a man better than a sheep? Wherefore it is lawful to do well on the sabbath days. But be not called "Rabbi": for one is your teacher, and all you are brethren. Neglecting the commandments of God, you hold to the tradition of men. Therefore, the Jews sought all the more to kill him, because he not only broke their sabbath, but also said that God was his Father, as though making himself equal with God.

After these things Jesus walked in Galilee: for he would not walk in Judea, because the Jews sought to kill him. Therefore, behold, I send to you prophets, and wise men, and scribes: and some of them you kill and crucify; and some of them you scourge in your synagogues, and persecute them from city to city: that upon you may come all the righteous blood shed upon the earth. Verily I say to you, "All these things shall come upon this generation of

Jerusalem, which kills the prophets and stones them which are sent to you.

How often I would have gathered your children together, but you would not allow it. Therefore, you are witnesses of yourselves, that you are the descendants of those which killed the prophets: fill up for yourselves then the measure of your fathers." Jesus went into the temple of God and cast out all of them that sold and bought in the temple and overthrew the tables of the moneychangers. Therefore, thus says the Lord GOD; "As the vine tree among the trees of the forest, which I have given to the fire for fuel, so will I give the inhabitants of Jerusalem." I will set my face against them; they shall go out from one fire, and another fire shall devour them; and you shall know that I am the LORD, when I set my face against them. I will make the land desolate, because they have committed a trespass, says the Lord GOD.

Then I will do among you what I have never done, and the like of which I will never do again, because of all your abominations! There shall come a smoke from the north, and none shall be alone at the appointed time. Then what agreement has the temple of God with idols? For you are the temple of the living God; as God has said, "I will dwell in them, and walk in them; and I will be their God, and they shall be my people." I now rejoice, for the sorrow that is according to God produces repentance without regret, to salvation; but the sorrow of the world produces death.

I will make an everlasting covenant with them, that I will not turn away from them, to do them good; but I will put the fear of me in their hearts, that they shall not depart from me. For thus says the LORD; "Like as I have brought all this great evil upon this people, so will I bring upon them all the good that I have promised them." But if you will not heed me and will not do all these commandments; but that you break my covenant, I will also do this to you: I will set my face against you, and you shall be slain before your enemies. If you will not yet for all this heed me, then I will punish you seven times more for your sins. Nevertheless, do not rejoice in this, that the spirits are subject to you, but rather rejoice because your names are written in heaven.

22. The Lowly

(Mt. 9:24; 2 Chr. 36:16; Mt. 27:30; Jb. 30:10; 9:23, 24; Jn. 19:1-3; Isa. 27:7, 8, 4; 41:14; Lk. 23:36; Mt. 27:34; Ps. 69:21; 109:4; 22:6-8; Mk. 15:32, 29, 30; Lk. 4:23; Jb. 25:4-6; Isa. 41:14; Jn. 5:26, 27; Isa. 31:3; 1 Cor. 1:19-21; 3:18-20)

Jesus said, "Make space: the girl is not dead but asleep;" but they laughed at him. They mocked the messengers of God, and despised his words, and misused his prophets, until the wrath of the LORD arose against those people, until there was no remedy. They spit on him, and took the reed, and smote him on the head.

They abhor me, they flee far from me, and spare not to spit in my face. If the scourge slays suddenly, he will laugh at the trial of the innocent. The earth is given into the hand of the wicked: he covers the faces of the judges thereof; if not, where, and who is he? Then Pilate therefore took Jesus and scourged him. The soldiers platted a crown of thorns, and put it on his head, and they put on him a purple robe, and said, "Hail, King of the Jews," and they smote him with their hands. Has he smitten him, as he smote those that smote him? Or is he slain according to the slaughter of them that are slain by him? In measure, when it shoots forth, you will debate with it: he stays his rough wind in the day of the east wind. Fury is not in me: who would set the briers and thorns against me in battle? I would go through them; I would burn them together.

Fear not, you worm Jacob, and you men of Israel; I will help you, says the LORD, and your redeemer, the Holy One of Israel. Then the soldiers also mocked him, they gave him vinegar to drink mingled with gall: and when he had tasted thereof, he would not drink. They gave me also ammonia in my meat; and in my thirst they gave me vinegar to drink. For my love they are my adversaries: but I pray.

But I am a worm, and no man; a reproach of men, and despised of the people. All they that see me laugh at me to scorn: they shoot from the lip, they shake their heads, saying, "He trusted on the LORD that he would deliver him: let him deliver him, seeing he delighted in him; let the Christ, the King of Israel, descend now from the cross, that we may see and believe." Even those who were crucified with him reviled him. Then they that passed by insulted him, wagging their heads, and saying, "Ah, you that destroy the temple, and build it in three days, save yourself, and come down from the cross." "Physician, heal yourself."

How then can man be righteous before God? Or how can he be pure who is born of a woman? If even the moon does not shine, and the stars are not pure in his sight, how much less man, a maggot, and a son of man, a larva? For as the Father has life in himself; so also has he given to the Son to have life in himself; and has given him authority to execute judgment, because he is the Son of Man.

Now the Egyptians are man, and not God; and their horses are flesh, and not spirit. When the LORD stretches out his hand, both he who helps will fall, and he who is helped will fall down; they all will perish together. For it is written, I will destroy the wisdom of the wise, and will bring to nothing the understanding of the prudent. Where is the wise? Where is the scribe? Where is the disputer of this world? Has God not made foolish the wisdom of this world? For after that in the wisdom of God the world by wisdom knew not God, it pleased God by the foolishness of preaching to save them that believe. Let no man deceive himself. If any man among you seems to be wise in this world, let him become a fool, that he may be wise. For the wisdom of this world is foolishness with God. He takes the wise in their own craftiness: and again, the Lord knows the thoughts of the wise, that they are futile.

23. The Elixir

(Jn. <u>2</u>:11, 9; Mk. <u>5</u>:35, 36, 39; Jn. <u>11</u>:11, 17, 39, 43, 44; <u>19</u>:30, 32, 33, 36; Ps. <u>34</u>:19, 20; Gen. <u>3</u>:15; Mk. <u>8</u>:12; Lk. <u>13</u>:33; <u>5</u>:31, 32; Mk. <u>16</u>:18; Ecc. <u>10</u>:1; Rev. <u>3</u>:1; Mt. <u>9</u>:13; Lk. <u>15</u>:7, 10; Isa. <u>29</u>:10; <u>7</u>:18; Mt. <u>27</u>:52, 53)

The beginning of *sorcery* Jesus did in Cana of Galilee and manifested forth his powers; and his disciples believed in him. When the ruler of the feast had tasted the *medicated wine*, he knew not what it was: but the servants which drew the water knew. Someone came from the ruler of the synagogue's house who said,

"Your daughter is dead." As soon as Jesus heard the word that was spoken, he said to the ruler of the synagogue, "Do not be afraid; only believe." When he came in, he said to them, "Why make this commotion and weep? The child is not dead, but '*sedated*.'" These things he said, and after that he said to them, "Our friend Lazarus is '*sedated*,' but I go that I may wake him up." So, when Jesus went, he found that he had already been in the tomb four days. Then the sister of the one who was *sedated*, said to him, "Lord, by this time there is a stench, for he has been four days." Jesus said, "Take away the stone." When he had said these things, he called out with a loud voice, "Lazarus, come forth." He who was *comatose* went forth, bound hand and foot with wrappings; and his face was wrapped around with a cloth. Jesus said to them, "Unbind him, and let him go." Therefore, when Jesus had received the *potion*, he said "It is finished." He bowed his head and lapsed into a *drug induced coma*. The soldiers therefore came and broke the legs of the first man who had been crucified with Jesus, and then those of the other. But when they came to Jesus and thought he was already dead, they did not break his legs. These things were done, that the scripture should be fulfilled: "A bone of him shall not be broken." Many are the afflictions of the righteous; but the LORD delivers him out of them all. He kept all his bones; not one of them was broken. But he shall wound your head, and you will bruise his heel.

He sighed deeply in his spirit, and said "Why does this generation seek after a sign? Verily I say to you, 'There shall no sign be given to this generation.'" "Nevertheless, I must walk today and tomorrow, and the day following: for it cannot be that a prophet perishes out of Jerusalem." Not those who are well need a medicine man, but those who are ailing. I have not come to call the righteous but sinners to repentance. With their hands they will pick up serpents, and if they drink anything deadly, it will not harm them. They shall lay hands upon the sick and they shall recover. Dead flies cause the ointment of the apothecary to exude a stinking odor: so does a little folly to the reputation of wisdom and honor.

I know your works, that you have a name that you live, and are dead. But go and learn this meaning, "I will have mercy, and not sacrifice": for I did not come to call the righteous, but sinners. There will be joy in heaven over one sinner who repents, more than over ninety-nine righteous persons who need no repentance. Likewise,

I tell you, there is joy in the presence of the *extraterrestrials* of God over one sinner who repents. But the LORD poured out upon you the spirit of deep sleep and closed your eyes: the prophets and your rulers, the seers he has covered. It shall come to pass in that day, that the LORD shall hiss for the fly that is in the uttermost part of the rivers of Egypt, and for the bee that is in the land of Syria. Then the graves were opened; and many bodies of the saints who were *sedated* arose, and came out of the graves after his resurrection, and went into the holy city, and appeared to many.

24. Ascension

(Exod. 3:2; Ac. 1:2, 3; Rev. 20:10, 14; Ac. 1:9, 11; 1 Thess. 4:16; Eph. 4:9, 10; Rom. 10:6, 7; 1 Cor. 13:3; Ac. 13:35; 2 Tim. 2:11, 12; Ps. 49:9; 1 Cor. 15:51, 53; 2 Tim. 2:14; Rev. 21:8; Isa. 30:33; Jer. 11:7, 8; Mt. 23:21, 22)

Behold the Angel of the LORD appeared in a blazing fire from the midst of a bush; and he looked, and behold, the bush was burning with fire, yet the bush was not consumed. Upon the day in which he was taken up, after he through the Holy Spirit had given commands to the apostles whom he had chosen, to whom he also presented himself **alive** after his suffering, by many infallible proofs, being seen by them during forty days and speaking of the things pertaining to the kingdom of God: the *serpent* that deceived them was cast into the lake of fire and brimstone, and death and hell were cast into the lake of fire. While they watched, he was taken up, and a cloud received him out of their sight.

This same Jesus, who was taken up from you into heaven, will so come in like manner as you saw him go into heaven. For the Lord himself will come down from heaven, with a loud command, with the voice of the archangel and with the trumpet call of God, and the dead in Christ will rise first. Now this, he ascended, is that he also descended into the lower parts of the earth [Septicemia]. He that descended is the same also that ascended far above all the heavens, that he might fill all things.

Do not say in your heart, "Who will ascend into heaven?" That is, to bring Christ down from above. Or "Who shall descend into the deep?" That is, to bring up Christ again from the dead. If I give all I possess to the poor and surrender my body to the flames, but have no compassion, I accomplished nothing. Therefore, he also says in another Psalm: "You will not allow your Holy One to see corruption." This is a faithful saying: for if we are *cremated* with him, we shall also rise with him; if we endure, we shall also reign with him. That he should still live forever, and not see corruption.

Behold, I tell you a mystery: we shall not all sleep, but we shall all evolve. For this corruptible must develop incorruption, and this mortal must develop immortality [gene therapy]. Remind them of these things, charging them before the Lord not to strive about words to no benefit, to the subverting of the hearers. But the fearful, and unbelieving, and abominable, and murderers, and prostitutes, and malpractitioners, and idolaters, and all frauds; their part is in the lake which burns with fire and brimstone, which is the second death.

For Tophet is ordained of old; yea, for the king it is prepared; he has made it deep and large: the pile thereof is fire and much wood; the breath of the LORD, like a stream of brimstone, does kindle it. For I earnestly exhorted your fathers in the day I brought them up out of the land of Egypt, until this day, rising early and exhorting, saying, "Obey my voice." Yet they did not obey or incline their ear, but everyone followed the imagination of his evil heart; therefore, I will bring upon them all the words of this covenant, which I commanded them to do, but which they have not done. He who swears by the temple, swears by it and by him who dwells in it; and he who swears by heaven, swears by the throne of God and by him who sits upon it.

25. Flight of Sacrifice

(Ac. 2:1; Isa. 48:20; Jer. 21:9; Lk. 9:24; Jer. 51:49; Isa. 48:22; 1 Tim. 6:9; Mk. 7:9; Ac. 7:51; Isa. 47:5; 28:18; Mk. 13:32)

Now when the day of Pentecost had fully arrived, they were all with one accord in one place. Go forth from Babylon! Flee from the Chaldeans! With a voice of singing, declare, proclaim this, utter it to the end of the earth; say, "The LORD has redeemed his servant,

Jacob." He that remains in this city shall die by the sword, and by the famine, and by the pestilence: but he that flees out, and falls to the Chaldeans that besiege you, he shall live, and his life shall be to him as his reward (traditors, 2 Thess 2:3). For whosoever will save his life shall lose it: but whosoever will lose his life for my sake, the same shall save it.

As Babylon has caused the slain of Israel to fall, so at Babylon shall fall the slain of all the earth. "There is no peace to the wicked," says the LORD. But they that covet wealth fall into temptation and a snare, and into many foolish and harmful desires, which plunge man into demise and perdition. All too well you reject the commandments of God, that you may keep your traditions. You always resist the Holy Spirit; as your fathers did, so do you. Sit in silence and go to darkness, O daughter of the Chaldeans: for you shall no more be called the lady of kingdoms.

Your covenant with death shall be disannulled, and your agreement with hell shall not stand; when the overflowing scourge shall pass through, then you shall be trodden down by it. But of that day and hour knows no man, not the angels in heaven, neither the Son, but only the LORD.

26. Rejection of National Israel

(Ezk. 36:4; 2 Ki. 17:17-20; Ezk. 7:2; Mal. 4:6; Gal. 3:13; 2 Cor. 5:21; Ac. 14:2; Jer. 9:25, 26; 2 Chr. 7:20-22; 24:20; 25:7, 8; Am. 2:5-7; Heb. 10:29; Mic. 3:10; Zec. 14:3, 4; Mt. 27:51, 54; Lk. 21:37)

Therefore, you mountains of Israel, hear the word of the Lord GOD. Thus says the Lord GOD to the mountains, and to the hills, to the rivers, and to the valleys, to the desolate wastes, and to the cities that are forsaken, which became a prey and derision to the residue of the heathen that surround them: for they caused their sons and their daughters to walk upon the fire, and used divination and enchantments, and sold themselves to do evil in the sight of the LORD, to provoke him to anger. Therefore, the LORD was very angry with Israel, and removed them out of his sight: there was none remaining but the tribe of Judah only.

But Judah kept not the commandments of the LORD their God but walked in the statutes of Israel which they made; and the LORD rejected all the seed of Israel, and afflicted them, and delivered them into the hand of spoilers, until he had cast them out of his sight. Thus says the Lord GOD to the land of Israel; "An end, the end is come upon the four corners of the land." Then I shall turn the heart of the fathers to the children, and the heart of the children to their fathers, unless I come and smite the earth with a curse. Christ redeemed us from the curse of the law by becoming a curse for us. As it is written: "Cursed is everyone who is hung on a tree." For our sake he made him to be sin who knew no sin, so that in him we might become the righteousness of God.

But the unbelieving Jews stirred up the Gentiles and poisoned their minds against the brethren. "Behold, the days are coming," says the Lord, "that I will punish all who are circumcised with the uncircumcised; Egypt, Judah, Edom, the people of Ammon, Moab, and all who are in the farthest corners, who dwell in the wilderness. For all these nations are uncircumcised and all the house of Israel are uncircumcised in their heart."

I will uproot Israel from my land, which I have given them, and will reject this temple I have consecrated for my name. I will make it a byword and an object of ridicule among all peoples. Though this temple is now so imposing, all who pass by will be appalled and say, "Why has the LORD done such a thing to this land and to this temple?" People will answer, "Because they have forsaken the LORD, the God of their fathers, who brought them out of Egypt, and have embraced lower gods, worshipping and serving them: that is why he brought all this catastrophe upon them."

Thus says God: "Why do you transgress the commandments of the LORD, so that you cannot prosper? Because you have forsaken the LORD, he also has forsaken you." Do not let the army of Israel go with you, for the LORD is not with Israel, God shall make you fall before the enemy; for God has power to help and to overthrow.

I will send fire upon Judah that will consume the fortresses of Jerusalem. They sell the righteous for silver, and the needy for a pair of sandals. They trample on the heads of the poor as upon the dust of the ground and they deny justice to the oppressed. Of how much worse punishment, do you consider, shall they be thought deserving, who have trodden down the Sons of God, and have accounted the blood of the covenant by which they are sanctified as an unholy thing, and have done spitefully against the Spirit of Christ? They establish Zion upon blood, and Jerusalem with iniquity. The LORD will go forth and fight against those nations, as when he fights on a day of battle.

In that day his feet will stand on the Mount of Olives, which is in front of Jerusalem on the east; and the Mount of Olives will be split in its middle from east to west by a very large valley, so that half of the mountain will move toward the north and the other half toward the south. Behold, the veil of the temple was torn in two from top to bottom, and the earth shook; and the rocks were split. Now, when they saw the earthquakes and the things that were happening, they became very frightened and said, "Truly this was the Son of God!" Each day Jesus was teaching at the temple, and every evening he went out to spend the night on the hill called the Mount of Olives.

27. Unifying Divisions

(Ezk. 22:19, 20; Rev. 21:2; Gal. 4:26; 1 Pet 3:5; 1 Tim. 2:13; 2 Cor. 11:2; Eph. 5:23; 1 Ki. 10:19; Zec. 4:14; Isa. 31:4; Zec. 4:2, 3; Rev. 11:4, 11; Eph. 2:15, 16; Lk. 16:26)

Therefore, thus says the Lord GOD; because you have all become dross, behold, therefore I will gather you into the midst of Jerusalem. As they gather silver, and brass, and iron, and lead, and tin, into the midst of the furnace, to blow the fire upon it, to melt it; so will I gather you in my anger and in my fury, and I will leave you there, and melt you.

The holy city, New Jerusalem, descended from God out of heaven, prepared as a bride adorned for her husband. This is allegorically speaking: for these are two covenants. As it is written, Abraham had two sons, one by a bondmaid, the other by a freewoman. But the Jerusalem above is free; she is our mother. So, brethren, we are not children of the bondwoman, but of the free. After this manner in the old times the holy women also, who trusted in God, adorned themselves, being in subjection to their own husbands.

For Adam was formed first, then Eve. I am jealous for you with a godly jealousy. I promised you to one husband, to Christ, so that I might present you as a pure virgin to him. For the husband is the head of the wife as Christ is the head of the denominations, his body; of which he is the savior.

There were six steps to the throne, and a round top on the throne at its back, and two lions standing beside the armrests. These are the two anointed ones, who stand beside the LORD of the entire earth. Like the lion and the young lion roaring on his prey: so shall the LORD of hosts come down to fight for mount Zion. There is a lampstand of solid gold with a bowl on top of it, and on the stand seven lamps with seven pipes to the seven lamps. Two olive trees are by it, one at the right of the bowl and the other at its left. These are the two olive trees and the two lampstands standing before the God of the earth [Christianity and Islam]. Now after the three-and-a-half days the breath of life from God entered them, and they stood on their feet, and great fear fell on those who saw them.

Having abolished in his flesh the enmity, even the law of statutes in ordinances; for to make in himself of two [theologians and seculars] one new man, so making peace; and that he might reconcile both to God in one body by the cross, having slain the enmity thereby. Beside all this, between us and you there is a great abyss: so that they which would pass from here to you cannot; neither can they pass from there to us.

28. Recompense of Unrighteousness

(1 Cor. 15:40; Hos. 4:6, 7; Ps. 37:14-16; 109:16, 17; 9:18; 72:12-14; Isa. 41:17; Ezk. 22:29; 2 Pet. 2:9, 10; Prov. 18:13; Ps. 78:59; 50:5, 7; Isa. 9:12; 10:20; Jer. 2:26, 28; 23:14, 39; Rev. 3:2, 3; 1 Jn. 2:9; Mt. 16:19)

There are celestial bodies, and terrestrial bodies: the glory of the celestial is one, and the glory of the terrestrial is another. My people are destroyed for lack of science: because you have rejected science, I will also reject you, that you shall be no priest to me: seeing you have forgotten the law of your God, I will also forget your children. As they were increased, so they sinned against me: therefore, I will change their glory into shame.

The wicked have drawn out the sword and have bent their bow to cast down the poor and needy, and to slay such as are of upright conversation. Their sword shall enter into their own heart, and their bows shall be broken. A little that a righteous man has is better than the riches of many wicked. Because that he remembered not to show mercy, but persecuted the poor and needy man, that he might even slay the broken in heart. As he loved cursing, so let it come to him: as he delighted not in blessing, so let it be far from him. For the needy shall not always be forgotten: the expectation of the poor shall not perish forever. For God shall deliver the needy when he cries; the poor also, and him that has no helper. He shall spare the poor and needy, and shall save the souls of the needy. He shall redeem their soul from deceit and violence: and precious shall their blood be in his sight. When the poor and needy seek water, and there is none, and their tongue fails for thirst, the LORD will hear them, the God of Israel will not forsake them.

The people of the land have used oppression, committed robbery, and mistreated the poor and needy; and they wrongfully oppress the stranger. But the Lord knows how to deliver the godly out of temptations and to reserve the unjust under punishment for the day of judgment, and especially those who walk according to the flesh in the lust of uncleanness and despise authority. They are presumptuous, self-willed, they are not afraid to speak evil of dignity. He who answers a matter before he hears it, to him it is folly and shame.

When God heard this, he was wroth, and greatly abhorred Israel. Gather my saints together to me; those that have made a covenant with me by sacrifice. Hear, O my people, and I will speak O Israel, and I will testify against you: I am God, even your God. The Syrians before, and the Philistines behind; and they shall devour Israel with gaping jaws. For all this his anger is not turned away, but his hand is stretched out still. Thus, it shall come to pass in that day, that the remnant of Israel, and such as have escaped of the house of Jacob, shall no more again stay upon him that smote them; but shall stay upon the LORD, the Holy One of Israel, in truth. As the thief is ashamed when he is found, so is the house of Israel ashamed;

they, their kings, their princes, their priests, and their prophets. But where are your gods that you have made for yourselves? Let them arise, if they can save you in the time of your trouble: for according to the number of your cities are your gods, O Judah.

I have seen also in the prophets of Jerusalem a horrible thing: they commit adultery and walk in lies: they strengthen also the hands of evildoers, that none returns from his wickedness. They are all of them to me as Sodom, and the inhabitants thereof as Gomorrah. Therefore, behold, I, even I, will utterly forget you, and I will forsake you, and the city that I gave you and your fathers, and cast you out of my presence. Be watchful, and strengthen the things which remain, that are ready to die: for I have not found your works replete before God. Remember therefore how you have received and heard, and hold fast, and reconsider. He that says he is of the light, and hates his brother, is in darkness even until now. Whatsoever you shall bind on earth shall be bound in heaven: and whatsoever you shall release on earth shall be released in heaven.

29. The Offering

(Jn. 10:7-9; Mt. 3:1, 2; Jn. 1:36; Lev. 23:5; Mk. 13:28; Mt. 26:2; Dan. 9:27; Heb. 13:12; 10:12; Ezk. 45:21; Jn. 6:48-50; 1 Cor. 5:6, 7; Isa. 52:14; Nah. 1:9)

Therefore, Jesus said again, "I tell you the truth, I am the gate for the congregations. Those who came before me were thieves and robbers, but the disciples did not listen to them. I am the gate; whoever enters through me will be saved. He will come in and go out and find dominion." In those days John the Baptist was preaching in the wilderness of Judea, and saying, "Repent, for the kingdom of heaven is at hand." Looking at Jesus as he walked, he said, "Behold the Lamb of God!" The LORD's Passover begins at twilight on the fourteenth day of the first month [the week of Easter]. Now learn the parable of a fig tree; "When its branch is yet tender, and puts forth leaves, you know that summer is near." You know that after two days is the Passover, and the Son of Man will be delivered up to be crucified. Then he shall confirm a covenant with many for one week; but in the middle of the week, he shall bring an end to sacrifice and offering. Therefore, Jesus also, that he could sanctify the people with his own blood, suffered outside the gate. But this man, after he had offered one sacrifice for sins forever, sat down at the right hand of God.

The Passover is a feast lasting seven days, during which you shall eat bread made without leavening: I am that bread of life. Your fathers did eat manna in the wilderness and are dead. But this is the bread which descends from heaven, that a man may eat thereof, and not die. Your boasting is not good. Do you not know that a little leaven raises the whole loaf? Remove the old leaven, that you may be a new loaf as this is unleavened. For Christ our Passover also has been sacrificed. Just as many were astonished at you, so his visage was marred more than any man, and his form more than the sons of man. What do you contrive against the LORD? He will make an utter end of it. Affliction will not rise up a second time.

30. The Foundation of the World

(2 Sam. 12:1-3; Lk. 16:21; 2 Sam. 12:4; Jn. 19:14; 2 Sam. 12:5, 6; Rev. 5:13; Mk. 9:12; Dan. 9:26; Mk. 14:27, 28; Dan. 11:4; Jn. 18:36; Isa. 53:7, 8; 57:1; Mic. 7:2; Isa. 53:12; Heb. 2:8; Ac. 1:7; Lk. 12:15; Jb. 2:4; Mt. 16:26; Ecc. 5:16; Lk. 22:36, 37; Mt. 10:34; Lk. 21:22; 24:44, 45; Isa. 28:19; Dan. 11:2, 3; Jas. 5:7; Rev. 22:14; Isa. 31:6, 9; Rev. 1:17; 22:13; 1:18; 6:8; 9:11; Mk. 13:27)

There were two men in a certain town, one rich and the other poor. The rich man had an exceptionally large number of sheep and cattle, but the poor man had nothing except one lamb he had bought. He raised it, and it grew up with him and his children. It shared his food, drank from his cup and even slept in his arms; and desperate to eat what fell from the rich man's table, even the dogs came and licked his sores. Then a traveler came to the rich man, who refused to take from his own flock and from his own herd to prepare one for the traveling man who had come to him; but he took the poor man's lamb and slaughtered it for the traveler who had come to him.

It was the preparation of the Passover, and about the sixth hour: and he said to the Jews, "Behold your King!" David burned with anger against the man and said, "As surely as the LORD lives, the man who did this deserves to die!" "He shall restore the lamb fourfold, because he did this thing, and because he had no pity." Thus, every creature which is in heaven and on the earth and under the earth and such as are in the sea, and all that are with them, I heard saying: "Blessing and honor and glory and power be to him who sits on the throne, and to the Lamb, forever and ever!" Thus, he answered and told them how it is written of the Son of Man, that he must suffer many things, and be set at naught. Then after the sixty-two weeks the Christ will be cut off and have nothing, and the people of the prince who is to come will destroy the city and the sanctuary, and it ends with a flood; even to the end there will be war: desolations are determined.

As Jesus said to them, "All of you shall be offended because of me this night: for it is written, 'I will smite the shepherd, and the sheep shall be scattered.' But after that I am risen." Then when he has arisen, his kingdom shall be broken up and divided toward the four winds of heaven, but not among his posterity nor according to his dominion with which he ruled; for his kingdom shall be uprooted, even for others beside those. Jesus answered, "My kingdom is not of this world. If my kingdom was of this world, then my servants would be fighting, that I might not be delivered to the Jews; but as it is, my kingdom Is not of this realm."

He was oppressed and he was afflicted, yet he opened not his mouth; he was led as a lamb to the slaughter, and as a sheep before its shearers is silent, so he opened not his mouth. Who will declare his generation? For he was cut off from the land of the living; for the transgressions of my people, he was stricken. The righteous perishes, and no man takes it to heart; merciful men are taken away, while no one considers that the righteous is taken away from evil. The good perished out of the earth: and there is none upright among men: they all lie in wait for blood; they hunt every man his brother with a net. He poured out his soul until death, and he was numbered with the transgressors; he suffered the sin of many and made intercession for the transgressors.

For in that he put all in subjection under him, he left nothing that is not put under him. But now we see not yet all things put under him. As he said to them, "It is not for you to know times or seasons which the LORD has placed in his own authority." "Take heed and beware of covetousness, for one's life does not consist in the abundance of the things he possesses. Skin for skin, yea, all that a man has will he give for his life. For what profit is it to a man if he gains the entire world, and loses his own soul? Or what will a man give in exchange for his soul?" This too is a grievous evil: as a man enters, so he departs, and what does he gain, since he strives for the wind?

Jesus said to them, "But now, he who has a money bag, let him take it, and likewise a knapsack; and he who has no sword, let him sell his garment and buy one. For I say to you that this which is written must still be accomplished in me. For the things concerning me have an end." "Do not suppose that I have come to bring peace to the earth. I come not to bring peace, but a sword." "For these are the days of vengeance, that all things that are written must be fulfilled." Now he says to them, "These are my words which I spoke to you while I was still with you, that all things which are written about me in the Law of Moses and the Prophets, and the Psalms must be fulfilled." Then he opened their minds to understand the scriptures. It shall be a vexation only to understand the report.

Now I will tell you the truth: "Behold, in Persia the fourth mighty king shall arise, who shall rule with great dominion. By his strength through his powers, he stirred up all against the realm of Grecia." Behold, the reaper waits for the precious fruit of the earth, and has long patience for it, until he receives the early and latter rain. Blessed are they that perfect their doctrine, that they may have right to the tree of life and may enter in through the gates into the city. "Return to him against whom the children of Israel have deeply revolted," says the LORD, whose fire is in Zion and his furnace in Jerusalem. When I saw him, I fell at his feet as dead. But he laid his right hand on me, saying to me, "Do not be afraid; I am Alaph thru Taw, the beginning and the end, the first and the last, he who lives and was dead, and behold: I am alive forevermore, and I have the keys of death and of hell." So, I looked, and behold, a grizzled horse; the name of him who sat on it was Death, and hell followed with him. They had as king over them the angel of the infinite void. Then shall he send his angels and shall gather together his chosen from the four winds, from the uttermost part of the earth to the uttermost part of heaven. Be patient therefore, until the coming of the Lord.

31. Sword of Condemnation

(Isa. 4:4; 8:12; 10:1, 2, 22, 23; Ezk. 6:10; Isa. 24:23; Mk. 8:38; Mic. 5:3; Isa. 9:6, 7; Nah. 1:2; Rom. 13:4; 8:34; 1 Jn. 1:9, 10; Jer. 2:35, 36; 1 Cor. 6:7, 8; Jer. 22:13; Mt. 25:45; Isa. 19:2, 4, 23; Ezk. 5:12)

Then the Lord shall have washed away the filth of the daughters of Zion and shall have purged the blood of Jerusalem from the midst thereof by the spirit of judgment, and by the spirit of burning. Say not, "A confederacy," to all of them to whom this people shall say, "A confederacy;" neither fear intimidation, nor be afraid.

Woe to those who make unjust laws, to those who issue oppressive decrees, to deprive the poor of their rights and withhold justice from the oppressed of my people, making widows their prey and robbing the fatherless. Though your people of Israel are like the sand by the sea, only a remnant will return. Destruction has been decreed, overwhelming and righteous. The Lord, the LORD Almighty, will carry out the destruction decreed upon the whole land. They shall know that I am the LORD, and that I have not said in vain that I would do this evil against them. Then the moon shall be confounded, and the sun ashamed, when the LORD of hosts shall reign in mount Zion, and in Jerusalem, and before his ancients gloriously.

Whosoever therefore shall be ashamed of me and of my words in this adulterous and sinful generation; of him also shall the Son of Man be ashamed, when he rises in the power of his LORD with the holy angels. Therefore, he shall give them up, until the time that she who is in labor has given birth; then the remnant of his brethren shall return to the children of Israel. For to us a child is born, to us a son is given, and the government will be on his shoulders. He will reign on David's throne and over his kingdom, establishing and upholding it with justice and righteousness from that time on and forever. The zeal of the LORD Almighty will accomplish this. God is zealous, and the LORD avenges; the LORD avenges, and is furious; the LORD will take vengeance on his adversaries, and he reserves wrath for his enemies.

For he is God's servant to you for good. But if you do wrong, be afraid, for he wields the sword, not in vain. He is God's servant, an agent of wrath to bring punishment on the wrongdoers. Who is he who condemns? It is Christ who died, and furthermore is also risen, who is even at the right hand of God, who also makes intercession for us. If we confess our sins, he is faithful and righteous to forgive us our sins and to cleanse us from all unrighteousness. If we say that we have not sinned, we called him a liar, and his word is not in us. Yet you said, "I am innocent; surely his anger is turned away from me." Behold, I will enter into judgment with you because you say, "I have not sinned."

Why do you go around so much changing your way? Now therefore there is utterly a fault among you because you go to law one with another. No, you do wrong, and defraud, and that your brethren. Woe to him who builds his house by unrighteousness and his chambers by injustice, who uses his neighbor's service without wages and gives him nothing for his work. Truly I say to you, "To the extent that you did it not to one of the least of these, you did it not to me."

I set the Egyptians against the Egyptians: and they fight every one against his brother, and every one against his neighbor; city against city, and kingdom against kingdom. Then the Egyptians I gave over into the hand of a cruel lord; and a fierce king to rule over them, says the Lord, the LORD of hosts. In that day shall there be a highway out of Egypt to Assyria, and the Assyrian shall come into Egypt, and the Egyptian into Assyria, and the Egyptians shall serve with the Assyrians. But the third part of you shall die with the pestilence, and with famine shall they be consumed in the midst of you: and a third part shall fall by the sword around you; and I will scatter a third part into all the winds, and I will draw out a sword after them.

32. Exporting Revolution

(Mt. 7:28; Jn. 12:42, 48; Mk. 3:29; 1 Thess. 5:3; Jn. 16:21; Rev. 12:17; 2:23; Hos. 2:4; 9:16; Lk. 21:23; Jer. 4:31; Isa. 52:2, 3; Rev. 12:2, 5, 13; Mic. 4:8; Lam. 4:22; Hos. 1:4, 5; Zec. 11:10, 11; Hos. 1:6; Rom. 1:25; Lam. 4:7; Hos. 1:8, 9; Jl. 3:14; Zec. 11:14; Jer. 34:10; Hos. 2:23; 1:11; Isa. 54:5)

It came to pass, when Jesus had ended these sayings, the people were astonished at his doctrine. Nevertheless, even among the leaders many believed in him, but because of the Pharisees they did not confess, or else they would be put out of the synagogue. He that rejects me, and accepts not my words, has one that judges him: the word that I have spoken, the same shall judge him in the last day. But he who blasphemes against the Holy Spirit never has forgiveness but is subject to eternal condemnation. While they are saying, "Peace and safety" then destruction will come upon them suddenly like birth pangs upon a woman with child; and they shall not escape.

Whenever a woman is in travail she has sorrow, because her hour has come; but when she gives birth to the child, she remembers the anguish no more, for joy that a child has been born into the world. The dragon was enraged with the woman and went to make war with the remnant of her seed, which keep the commandments of God, and have the testimony of Jesus Christ. I will kill her children with death, and all the churches shall know that I am he who searches the motivation and intent, and I will give to each one of you according to your works. I will not have mercy on her children, for they are the children of harlotry. Their root is dried up, they shall yield no fruit: yes, though they bring forth, yet will I slay even the beloved in their womb. But woe to those who are pregnant and to those who are nursing babies in those days! For there will be great distress in the land and wrath upon these people. For I have heard a voice as of a woman in labor, the anguish as of her who brings forth her first child, the voice of the daughter of Zion bewailing herself; she spreads her hands, saying, "Woe is me now, for my soul is weary because of murderers!"

Shake yourself from the dust, rise up, O captive Jerusalem; loosen yourself from the chains around your neck, O captive daughter of Zion. For thus says the LORD, "You were sold for nothing, and you will be redeemed without money." Then being with child, she cried out in labor and in pain to give birth. She bore a male child who was to rule all nations with a rod of iron, and her child was caught up to God and his throne. Now when the dragon saw that he had been sent down to the earth, he persecuted the woman who gave birth to the male child. Then you, O tower of the flock, the stronghold of the daughter of Zion, to you shall it come, even the former dominion shall come, the kingdom of the daughter of Jerusalem. The punishment of your iniquity is accomplished, O daughter of Zion; he will no longer send you into captivity. He will punish your iniquity; he will uncover your sins. Call his name Jezreel, for in a short time I will avenge the bloodshed of Jezreel on the house of subsistence and bring an end to the kingdom of the house of Israel. It shall come to pass in that day that I will break the bow of Israel in the valley of Jezreel. I took my staff of approval, and cut it asunder, that I might break my covenant which I had made with all the people. It was broken in that day: and so, the poor of the flock that waited upon me knew that it was the word of the LORD. Then she conceived again and bore a daughter. Then God said: "Call her name Loruhamah, for I will no longer have mercy on the house of Israel, but I will utterly take them away"; who changed the truth of God into a lie and worshipped and served the creature more than the creator, who is blessed forever.

Her Nazarites were whiter than milk, and polished like sapphire. Now when she had weaned Loruhamah, she conceived and bore a son. Then God said: "Call his name Loammi, for you are not my people, and I will not be your God." Multitudes, in the valley of decision: for the day of the LORD is near in the valley of decision. Then I cut asunder my staff of bondage, that I might break the brotherhood between Israel and Judah [north and south, rich and poor]. Now when all the princes, and all the people, which had entered into the covenant, heard that everyone should let his manservant, and everyone his maidservant, go free, that none should serve them anymore, then they obeyed, and let them go. Then I will sow her for myself in the earth, and I will have mercy on her who had not obtained mercy; then I will say to those who were not my people, "You are my people" and they shall say, "You are my God." Then shall the children of Judah and the children of Israel be gathered together, and appoint themselves one head, and they shall rise up out of the land: for great shall be the day of Jezreel. God of the whole earth shall he be called.

33. The Old World

(Mk. 9:4,8; Dan. 8:3; Lk. 23:27, 32, 43; Dan. 8:20; Jn. 19:15; Lk. 2:2; Dan. 8:21, 6, 7; Rev. 11:8; Dan. 8:7, 8; 7:3, 7, 8; Rev. 13:11; Dan. 8:10; Rev. 13:2; Jer. 21:10; Ezk. 38:10; Jb. 41:27, 31-33; Dan. 11:32; Prov. 26:24-28; Rev. 11:3; Dan. 12:11, 12; 8:14; Mt. 12:42; Dan. 11:7, 9; Rev. 10:2, 3; Jer. 6:10; Isa. 28:13; 2 Tim. 3:16; Mk. 13:10)

There before them were the apparitions of Elijah and Moses, who were talking with Jesus. All at once they looked around and saw no one with them anymore, except Jesus alone. Then I lifted my eyes and saw, and there, standing beside the river, was a ram which had two horns, and the two horns were high; but one was higher than the other, and the higher one came up last. A great multitude of the people followed him, and women also, who mourned and lamented him. There were also two others, malefactors, led with him to be put to death. Then Jesus said to them, "Verily I say to you, 'Today you shall be with me in paradise.'" The ram which you saw, has the two horns, which are the kings of Media and Persia. The chief priests answered, "We have no king but Caesar." It was the first enrollment. The male goat is the kingdom of Greece. The large horn that is between its eyes is the first king. Then he came to the ram that had two horns, which I had seen standing beside the river, and ran at him with furious power. There I saw him confronting the ram; he was moved with rage against him, attacked the ram, and broke his two horns. Their bodies will lie in the street of the great city, which is figuratively called Sodom and Egypt, where also their Lord was crucified. There was no power in the ram to withstand him, but he cast him down to the ground and trampled him; and there was no one that could deliver the ram from his hand. Therefore, the male goat grew very great; but when he became strong, the large horn was broken, and in place of it four notable ones came up toward the four winds of heaven [Monarchy, Democracy, Communism, Capitalism]. The four great beasts came up from the sea, diverse one from another.

After that, in my night visions I looked, and there before me was the fourth beast. I was considering the horns, and there was another little horn, coming up among them, before whom three of the first horns were plucked out by the roots: and there, in this horn, were eyes like the eyes of a man, and a mouth speaking boastful words [Trump]. I saw that beast coming up out of the earth; and he had two horns like a lamb, and he spoke as a dragon [Biden]. It grew up to the host of heaven; and it cast down some of the host and some of the stars to the ground and trampled them. The beast I saw resembled a leopard but had feet like those of a bear and a mouth like that of a lion. The dragon gave the beast his power and his throne and great authority. "For I have set my face against this city for adversity and not for good," says the LORD. "It was given into the hand of the King of Babylon, and it shall burn with fire."

This is what the Lord GOD says: "In that day, thoughts arise in your mind, and you devised an evil scheme."

He regards iron as straw, and bronze as rotten wood. He makes the depths churn like a boiling caldron and stirs up the sea like a pot of ointment. Behind him he leaves a glistening wake; nothing on earth is his equal, a creature without fear. Such as do wickedly against the covenant shall he corrupt by flatteries. He that hates, dissembles with his lips, and lays up deceit within him. When he speaks fairly, believe him not: for there are seven abominations in his heart. Whose hatred is covered by deceit, his wickedness shall be shown before the whole audience. Whoso digs a pit shall fall therein: and he that rolls the stone, it will return upon him. A lying tongue hates those who are afflicted by it; and a flattering mouth works ruin. But I will give power to my two witnesses, and they will prophesy one thousand two hundred and sixty days, clothed in sackcloth. From the time that the continuation shall be interrupted, and the abomination of desolation is set up, there shall be one thousand two hundred and ninety days. Blessed is he who waits and comes to the one thousand three hundred and thirty-five days. Two thousand three hundred days; then the sanctuary shall be cleansed.

The Queen of the South will rise at the judgment with this generation and condemn it; for she came from the ends of the earth to listen to Solomon's wisdom, and now one greater than Solomon is here. But from a branch of her roots, one shall arise in his place, who shall come with an army, enter the fortress of the king of the north, and deal with them and prevail. So, the king of the south shall come into his kingdom and shall return into his own land. He had a little book open in his hand, and he set his right foot on the sea and his left foot on the land, and cried with a loud voice, as when a lion roars. When he cried out, seven thunders uttered their voices.

To whom shall I speak and give warning, that they may hear? Behold, the word of the LORD is a reproach to them; they have no delight in it. The word of the LORD was to them, precept upon precept, precept upon precept, line upon line, line upon line; here a little, there a little, that they might go and fall backward, and be broken and snared and caught. All Scripture is inspired by

God, and is beneficial for doctrine, for reproof, for correction, for instruction in righteousness; that the servants of God may be complete, thoroughly prepared for every good work. And the good word must first be published among all nations.

34. The New World

(Rev. 19:11, 14; 9:7-9, 17; 14:5; 15:5; 14:13; Mk. 9:40; Ezk. 26:15-17; 38:8; Rev. 7:14; Isa. 19:20)

Now I saw heaven opened, and behold, a white horse: and he who sat on him was called faithful and true, and in righteousness he judges and makes war. The armies in heaven, clothed in fine linen, white and clean, followed him on white horses, like horses prepared for battle. On their heads were crowns like gold, and their faces were like faces of men. Their hair was cut like women's hair, and their teeth were like lions' teeth. They had breastplates like iron, and the sound of their wings was like the sound of chariots with many horses running into battle. Thus, I saw the horses in the vision: those who sat on them had breastplates of fire, hyacinth blue, and sulfur; and the heads of the horses were like the heads of lions; and out of their mouths came fire, smoke, and brimstone. In their mouth was found no deceit, for they are without fault before the throne of God.

After this I looked and in heaven the temple, that is, the tabernacle of the testimony, was opened. Then I heard a voice from heaven, saying, "Write, 'Blessed are the dead who die in the Lord from now on!'" "Yea," says the Spirit, "that they may rest from their labors, for their deeds follow with them." For he who is not against us is on our side. Then shall the islands shake at the sound of your fall, when the wounded cry, when the slaughter is fulfilled in your midst. Then all the princes of the coast will step down from their thrones. Clothed with terror, they will sit on the ground, trembling every moment, appalled at you. They shall take up a lamentation for you, and say to you, "How are you destroyed, that was inhabited of seafaring men, the renowned city, which was strong in the sea, she and her inhabitants, which cause their horror to be on all that haunt it."

After many days you shall be visited: in the latter years you shall come into the land that is brought back from the sword, and is gathered out of many people, against the mountains of Israel, which have always been waste: but it is brought forth out of the nations, and they shall dwell safely all of them. These are they that return from the great tribulation, and they washed their robes, and made them white in the blood of Christ. They will cry to the LORD because of the oppressors, and he will send them a savior and a mighty one, and he will deliver them: and they shall return even to the LORD, and he shall be entreated of them, and shall heal them.

35. Era of Healing

(Mt. 4:23, 24; 15:30, 31; Mk. 6:13; Lk. 4:40; 6:18, 19; 9:11; Mk. 16:15-19; Ac. 4:13; Isa. 35:5, 6; Ps. 24:3-5)

Jesus went about all Galilee, teaching in their synagogues, and preaching the gospel of the kingdom, and healing all manner of sickness and all manner of disease among the people; and his reputation went throughout all Syria: and they brought to him all sick people that were taken with diverse diseases and ailments, and those which were possessed with devils, and those which were lunatics, and those that had the palsy; and he healed them. Multitudes came to him, having with them those that were lame, blind, dumb, maimed, and many others, and cast them down at Jesus' feet; and he healed them. Inasmuch that the multitude wondered, when they saw the dumb to speak, the maimed to be whole, the lame to walk, and the blind to see: they glorified the God of Israel. Then they cast out many devils, and anointed with balm many that were sick, and healed them. Now when the sun was setting, all they that had any sick with diverse diseases brought them to him; and he laid his hands on every one of them and healed them. They that were vexed with unclean spirits: even they were healed. The whole multitude sought to touch him: for there went virtue out of him and healed them all. Then the people, when they knew it, followed him: and he received them, and spoke to them of the kingdom of God, and healed them that had need of healing [naturopathic holistic medicine].

These signs shall follow them that believe; "In my name shall they cast out devils; they shall speak with new languages; they shall pick up serpents; and if they drink any deadly thing, it shall not harm them. They shall lay hands on the sick, and they shall recover."

So then after the Lord had spoken to them, he was received up into heaven, and sat at the right hand of God. Now when they saw the boldness of Peter and John, and perceived that they were uneducated and untrained men, they were amazed; and they noted that they had been with Jesus.

Then the eyes of the blind shall be opened, and the ears of the deaf shall be unstopped. Then the lame shall leap like a deer, and the tongue of the dumb sing.

For waters shall burst forth in the wilderness, and streams in the desert. Who may ascend into the hill of the LORD, and who may stand in his holy place? He who has clean hands and a pure heart, who has not lifted up his soul to falsehood, and has not sworn deceitfully. He shall receive a blessing from the LORD and righteousness from the God of his salvation.

36. Second Resurrection

(Jn. 5:28, 29; Rev. 20:5, 7-9; Lk. 17:29, 30; Ps. 11:6; 2 Thess. 1:9; Rev. 2:23; Jn. 8:15, 16; Lk. 12:5; Jn. 5:43; Jer. 32:27)

Do not marvel at this; for the hour is coming in which all who are in the graves will hear his voice and come forth: those who have done good, to the resurrection of life, and those who have done evil, to the resurrection of condemnation. But the remainder of the dead did not live again until the thousand years were finished. When the thousand years are expired, Satan shall be released from his prison, and shall go out to deceive the nations which are in the four quarters of the earth, Gog and Magog, to gather them together to battle: the number of whom is as the sand of the sea. They marched across the breadth of the earth and surrounded the shelter of God's people, the city he loves. But fire came down from heaven and devoured them.

The same day that Lot went out of Sodom it rained fire and brimstone from heaven and destroyed them all. Even thus shall it be in the day when the Son of Man is revealed. On the wicked he will rain fiery coals and burning sulfur; a scorching wind will be their allotment. These shall be punished with everlasting destruction from the presence of the Lord and from the glory of his power. I am he, which searches the reins and hearts: and I will give to every one of you according to your works.

You judge after the flesh; I judge no one, and yet if I judge, my judgment is true: for I am not alone, but it is I and the LORD that sent me. But I warn you whom to fear: fear the one who after he has killed, has authority to cast into hell; yes, I tell you, fear him. I came to you in the LORD's name, and you received me not: if another shall come to you in his own name, him you will receive. Behold, I am the LORD, the God of all flesh: is there anything too difficult for me?

37. The Rise of Dominion

(Mt. 4:4; 23:20; Jn. 4:32; Mt. 10:35, 36, 37, Heb. 5:12; 1 Cor. 14:34; Ps. 29:4, 7, 8; Mt. 13:33; Heb. 9:22; 1 Cor. 5:6; Gen. 2:16, 17; 3:3, 4, 13, 14, 16-19; Mk. 8:15; Lev. 17:11; Heb. 10:26)

It is written, "Man shall not live by bread alone, but by every word that proceeds from the mouth of God." Therefore, anyone who swears by the altar swears by it and by everything on it. I have food to eat that you know not of. For I have come to set a man against his father, a daughter against her mother, and a daughter-in-law against her mother-in-law; and a man's enemies will be those of his own household. He who loves father or mother more than me is not worthy of me. And he who loves son or daughter more than me is not worthy of me.

You have need of one to teach you again what is the beginning of the principles from the oracles of God. The women keep silent in the churches, for they are not permitted to preach, but are to be submissive, as the law also says. The voice of the LORD is powerful; the voice of the LORD is majestic. The voice of the LORD strikes flames of fire. The voice of the LORD shakes the wilderness. The kingdom of heaven is like yeast that a woman took and mixed into a large amount of flour until it worked all through the dough. Do you not know that a little leaven raises the whole loaf?

Of every tree of the garden, you may freely eat; but of the tree of the knowledge of good and evil you shall not eat, for in the day that you eat of it you shall surely die. God has said, "You shall not eat it, nor shall you touch it, lest you die." But the serpent said to the woman, "You will not surely die" [Seed of eras nigh]. The LORD God said to the woman, "What is this you have done?" Then the woman said, "The serpent deceived me, and I ate it." So, the LORD God said to the serpent: "I will put enmity between you and the woman, and between your seed and her seed." To the woman he said: "I will greatly multiply your sorrow and your conception; in pain you shall bring forth children; your desire shall be for your husband, and he shall rule over you." Then to the man he said, "Because you have heeded the voice of your wife, and have eaten from the source of which I commanded you, saying, 'You shall not eat of it': cursed is the ground for your sake; in strife you shall eat of it all the days of your life. Both thorns and thistles it shall bring forth for you, and you shall eat the herb of the field. In the sweat of your face, you shall eat bread until you return to the ground: out of it you were taken; dust you are, and to dust you shall return." Thus, he charged them, saying, "Take heed, beware of the leaven of the Pharisees, and of the leaven of Herod." Almost all things are by the law purged with blood; and without shedding of blood is no remission. For the life of the flesh is in the blood, and I have given it to you upon the altar to make atonement for your souls; for it is the blood that makes atonement for the soul. But if we sin willingly after we receive the knowledge of the truth, there no longer remains a sacrifice for sins.

38. The Cup of Wrath

(Judg. 13:3, 5; Lk. 1:14-16; 7:33; Hab. 1:4; Rev. 3:12; Lev. 21:12; Ps. 112:6; Hab. 1:5; Jn. 12:47; Isa. 33:24; Lk 22:20; Jer. 25:29; Mk. 14:36; Jer. 25:28; Mk. 14:23; Deut. 21:9; 2 Tim. 2:26; Rev. 16:6)

The angel of the LORD appeared to a woman, and said to her, "Behold now, you are barren, and borne not: but you shall conceive, and bear a son. Also, you will have joy and gladness; and many shall rejoice at his birth. For he shall be great in the sight of the Lord and shall drink neither wine nor hard liquor; and he shall be filled with the Holy Spirit, even from his mother's womb. Then many of the children of Israel shall he turn to the Lord their God."

John the Baptist came neither eating bread nor drinking wine; but you say, "He is of the devil." Therefore, the law is delayed, and judgment never goes forth: for the wicked surround the righteous; therefore, wrong judgment prevails. But he who overcomes, I will make him a pillar in the temple of my God, and he will not go out from it anymore; and I will write upon him the name of my God, and the name of the city of my God, *New Jerusalem*, which comes down out of heaven from my God, and my new name [*Jesus Abaddon Christ*]. Neither shall he go out of the sanctuary, nor profane the sanctuary of his God; for the consecration of the anointing oil of his God is upon him: I am the LORD. Surely, he shall not be removed forever: the righteous shall be in everlasting remembrance.

Behold, you among the heathen, and regard, and wonder marvelously: for I will work a work in your days, which you will not believe, though it is told to you. If anyone hears my words, and believes not, I judge him not: for I came not to judge the world, but to save the world. The inhabitant shall not say, "I am sick": the people that dwell therein shall be forgiven their iniquity. This cup is the new covenant in my blood, which is shed for you. For, lo, I begin to bring evil on the city, which is called by my name, and should you be utterly unpunished? You shall not be unpunished: for I will call for a sword upon all the inhabitants of the earth, says the LORD of hosts. Allah, Father, all things are possible for you. Take this cup from me; nevertheless, not what I will, but what you will.

And it shall be, if they refuse to take the cup at your hand to drink, then shall you say to them, "Thus says the LORD of hosts; 'You shall certainly drink.'" Then he took the cup, and when he had given thanks he gave it to them, and they all drank from it. So, you shall remove the guilt of innocent blood from your midst, when you do what is right in the eyes of the LORD; that they may recover themselves out of the snare of their enemy, who are taken captive by him at his will. They shed the blood of saints and prophets; thus, you gave them blood to drink; for they are deserving.

39. Prohibitions

(Jer. 35:6, 16, 17, 15, 19; Lk. 15:22, 32; Mk. 4:17; Mt. 11:6; Lk. 8:15; 2 Tim. 2:15; Eph. 2:20, 21; 1 Cor. 3:4, 11; 1 Jn. 2:1)

But some said, "We will not drink wine, for Jonadab the son of Rechab, our father, commanded us, saying, 'You shall drink no wine, you nor your sons, forever.'" Surely the sons of Jonadab the son of Rechab have performed the commandment of their father, which he commanded them, but this people have not obeyed me. Therefore thus says the LORD God of forces, the God of Israel: "Behold, I will bring on Judah and on all the inhabitants of Jerusalem all the doom that I have pronounced against them; because I have spoken to them but they have not heard, and I have called to them but they have not answered." "I have also sent to you all my servants the prophets, rising up early and sending them, saying, 'Turn now everyone from his evil way, amend your doings, and do not go after lower gods to serve them; then you will dwell in the land which I have given you and your fathers.' But you have not inclined your ear, nor obeyed me."

Therefore, thus says the LORD of hosts, the God of Israel: "Jonadab the son of Rechab shall not lack a man to stand before me forever." But the father said to his servants, "Bring forth the best robe, and put it on him; and put a ring on his hand, and shoes on his feet. It was appropriate that we should rejoice and be glad: for this your brother was dead, and is alive again; and was lost, and is found." They have no root in themselves, and so endure but for a time: afterward, when affliction or persecution arises for the word's sake, immediately they are offended. Blessed is he, whosoever shall not be offended in me. But that on the good ground are they, which in an honest and good heart, having heard the deliberation, keep it, and bring forth fruit with patience.

Be diligent to present yourself approved to God, a worker who does not need to be ashamed, rightly dividing the word of truth. Having been built on the foundation of the apostles and prophets, Jesus Christ himself being the chief corner stone, in whom the whole building, being tightly framed together, expands into a holy temple in the Lord. For when one says, "I am of Paul," and another, "I follow Apollos," are you not man-faced? For no one can lay any foundation other than the one already laid, which is Jesus Christ. These things I write to you, that you sin not. Yet if any man sins, we have an advocate with the LORD, Jesus Christ the righteous.

40. Bread of Life

(Exod. 13:7; Lev. 3:17; Deut. 14:3; Lev. 19:26; Ti. 1:12; 1 Cor. 11:29-31; 1 Tim. 5:22, 23; Ti. 1:13, 14; 1 Cor. 8:10, 13; Jn. 6:33, 48-50)

Unleavened bread shall be eaten seven days. No leavened bread shall be used among you, nor shall leaven be used among you in all your quarters. This shall be a perpetual enactment throughout your generations in all your dwellings. You shall eat neither animal fat nor blood. You shall not eat any detestable thing. Do not consume any food containing *cholesterol*.

Cretans are always liars, evil brutes, bloat bellies. For he that eats and drinks, eats and drinks judgment into himself, if he discerns not the body. For this cause many among you are weak and sickly, and not a few sleep. But if we discern ourselves, we should not be judged. Do not share in the sins of others. Keep yourself pure. Stop drinking water only and use a little wine because of your stomach and your frequent illnesses. This testimony is true. For this cause, reprove them decisively that they may be valid in the faith, not adhering to Jewish myths and instructions of men who turn away from the truth. If anyone with a weak conscience sees you that have this knowledge eating in an idol's temple, would he not be emboldened to eat what is sacrificed to idols? Therefore, if what I eat causes my brother to fall into sin, I will never eat meat again, so that I will not cause him to fall. [Organic vegan standards are recommended.] For the bread of God is he who comes down from heaven and gives life to the world. I am the bread of life. Your fathers ate manna in the wilderness and are dead. But this is the bread which comes down from heaven, that one may eat of it and not die. [Whole multigrain required, and no refined carbohydrates.]

41. Prayer of the Heart

(Mt. 6:7, 8; Mk. 12:38-40; Prov. 4:14-16; 1 Pet. 4:4; 2 Tim. 2:23; Mt. 20:16, 15; 1 Cor. 6:12; Lk. 23:34; Isa. 55:7, 8; Jl. 3:21; Jd. 1:10; Lk. 1:51; Jer. 7:24; 17:9; Mk. 10:21; Jn. 16:33)

When you pray, do not use vain repetitions as the heathen do. For they think that they will be heard for their many words. Therefore, do not be like them, for the LORD knows the things you have need of before you ask him. Beware of the scribes, who desire to go around in long robes, greetings in the marketplaces, the first seats in the synagogues, and the foremost places at feasts, who devour widows' houses and for a pretense make long prayers. These will receive greater condemnation. Enter not into the path of the wicked, walk not in the way of evil men. Avoid it, pass not by it; turn from it, and pass on. For they sleep not, except they do evil; and their sleep is taken away, unless they cause some to fall. Wherein they think it strange that you run not with them to the same excess of disruption, speaking evil of you. But avoid foolish and ignorant disputes, knowing that they generate strife.

So, the last will be first, and the first last. For many are called, but few chosen. Is it not lawful for me to do what I wish with my own things? Or is your eye evil because I am good? All things are lawful for me; but not all things are expedient. All things are lawful for me; but I will not be brought under the power of any. Then said Jesus, "LORD, forgive them; for they know not what they do." Let the wicked forsake his way, and the unrighteous man his thoughts; let him return to the LORD, and he will have mercy on him; and to our God, for he will abundantly pardon. "For my thoughts are not your thoughts, nor are your ways my ways," says the LORD. For I will cleanse their blood that I have not cleansed: for the LORD dwells in Zion.

But these men revile the things which they do not understand; and the things which they know by instinct, like unreasoning animals, by these things they are destroyed. He has shown strength with his arm; he has scattered the proud in the imagination of their hearts. Yet they did not obey or incline their ear but walked in counsels of the imagination of their evil heart and went backward and not forward. The heart is deceitful above all things, and desperately wicked; who can know it?

One thing you lack: go your way, sell whatever you have and give to the poor, and you will have treasure in heaven; and come, take up the cross, and follow me. These things I have spoken to you, that in me you might have peace. In the world you will have tribulation; but be courageous, I have overcome the world.

42. Tithes for the Poor

(Ps. 110:4; Heb. 6:20; 7:5; Ac. 7:53; Heb. 7:6-8; Ac. 20:35; Ti. 3:9; 1 Tim. 1:4, 5; Rom. 12:18)

The LORD has sworn and will not relent, "You are a priest forever according to the order of Melchizedek." Jesus, who went before us, has entered on our behalf. He has become the high priest forever, in the order of Melchizedek. Indeed, those who are of the sons of Levi, who received the priesthood, had authority to receive tithes from the people according to the law, that is, from their brethren, who have received the law by the disposition of angels, and have not kept it. But he whose genealogy is not derived from them received tithes and blessed him who had the promises. Now beyond all contradiction the lesser is blessed by the greater. Here mortal men receive tithes, but there he receives them, of whom it is witnessed that he lives.

I have shown you in every way, by laboring like this, that you must support the weak. So, remember the words of the Lord Jesus, that he said, "It is more blessed to give than to receive." But avoid foolish disputes, genealogies, contentions, and strivings about the law; for they are unprofitable and vain. Nor give heed to fables and endless genealogies, which cause disputes rather than godly edification which is in faith. Now the purpose of the commandments is love from a pure heart, from a good conscience, and from sincere faith. If it is possible, to the best of your ability, live at peace with all people.

43. Charity by Faith

(Jas. 2:12, 13, 15-17; 1 Jn. 3:17; Jn. 5:42; Prov. 30:12, 8; 31:6-9; 1 Pet. 4:8; Lk. 9:62; 1 Cor. 9:10)

Speak and act as those who shall be judged by the law of freedom, because judgment without mercy will be shown to anyone who has not been merciful. Mercy triumphs over judgment. If anyone is without clothing and in need of daily food, and any of you says to them, "Go in peace, be warmed and filled," and yet you do not give them what is needed for the body, what benefit is that? Even so faith if it has no works, is dead, by itself. But whoever has this world's goods, and sees another in need, but closes off *compassion* from him, how does the love of God abide in him? But I know you, that the love of God, you have not in yourselves.

There is a generation that is pure in its own eyes yet is not washed from its filthiness. Remove far from me falsehood and lies; give me neither poverty nor riches; feed me with the food that is needful for me. Give beer to those who are despondent, and wine to those who are in anguish; let them drink and forget their poverty and remember their misery no more. Speak up for those who cannot speak for themselves, for the rights of all who are destitute. Speak up and judge fairly; defend the rights of the poor and needy. Above all things have extensive charity among yourselves: for charity shall cover a multitude of sins. No one, having put his hand to the plow, and looking back, is welcome in the kingdom of God. He who plows should plow in hope, and he who threshes in hope should partake.

44. Real World Treachery

(Rom. 7:23; Jl. 3:5; Ezk. 33:17; 2 Cor. 8:13, 14; Mal. 3:8; Jer. 4:22; Hos. 2:16; Mt. 26:41; Jn. 4:34, 35; Gal. 6:7, 8; Lk. 19:22, 23; 16:9; 2 Tim. 3:1-5; Ps. 109:5; Isa. 24:16; Nah. 3:14, 15)

But I see another law in my members, warring against the law of my mind, and bringing me into captivity to the law of sin which is in my members. For you took my silver and my gold and carried off my finest treasures to your temples. Yet the children of your people say, "The way of the Lord is not fair." But as for them, their way is not fair. Not that othersmight be relieved while you are pressured, but that there might be equality. Will a man rob God? Yet you have robbed me! But you say, "In what way have we robbed you?" In fees and royalties. My people are foolish, they have not known me. They are silly children, and they have no understanding. They are wise to do evil, but to do good they have no knowledge. Yet "It will come about in that day," declares the LORD, "that you will call me 'family' and will no longer call me 'mastery.'"

Watch and pray, that you enter not into temptation: the spirit indeed is willing, but the flesh is weak. My food is to do the will of him that sent me, and to finish his work. Do you not say, there are yet four months, then comes harvest? Behold, I say to you, "Lift up your eyes, and look on the fields; for they are white already to harvest." Be not deceived; God is not mocked: for whatever a man sows, that shall he also reap. For he that sows to his flesh shall of the flesh reap corruption; but he that sows to the Spirit shall of the Spirit reap life everlasting.

"By your own words I will judge you, corrupt servants. You did know that I am an exacting man, taking up what I did not lay down, and reaping what I did not sow. Then why did you not put the money in the bank, and having returned, I would have collected it with interest?" I say to you, "Make yourselves friends with the wealthy of unrighteousness; that, when you fail, they may receive you into everlasting habitations."

But know this, that in the last days perilous times will come. They repay me evil for good, and hatred for my friendship. From the uttermost part of the earth have we heard songs, even power to the righteous. But I said, "My leanness, my leanness, woe to me!" The treacherous dealers have dealt treacherously; yea, the treacherous dealers have dealt very treacherously. Draw water for the siege, strengthen your defenses! Work the clay, tread the mortar, repair the brickwork. There the fire will devour you; the sword will cut you down and, like locusts, consume you.

45. Fires of Destitution

(Isa. 9:15; Ezk. 14:9; Jer. 5:31; Rev. 17:13; Jer. 44:11; Isa. 47:14, 15; Am. 6:7; 3:15; Zec. 1:12; Ezk 7:5-7; Jer 21:12)

The ancient and honorable, is the head; and the prophet that teaches lies, is the tail. If a prophet is deceived when he has spoken a thing, I the LORD have deceived that prophet, and will destroy him from the midst of my people Israel. Their prophets prophesy falsely, and the priests rule by their means; and my people love it: what will you do in the end thereof? They have one purpose and give their power and authority to the beast. Therefore, thus says the LORD of hosts, the God of Israel: "Behold, I will set my face against you for evil, and to cut off all Judaism. Behold, they will be as stubble, the fire shall burn them; they will not deliver themselves from the power of the flame: there shall be no coals to warm at, nor fire to sit before it." Therefore, they shall be with you, with whom you worked since your youth, even the travelers: they shall wander everyone back to his area and none shall save you.

Therefore, you will be among the first to go into exile; your feasting and lounging will end. I will tear down the winter house along with the summer house; the houses decorated with ivory will be destroyed and all their mansions will be demolished. Then the angel of the LORD answered and said, "O LORD of hosts, how long will you not have mercy on Jerusalem and on the cities of Judah, against which you were angry these seventy years?" Thus says the Lord GOD; "An evil, an only evil, behold, is come." "An end is come, the end has come: it watches for you; behold, it has come." The morning has come to you, O you that dwell in the land: the time is come, the day of trouble is near, and not the sounding again of the mountains. O house of David! Thus says the LORD: "Execute judgment in the morning; and deliver him who is plundered out of the hand of the oppressor, lest my fury goes forth like fire and burns so that no one can quench it, because of the evil of your doings."

46. Vengeance Against Ungodliness

(Isa. 13:19; Jd. 1:7; Ps. 137:8; Prov. 28:15; Rev. 17:18, 5; Lam. 1:5; 2:5; Mt. 5:25; Rev. 5:5; 1 Pet. 5:8; 1 Cor. 10:10, 11; Isa. 63:8-10; 14:29; Jer. 8:17; Zec. 9:14; Lk. 17:24, 25; 10:18; Isa. 8:13, 14; Mk. 12:10; Ps. 118:23; Lk. 20:18; Mt. 24:37; Jb. 22:16; Dan. 11:22; Rev. 12:15; 2 Pet. 2:5; Nah. 1:8; Num. 5:24; Zec. 9:4; Mal. 3:9; Isa. 24:6; Lk. 10:14; Lam. 4:11; Zec. 9:13; Am. 7:4; Mic. 1:4; Hab. 2:14; Mal. 4:2; Heb. 12:29; Rev. 22:16; Ac. 13:23; Heb. 2:4; Mt. 13:43)

Babylon, the glory of kingdoms, the beauty of the Chaldeans' pride, will be as when God overthrew Sodom and Gomorrah. As the USA and Britain, and the cities about them in like manner, giving themselves over to fornication, and going after strange flesh, are set forth for an example, suffering the vengeance of eternal fire. O daughter of Babylon, who are to be destroyed, delighted is the one who repays you as you have served us; like a roaring lion and a charging bear is a wicked ruler over poor people. The woman I saw is the great city that rules over the kings of the earth; and upon her forehead was a name written: "Secrecy, Babylon the Great, the Mother of Harlots and Abominations of the Earth." Her adversaries have become the masters, her enemies prosper; for the LORD has afflicted her because of the multitude of her transgressions. Her children have gone into captivity before the enemy. The Lord was as an enemy, he devoured Israel, he devoured all its palaces; he has destroyed its strongholds and has increased mourning and lamentation in the daughter of Judah. Agree with your adversary quickly, while you are in the way with him, or else your adversary delivers you to the judge, the judge to the officer, and you are thrown into prison.

One of the elders said to me," Weep not; behold, the lion that is of the tribe of Judah, the root of David, has overcome to open the book and the seven seals thereof." Be sober and vigilant. Your diabolical enemy prowls around as a roaring lion seeking someone to consume. Neither murmur, as some of them murmured, and perished by the destroyer. Now these things happened to them by way of example; and they were written for our admonition, upon whom the fulfillment of the ages is attained. For he said, "Surely they are my people, children that will not lie": so, he was their savior. In all their affliction he was afflicted, and the angel of his presence saved them: in his love and in his pity, he redeemed them; he bare them, and carried them all the days of old. But they rebelled, and vexed his Holy Spirit: therefore, he turned to be their enemy, and he fought against them. From the serpent's root a viper will come forth, and its fruit will be a flying serpent. "For behold, I will send serpents among you, vipers which cannot be charmed, and they shall bite you," says the LORD. Then the LORD will be seen over them, and his arrow will go forth like lightning. The Lord GOD will blow the trumpet and go with whirlwinds from the south. "For as the lightning that flashes out of one part under heaven shines to the other part under heaven, so also the Son of Man will be in his day. But first he must suffer many things and be rejected by this generation." As he said to them, "I beheld Satan as lightning strike from heaven." The LORD of hosts, him you shall hallow; let him be your fear and let him be your dread. He will be as a sanctuary, but a stone of stumbling and a rock of offense to both the houses of Israel, as a trap and a snare to the inhabitants of Jerusalem. Have you not read the scripture? "The stone which the builders rejected, the same was made the head of the corner." The LORD has done this, and it is marvelous in our eyes. Everyone who falls on that stone will be broken to pieces, but he on whom it falls will be crushed. But as the days of Noah, so will the coming of the Son of Man be. They were carried off before their time, their foundations washed away by a flood. With the arms of a flood shall they be overflown from before him, and shall be broken, yea, also the prince of the covenant. The serpent cast out of his mouth water as a flood after the woman, that he might cause her to be carried away in the flood, and spared not the old world, but saved Noah the eighth person, a preacher of righteousness, bringing in the flood upon the world of the ungodly. But with an overrunning flood he will make an utter end of the place thereof, and darkness shall pursue his enemies. Then he shall make the woman drink the bitter water that brings a curse, and the water that brings the curse shall enter her to become bitter. Behold, the LORD will cast her out; he will destroy her power in the sea, and she will be devoured by fire.

You are cursed with a curse, for you have robbed me, even this whole nation. Therefore, the curse devoured the earth, and those who dwell in it are desolate. Therefore, the inhabitants of the earth are burned, and few men remain. But it shall be more tolerable for Tyre and Sidon at the judgment, than for you. The LORD accomplished his fury; he poured out his fierce anger, and kindled a fire in Zion, and it devoured the foundations thereof. For I have bent the South, my bow, fitted the bow with double fruit, and raised up your sons, O Zion, against your sons, O Greece, and made you like the sword of a mighty man. Thus, the Lord GOD showed me: behold, the Lord GOD called for conflict by fire, and it consumed the great deep and devoured the territory. The mountains will melt under him, and the valleys will split like wax before the fire, like waters poured down a steep place. For the earth shall be filled with the knowledge of the heaviness of the LORD, as the waters cover the sea. But for you that fear my name shall the Sun of Righteousness arise with healing in its wings. For our God is a consuming fire. "I, Jesus, sent my messenger to prophesy to you these things for the congregations. 'I am the root and the offspring of David, the bright morning star.'" From the descendants of this man, according to promise, God has brought to Israel the savior, *Jesus*. God also testifies to it by signs, wonders and various miracles, and virtues of the Holy Spirit according to his own will. Then the righteous shall shine forth as the sun in the kingdom of their LORD.

47. The Vanquished

(Hos. 2:2; Zeph. 3:1-5; Rom. 16:17; Ti. 1:16; Jer. 11:9; Isa. 65:2, 3; Zec. 1:15; Gal. 4:17; Zec. 8:14; Jer. 23:21, 22; Ezk. 22:25; Jer. 5:5; Isa. 24:5; Ezk. 32:7, 8, 15; 39:11; Dan. 7:26, 25; Hab. 2:3; Heb. 10:39; Ezk. 34:12; Mk. 13:27; Rev. 10:5, 6; Dan. 7:28)

Contend with your mother, contend, for she is not my wife, and I am not her husband. Woe to the city of oppressors, rebellious and defiled! She obeys no one, she accepts no correction. She trusts not in the LORD; she does not draw near to her God. Her officials are roaring lions, her rulers are evening wolves, who leave nothing for the morning. Her prophets are arrogant; they are treacherous men. Her priests profane the sanctuary and do violence to the law. The LORD within her is righteous; he does no wrong. Morning by morning he dispenses his justice, and every new day he does not fail, yet the unrighteous know no shame.

Now I urge you, brethren, note those who cause divisions and offenses, contrary to the doctrine which you learned, and avoid them. They claim to know God, but by their actions they deny him. They are detestable, disobedient, and unfit for doing anything good. The LORD said to me, "A conspiracy has been found among the men of Judah and among the inhabitants of Jerusalem." I have stretched out my hands all day long to a rebellious people, who walk in a way that is not good, according to their own thoughts; a people who provoke me to anger continually to my face. I am very displeased with the heathen that are at ease: for I was but a little displeased, and they helped forward the affliction. They zealously affect you, but not well; yea, they would exclude you, that you might affect them. For thus says the LORD of hosts, "As I thought to punish you, when your fathers provoked me to wrath," says the LORD of hosts, "and I repented not: I have not sent these prophets, yet they ran; I have not spoken to them, yet they prophesied. But if they stood in my counsel and caused my people to hear my words, then they should have turned them from their evil way, and from the evil of their doings." There is a conspiracy of her prophets in the midst thereof.

I will go to the great men and speak to them, for they have known the way of the LORD, the judgment of their God. But these have altogether broken the yoke and burst the bonds. The earth is also defiled under its inhabitants because they have transgressed the laws, evaded the ordinance, broken the everlasting covenant.

When I shall cause your termination, I will cover the heaven, and make the stars thereof dark; I will cover the sun with a cloud, and the moon shall not give its light. All the bright lights of heaven will I make dark over you, and set darkness upon your land, says the Lord GOD. The country shall be destitute of that whereof it was full, when I shall smite all of them that dwell therein, then shall they know that I am the LORD.

It shall come to pass in that day, that I will give to Gog a place there, of graves in Israel, at the valley of the trespassers on the east of the sea; and it shall stop the trespass. There shall they bury *Rome* and all its multitude: and they shall call it *the valley of great tribulation*. But the judgment shall sit, and they shall take away his dominion, to consume and to destroy it until the end. They shall be given into his hand until a time and times and the dividing of time. For the vision is yet for an appointed time; but at the end it will speak, and it will not lie. Though it tarries, wait for it; because it will surely come, it will not delay. But we are not of them who draw back into perdition; but of them that believe to the saving of the soul.

As a shepherd seeks out his flock in the day that he is among his people that are scattered; so, will I seek out my people, and will deliver them out of all places where they were scattered in the cloudy and dark day. Then he will send his angels and gather together his chosen ones from the four winds, from the farthest part of earth to the farthest part of heaven. The angel which I saw stand upon the sea and upon the earth swore by him that lives for ever and ever, that there should be time no longer. Hitherto is the end of the matter.

48. National Liability

(Rev. 12:1; 17:4; Obad. 1:4; Ezk. 39:3; Jer. 4:30; Isa. 1:4; Hos. 13:8; Jer. 6:7; Am. 9:2; Jer. 48:40, 39; Isa. 10:10, 11; Ezk. 23:40; Isa. 28:4; 13:2; Jer. 2:7; 5:7; Rev. 18:16; Isa. 3:1, 3; Jer. 22:19; Jb. 40:15; Ezk. 38:9; Isa. 29:5, 6; 31:2; 9:17)

Then there appeared a great wonder in heaven; a woman clothed with the sun, and the moon under her feet, and upon her head a crown of twelve stars. And the woman was arrayed in purple and scarlet, and adorned with gold and precious stones and pearls, having a golden cup in her hand full of the abominations and filthiness of her fornication. "Though you soar like the eagle and build your nest among the stars, from there I will bring you down," declares the LORD. Then I will strike your bow from your left hand and make your arrows drop from your right hand. Then you, O desolate one, what will you do? Although you dress in scarlet, although you decorate yourself with ornaments of gold, although you smear your eyes with paint, in vain you make yourself beautiful; your lovers despise you; they seek your life.

Ah sinful nation, a people laden with iniquity, a seed of evildoers, children that are corrupters: they have forsaken the LORD, they have provoked the Holy One of Israel to anger, they are gone away backward. I will meet them like a bear bereaved of its whelps; the wild beast shall tear them. As a fountain casts out its waters, so she casts out her wickedness: violence and spoil is heard in her; before me continually are grief and wounds. Though they dig down to the depths of the grave, from there my hand will take them. Though they climb up to the heavens, from there I will bring them down. For thus says the LORD; "Behold, he shall fly as an eagle, and shall spread his wings over Moab. They shall howl, saying, 'How is it broken down!' How they have turned their back with shame! So, they shall be in derision and dismay to all of them about him."

As my hand has found the kingdoms of the idols, and whose graven images did exceed those of Jerusalem and of Samaria; shall I not, as I have done to Samaria and her idols, so do to Jerusalem and her idols? Furthermore, you sent for men to come from afar, to whom a messenger was sent; and there they came, and you washed yourself for them, painted your eyes, and adorned yourself with ornaments. But the glorious beauty is a fading flag which is at the head of the verdant valley, like the first fruit before the summer. Lift up a banner on the high mountain, raise your voice to them; wave your hand, that they may enter the gates of the nobles. I brought you into a plentiful country, to eat the fruit thereof and the goodness thereof; but when you entered, you defiled my land, and made my heritage an abomination. How shall I pardon you for this? Your children have forsaken me and sworn by those that are not gods. Cry out: woe! Woe, O great city, dressed in fine linen purple and scarlet.

For behold, the Lord, the LORD Almighty, takes away from Jerusalem and Judah both supply and support: all supplies of food and all supplies of water, the captain of fifty, and the honorable person, and the counselor, and the cunning artisan, and the eloquent orator. He shall be buried with the burial of an ass, drawn and cast forth beyond the gates of Jerusalem. Behold then the behemoth, which I made with you; he eats grass like an ox. You and all your troops and the many nations with you will go up, advancing like a storm; you will be like a swarm covering the land. But the multitude of your enemies shall become like fine dust, and the multitude of your ruthless ones like the chaff which blows away; and it shall happen instantly, suddenly. From the LORD of hosts, you will be punished with thunder and earthquake, loud noise, whirlwind, tempest, and the flame of a consuming fire. Yet he is wise and will bring disaster, and does not retract his words, but will arise against the house of evildoers, and against the help of the workers of iniquity. For everyone is a hypocrite and an evildoer, and every mouth speaks folly. For all this his anger is not turned away, but his hand is stretched out still.

49. The Premonition

(Jer. 5:14; Mt. 10:18; 2 Ki. 1:10; Isa. 10:17; Mt. 24:22; Isa. 54:8)

Therefore, thus says the LORD Almighty God: "Because you speak this word, behold, I will make my words in your mouth fire, and this people wood, and it shall devour them." You will be brought before governors and kings for my sake, for a testimony to them and to the nations. Elijah answered and said to the captain of fifty, "If I am a man of God, let fire come down from heaven and consume you and your fifty." Then fire came down from heaven and consumed him and his fifty. The light of Israel will become a fire and his Holy One a flame, and it will burn and devour his thorns and his briars in a single day: and unless those days were shortened, no flesh would be saved; but for the sake of the chosen, those days will be shortened. In a little wrath I hid my face from you for a moment; but with everlasting kindness I will have mercy on you, says the LORD your redeemer.

50. Global Hegemony

(Ezk. 38:2, 3, 15; 39:6, 2; 22:12; Isa. 2:20, 21, 18; Gen. 11:9; 13:17; 1 Ki. 11:6; 2 Tim. 3:6; Prov. 12:4; 28:8; 1 Ki. 10:14, 15; Rev. 17:3, 4; Dan. 7:19; Rev. 13:1, 17, 16; Mt. 22:20, 21; Jb. 41:34, 20, 21; Mt. 5:30)

Son of man, set your face against Gog, of the land of Magog, the chief prince of Meshech and Tubal; prophesy against him and say: "This is what the Sovereign LORD says: 'I am against you, O *GOP*, chief prince of *Democrats* and *Republicans*; you will come from your place out of the north, you and many peoples with you, a great company and a mighty army, and I shall send fire upon Magog and those who inhabit the coastlands securely; and they will know that I am the LORD.' 'I will turn you back, and leave but the sixth part of you, and will cause you to come up from the north parts and will bring you upon the mountains of Israel.'" "In you they have taken bribes to shed blood; you have taken interest and profits, and you have injured your neighbors for gain by oppression, and you have forgotten me," declares the Lord GOD.

In that day, a man shall cast his idols of silver, and his idols of gold, which they made each one for himself to worship, to the moles and the bats for fear of the LORD, when he arises to shake terribly the earth. The idols he shall utterly abolish. Therefore, its name is called Babel, because there the LORD confused the language of all the earth; and from there the LORD scattered them abroad over the face of all the earth. Arise, walk in the land through its length and its width, for I give it to you.

But Solomon did evil in the sight of the LORD and went not fully after the LORD, as did David his father. Of this sort are they which creep into houses, and lead captive foolish women laden with sins, led away with diverse lusts. An assertive woman is a crown for her husband; but she who causes shame is like decay in his bones. He who increases his wealth by interest and usury, gathers it for him who is gracious to the poor. The weight of the gold that Solomon received yearly was six hundred and sixty-six talents, besides the traders, and traffic of the merchants, and of all the kings of Arabia, and of the governors of the country.

So, he carried me away in the Spirit into the wilderness, and I saw a woman sitting on a scarlet beast which was full of names of blasphemy, having seven heads and ten horns. The woman was arrayed in purple and scarlet and adorned with gold and precious stones. Then I wished to know the truth about the fourth beast, which was different from all the others, exceedingly dreadful, with its teeth of iron and its nails of bronze, which devoured, broke in pieces, and trampled the residue with its feet. Then I stood on the sand of the sea, and I saw a beast rising up out of the sea, having seven heads and ten horns, and on his horns ten crowns [G20: Argentina, Australia, Brazil, Canada, China, European Union. France, Germany, India, Indonesia, Italy, Japan, Republic of Korea,

Mexico, Russia, Saudi Arabia, South Africa, Turkey, the United Kingdom, the United States], and on his heads a blasphemous name so that no one could buy or sell unless he had the mark, which is the name of the beast or the number of his name [USD global reserve currency]: causing all, both small and great, rich and poor, free and bond, to receive a mark in their right hand, or in their foreheads. And Jesus said to them, "Whose image and inscription is this?" They said to him, "Caesar's." And he said to them, "Render therefore to Caesar the things that are Caesar's, and to God the things that are God's." He beholds every high thing; he is king over all the children of pride. Out of his nostrils goes smoke, as out of a seething caldron and quagmire. His breath kindles coal, and a flame shoots out of his mouth. If your right hand causes you to sin, cut it off and throw it away. It is better for you to lose one part of your body than for your whole body to go to hell.

51. The Repression That Causes Poverty

(Dan. 11:20; Rev. 17:10; 13:12, 15, 6, 7; Dan. 11:29; Rev. 17:6; 18:6, 7; Mt. 21:13; Jn. 2:16; Jer. 15:13; Ezk. 11:21; 7:4; Mt. 12:43, 44; Rev. 16:15; Mt. 23:38; 24:15-18, Lk. 19:43, 44)

Then shall stand up in his estate a raiser of taxes in the glory of the kingdom: but within few days he shall be shattered, neither in anger, nor in battle. There were also seven kings: five have fallen, one is, the other had not yet come, and he must continue a short term. He exercised all the authority of the first beast on his behalf and made the earth and its inhabitants worship the first beast, whose fatal wound had been healed. He was granted power to give breath to the image of the beast, that the image of the beast should both speak and cause as many as would not worship the image of the beast to be killed. Then he opened his mouth in blasphemy against God, to blaspheme his name, his tabernacle, and those who dwell in heaven. It was granted to him to make war with the saints and to overcome them. Authority was given to him over every tribe, language, and nation.

At the appointed time he shall return and go toward the South, but it shall not be like the former or the latter. Then I saw the woman drunken with the blood of the saints, and with the blood of the martyrs of Jesus. Recompense to her as she rendered to you and repay her double according to her works; in the cup which she has filled, fill double to her. In the measure that she glorified herself and lived luxuriously, in the same measure give her torment and sorrow. As he said to them, "It is written, 'my house shall be called a house of prayer,' but you have made it a den of thieves." "Take these things away! Do not make the LORD's house a house of merchandise!" Your wealth and your treasures I will give as plunder without price, because of all your sins, throughout your territories.

But as for those whose hearts are devoted to their vile images and detestable idols, I will bring down on their own heads what they have done, and my eye shall not spare you, neither will I have pity: but I will recompense your ways upon you, and your abominations shall be in the midst of you: and you shall know that I am the LORD. When the unclean spirit is gone out of a man, he walks through dry places, seeking rest but finds none. Then he said, "I will return into my house from where I went out"; and when he returns, he finds it empty, swept, and garnished. Behold, I come as a thief. Behold, your house is left desolate to you. When you therefore shall see the abomination of desolation stand in the holy place, then let them who are in Judea flee into the mountains: let him which is on the housetop not come down to take anything out of his house; neither let him which is in the field return back to take his clothes. For days will come upon you when your enemies will build an embankment around you, surround you and close you in on every side, and level you and your children within you, to the ground; and they will not leave in you one stone upon another, because you did not know the time of your visitation.

52. Empathy and Compassion

(Jn. 4:7, 9; 8:48, 49; 10:33; Lk. 10:33; Jn. 8:10, 11; Jer. 2:13; Zec. 14:8; Jn. 7:38)

A woman of Samaria came to draw water. Jesus said to her, "Give me a drink." Then the woman of Samaria said to him, "How is it that you, being a Jew, ask a drink from me, a Samaritan woman?" For Jews have no involvement with Samaritans. But the Jews answered and said to him, "Do we not say rightly that you are a Samaritan and are of the devil?" Jesus answered, "I am not of the devil." Again, the Jews answered him, saying, "For a good work we do not stone you, but for blasphemy because you, being 'the devil,' make yourself God." But a certain Samaritan, as he journeyed, went where he was; and when he saw him, he had compassion. When Jesus had raised himself up and saw no one but the woman, he said to her, "Woman, where are those accusers of yours? Has no one condemned you?" She said, "No one, Lord." Then Jesus said to her, "Neither do I condemn you; go and sin no more."

For my people have committed two evils: and they have forsaken me the fountain of living waters, to cut for themselves cisterns, broken cisterns, which can hold no water. It shall be in that day, that living waters shall go out from Jerusalem; half of them toward the former sea, and half of them toward the latter sea: in summer and in winter shall it be. He who believes in me, as the scripture said, "From in his soul shall flow rivers of living water."

53. Perilous Times

(Isa. 1:18; 23:17; Jn. 18:23; Ac. 23:3; 2 Cor. 4:8, 9, 11, 13; Prov. 20:30; Heb. 9:22; Isa. 24:1, 2; Mt. 23:27, 28, 25; Lk 11:39)

"Come now, and let us reason together," says the LORD. Though your sins are like scarlet, they shall be as white as snow. It shall be, at the end of seventy years, that the LORD will visit. If I said something wrong, explain as to what is wrong; but if I spoke the truth, why did you strike me? God will strike you, you whitewashed wall. You sit there to judge me according to the law, yet you yourself violate the law by commanding that I be struck! We are pressured on every side, but not crushed; perplexed, but not in despair; persecuted, but not abandoned; struck down, but not destroyed. For we who are alive are always being given over to death for Jesus' sake. It is written: "I believed; therefore I have spoken." With that same spirit of faith we also believe and therefore speak. The blueness of a wound cleanses away evil: so do stripes the inward parts of the belly. Almost all things are by the law purged with blood; and without shedding of blood is no remission.

Behold, the LORD lays the earth waste, devastates it, distorts its surface, and scatters its inhabitants. The people will be like the priest, the servant like his master, the maid like her mistress, the buyer like the seller, the lender like the borrower, the creditor like the debtor. Woe to you, hypocrites! For you are like whited sepulchers, which indeed appear beautiful outward, but are within full of dead men's bones, and of all uncleanness. Even so you also outwardly appear righteous to man, but within you are full of hypocrisy, iniquity, extortion, excess, greed, and wickedness!

54. The Arbiter of Sanctions

(Lk. 12:49; Hos. 11:9; Jer. 51:8, 9, 37; Rev. 18:11; Lk. 14:28-30; 13:4, 5; Mal. 2:13; Ezk. 38:10-12, 5; Nah. 3:8, 9, 16; Eph. 2:10; Ezk. 1:4; Isa. 14:19; Jd. 1:4; Isa. 41:2-4)

I come to send fire on the earth; and what will I do, if it is already kindled? I will not enter into the city. Babylon is suddenly fallen and destroyed: howl for her; take balm for her pain, if so be she may be healed. We would have healed Babylon, but she is not healed. Forsake her and let us go everyone into his own country: for her judgment reaches into heaven and is lifted up even to the skies. Babylon shall become heaps, a dwelling place for dragons, an astonishment, and a hissing, without an inhabitant. The merchants of the earth will weep and mourn over her, for no one buys their merchandise anymore. For which of you, intending to build a tower, does not sit down first and count the cost, whether he has enough to finish it? Otherwise, when he has laid a foundation, and is not able to finish, all who observe it begin to ridicule him, saying, "This man began to build and was not able to finish." Or those on whom the tower fell and killed them, do you think that they were worse sinners than all others who dwell in Jerusalem? I tell you, no; but unless you repent you shall all likewise perish. This you have done again, covering the altar of the LORD with tears, with weeping, and with crying out, inasmuch that he regards not the offering anymore, nor receives it with good will at your hand.

Thus says the Lord GOD, "It will come about on that day, that thoughts will enter into your mind, and you will devise an evil plan." [Politics are hypocrisy.] You will say, "I will go up against the land of unwalled villages. I will go against those who are at rest, that live securely, all of them living without walls and having no bars or gates," to take a spoil and to take a prey; to turn your hand upon the desolate places that are now inhabited, and upon the people that are gathered out of the nations. Persia, Ethiopia, and Libya with them; all of them with shield and helmet. Are you better than they that were situated by the river, that had the waters around her, whose rampart was the sea, whose wall was the sea? Ethiopia and Egypt were her strength, and it was boundless. You increased the number of your merchants until they are more than the stars of the sky.

For we are his workmanship, created in Christ Jesus for good works, which God preordained that we should walk in them. I looked, and behold, a whirlwind came out of the north, a great cloud, and a fire enfolding itself, and a brightness was about it. But you have been cast out of your tomb like an abominable branch, clothed with the slain who are pierced with a sword, who go down to the stones of the pit, like a trampled corpse. For there are certain men crept in unaware, who were before preordained to this condemnation, ungodly men, turning the grace of our God into lasciviousness, and denying the only King, our Lord Jesus Christ.

Who raised up one from the east? Who in righteousness called him to his feet? Who gave the nations before him, and made him rule over kings? Who gave them as the dust to his sword, as driven stubble to his bow? Who pursued them and passed safely by the way that he had not gone with his feet? Who has performed and done it, calling the generations from the beginning? I, the LORD, am the first and the last; I am he.

55. Infiltration of Jurisdiction

(Dan. 9:24; Rev. 16:18; Dan. 7:7; Rev. 17:3, 9, 8; Dan. 7:12; Rev. 14:11; Jl. 2:20; Rev. 17:7; Mt. 9:4, 5; 17:17; 12:45, 39)

Seventy weeks are determined for your people and for your holy city. Then there were noises and thundering and lightning; and there was a great earthquake, such a mighty and great earthquake as had not occurred since men were on the earth. After that, in my vision at night I looked, and there before me was the fourth beast, terrifying and frightening and very powerful. It had large iron teeth; it crushed and devoured its victims and trampled underfoot whatever remained. It was different from all the former beasts, and it had ten horns.

I saw a woman sitting on the scarlet beast full of names of blasphemy, having seven heads and ten horns. Here is the mind having wisdom: the seven heads are seven mountains, where the woman sits upon them. The beast that you saw was, and is not, and will ascend out of the bottomless pit and go into perdition. And those who dwell on the earth will marvel, whose names are not written in the Book of Life from the foundation of the world, when they see the beast that was, and is not, and yet is. As for the other beasts, they had their dominion taken away, yet their lives were prolonged for a season and a time. The smoke of their torment ascends forever and ever; and they have no rest day or night, who worshipped the beast and his image, and whoever received the mark of his name.

But I will remove far off from you the northern army and will drive it into a land barren and desolate, its forepart into the eastern sea, and its latter part into the western sea; and its stench shall come up, and its ill savor shall come up, because it has done astonishing things. But the angel said to me, "Why do you wonder? I will tell you the mystery of the woman and of the beast that carries her, that has the seven heads and ten horns." [Seven richest nations and ten industrial democracies: G-7 Canada, European Union, France, Germany, Italy, Japan, United Kingdom, and the United States. G-10 Belgium, Canada, France, Germany, Italy, Japan, Netherlands, Sweden, Switzerland, and the United Kingdom]. [Currency is their weapon, and they persecute by deprivation with arbitrary enumeration as their standard of repression.]

Why are you imagining evil in your hearts? For which is easier, to say, "Your sins are forgiven," or to say, "Rise, and walk"? O faithless and perverse generation, how long shall I be with you? How long must I suffer you? The last state of a man is worse than the first. So shall it also be with this wicked generation. An evil and adulterous generation seeks after a sign, but no sign will be given to it.

56. Exploitation Subterfuge

(Dan. 9:27; Exod. 25:19, 20; Heb. 9:5; Dan. 11:39; Jer. 51:42, 43; 2:14; Gal. 4:1-3; Ac. 15:19, 20; Rev. 2:20, 21; 18:2)

But, on the wing of abominations is one who makes desolate, even until the consummation, which is determined, is poured out on the desolate. Of the mercy seat shall he make the cherubim on the two ends thereof. The cherubim shall stretch forth their wings on high, covering the mercy seat with their wings. Over it the mummies of gold, shadowed the mercy seat. Thus shall he do in the strongholds with a strange god, whom he shall acknowledge and increase with glory: and he shall cause them to rule over many and shall divide the land for gain. The sea has come up over Babylon; she is covered with the multitude of its waves. Her cities are a desolation, a dry land, and a wilderness; a land where no one dwells, through which no son of man passes.

Is Jacob a servant? Is he a homeborn slave? Why is he plundered? Now I say that the heir, as long as he is a child, differs nothing from a servant, though he is lord of all; but is under tutors and governors until the time appointed of the father. Even so we, when we were children, were in bondage under the elements of the world. Therefore, it is my judgment that we do not trouble those who are turning to God from among the seculars, but that we write to them that they abstain from things contaminated by idols and from fornication, and from what is strangled, and from blood. Also, I hold other things against you, because you justify that woman *the USA* that calls herself a prophetess to teach and mislead my servants to commit fornication, and to eat things sacrificed to idols. I gave her space and time to repent of her fornication: but she repented not. Babylon the great has fallen, is fallen, and has become the habitation of sinners and a haven for every unclean, violent, and hateful *felon*.

57. Faithless Denialism

(1 Cor. 5:9; Ac. 13:10; 2 Thess. 2:5-7; 1 Jn. 2:22, 23; Jn. 13:20; Jer. 9:6; Mt. 12:30; Rev. 13:3; Jer. 51:17, 29, 28)

Do you not remember that when I was still with you, I told you these things? I wrote to you in an epistle not to collaborate with fornicators. But you are full of all deception and recklessness, you children of evil and enemies of everything that is right. Will you never stop perverting the right ways of the Lord? The mystery of transgression is already in effect for him who now merely presides, until he is taken out of the way. But you now know what was withheld, that he may be revealed in his own time, who the deceiver is, he who denies that Jesus is the Messiah. He is antichrist (antigod) who denies the LORD and the Son. Whoever denies the Son does not have the LORD either; he who acknowledges the Son has the LORD also. He who receives whomever I send receives me; and he who receives me receives him who sent me.

You dwell in the midst of deception; in their deceit they refuse to acknowledge me, declares the LORD. He who is not with me is against me, and he who does not gather with me scatters abroad. I saw one of his heads as it was wounded to death; and his deadly wound was healed: and all the world wondered after the beast. Every human is senseless and without knowledge; every goldsmith is shamed by his idols. His images are a deception; they have no breath in them. The land will tremble in sorrow; for every purpose of the LORD shall be performed against Babylon, to make the land of Babylon a desolation without inhabitant. Prepare against her the nations, with the kings of the Medes, its governors and all its rulers, all the land of his dominion.

58. Numbered to the Sword

(Dan. 5:26-28; Rev. 11:5-7; 14:9, 10; 16:2; 17:16, 17; Jer. 19:12; Ezk. 26:21; Jer. 51:25; Ezk. 6:6, 7; Rev. 2:16; Mt. 12:31; Isa. 30:9; Lev. 24:16, 17; Rom. 2:12; Mt. 12:32; Rev. 17:3; 13:1; 18:4, 5; Ac. 8:22, 23; Jer. 6:10; Rev. 13:10)

God numbered your kingdom and finished it. You are weighed in the balances and are found insufficient. Your kingdom is divided and given to the Medes and Persians. If anyone tries to harm them, fire comes from their mouths and devours their enemies: this is how anyone who wants to harm them must die. These have power to shut heaven, so that no rain falls in the days of their prophecy; and they have power over waters to turn them to blood, and to strike the earth with all plagues, as often as they desire. Now when they finish their testimony, the beast that ascends out of the bottomless pit [profits from debt] makes war against them, overcomes them, and kills them. If anyone worships the beast and his image, or received his mark in his forehead, or in his hand, the same shall be tormented with fire and brimstone in the presence of the holy angels, and in the presence of the Christ. Thus, grievous and painful sores broke out on the people who had the mark of the beast and worshipped his image. Then the ten horns which you saw upon the beast, these shall hate the whore, and shall make her desolate and exposed, and shall eat her flesh and burn her with fire [riots]. For God put in their hearts to fulfill his will, and to agree and give their kingdom to the beast, until the words of God shall be fulfilled. "Thus, will I do to this place," says the LORD, "and to the inhabitants thereof, and make this city as Tophet." "I will make you the horror, and you shall be no more; though you are sought for, you will never be found again," says the Lord GOD.

"Behold, I am against you, O destroying mountain," says the LORD, "which is destroying all the earth: and I will make you a burnt mountain." In all your dwelling places the cities shall be laid waste, and the high places shall be desolate; that your altars may be laid waste and made desolate, your idols may be broken and cease, your images may be cut down, and your works may be abolished. The slain shall fall in the midst of you, and you shall know that I am the LORD.

Repent therefore, or else I am coming to you quickly and I will make war against them with the sword of my mouth. Wherefore I say to you, "All manner of sin and blasphemy shall be forgiven to man: but the blasphemy against the Holy Ghost shall not be forgiven to man." These are rebellious people, deceitful children, unwilling to listen to the LORD's instruction. Whoever blasphemes the name of the LORD shall surely be put to death, the stranger as well as one who is born in the land. When he blasphemes the name of the LORD, he shall be put to death.

Whoever murders anyone shall surely be put to death. For as many as have sinned without law shall also perish without law: and as many as have sinned under the law shall be judged by the law. Anyone who speaks a word against the Son of Man will be forgiven, but anyone who speaks against the Holy Spirit will not be forgiven, neither in this era nor in the future.

I saw a woman sit on a scarlet-colored beast, full of names of blasphemy, [citizens who are registered to vote, all politicians, government employees, members of the armed services] having seven heads and ten horns. and upon his horns ten crowns [G20], and upon his heads the name of blasphemy [USA]. And I heard another voice from heaven, saying, "Come out of her, my people, that you be not partakers of her sins, and that you receive not of her plagues. For her sins have reached to heaven, and God has remembered her iniquities." (Rev 2:22,23.) Repent therefore of this your wickedness and pray God if perhaps the thought of your heart might be forgiven to you. For I perceive that you are full of bitterness and bound by iniquity.

To whom shall I speak and give warning, that they may hear? Behold, their ears are closed, and they cannot listen. Behold, the word of the LORD has become a reproach to them; they have no delight in it. He who leads into captivity shall go into captivity; he who kills with the sword must be killed by the sword. Here is the patience and the faith of the sacred.

59. Bereavement of Possession

(Isa. 3:14, 15; Hos. 3:4; Ezk. 7:13, 19-21, 24, 18; Isa. 3:24; 7:20; Prov. 16:4, 5; Jb. 40:11, 12; Ps. 94:23; 12:5; 18:47)

The LORD enters into judgment against the elders and leaders of his people: "It is you who have ruined my vineyard; the plunder from the poor is in your houses. What do you mean by crushing my people and grinding the faces of the poor?" declares the Lord, the LORD Almighty. For they shall abide many days without a king, and without a prince, and without a sacrifice, and without an image, and without an ephod, and without teraphim. They will throw their silver into the streets, and their gold will be an unclean thing. For the seller shall not return to what has been sold, though he may still be alive; for the vision concerns the whole multitude, and it shall not turn back; no one will strengthen himself living in iniquity. They were proud of their beautiful jewelry and used it to make their detestable idols and vile images. I will hand it all over as plunder to foreigners and as loot to the wicked of the earth: I will bring the most wicked of the nations to take possession of their houses; I will put an end to the pride of the mighty, and their sanctuaries will be desecrated. They shall also gird themselves with sackcloth, and horror shall cover them; shame shall be upon all faces, and baldness upon all their heads. Instead of fragrance there will be a stench; instead of a sash, a rope; instead of well-dressed hair, baldness; instead of fine clothing, sackcloth; instead of beauty, scaring. In that day, the Lord will shave with a razor purchased from beyond the river; it shaves the head and the hair of their legs and takes off your beards also.

The LORD has made all for himself, even the wicked for the day of evil. Every one that is proud in heart is an abomination to the LORD. Disperse the rage of your wrath; behold everyone who is proud, and abase him, bring him low; tread down the wicked in their place. He shall bring upon them their own iniquity and shall cut them off in their own wickedness; yea, the LORD our God shall cut them off. For the oppression of the poor, for the sighing of the needy, now I will arise, says the LORD. It is God who avenges me and subdues the peoples under me.

60. Declaration of Fulfillment

(2 Thess. 2:2; 2 Chr. 5:7; Mt. 24:14, 30; 13:17; Mk. 16:15, 16; Heb. 9:3; Jn. 10:35; Exod. 19:11)

Do not become easily unsettled or alarmed either by spirit or by word or by letter, as if from us, as though the day of the Lord has already occurred. The apostles brought in the ark of the covenant of the LORD into his place, to the oracle of the caves, into the most holy place, even under the wings of *darkness*. This covenant of the kingdom shall be published in all the world for a witness to all nations; and then shall the end come.

Then shall appear the sign of the Son of Man in heaven [nuclear mushroom clouds]: and then shall all the tribes of the earth mourn, and they shall see the Son of Man returning in the clouds of the heavens with power and great glory. For truly I say to you, that many prophets and righteous men desired to see what you see and did not see it; and to hear what you hear and did not hear it.

Go into all the world and teach the covenant to every creature. He who believes and is indoctrinated will be saved; but he who does not believe will be condemned. Then after the second veil, the tabernacle is called the holiest of all, and scripture cannot be broken. Be ready against the third day: for the third day the LORD will come down in the sight of all the people upon mount Sinai.

61. The Aftermath

(Prov. 16:19; Mt. 11:29, 30; Lk. 14:11; Mt. 25:34; 7:13, 14; Lk. 6:26; Jn. 15:16; Mk. 13:27; 22:14; Num. 26:4)

Better to be of a humble spirit with the lowly, than to divide the spoil with the proud. Take my yoke upon you and learn of me; for I am meek and lowly in heart: and you shall find rest in your souls. For my yoke is easy, and my burden is light. For whoever exalts himself will be humbled, and he who humbles himself will be exalted. Then the king will say to those on his right hand, "Come, you blessed of the LORD, inherit the kingdom prepared for you from the foundation of the world." Enter by the narrow gate; for wide is the gate and broad is the way that leads to destruction, and there are many who go in by it. Because narrow is the gate and restricted is the way which leads to life, and few there are who find it. Woe to you when the people speak well of you, for so did their fathers to the false prophets. You did not choose me, but I chose you and appointed you. He will send his angels and gather his select from the four winds, from the ends of the earth to the ends of the heavens. For many are called, but few are chosen. Take a census of the people from twenty years old and above, exactly as the LORD commanded.

The LORD said, "Go through the midst of the city, through the midst of Jerusalem, and put a mark on the foreheads of those who grieve and lament over all the detestable things that are being committed in its midst." Then I saw another angel coming up from the east, having the seal of the living God. He called out in a loud voice to the four angels who had been given power to harm the land and the sea: "Do not harm the land or the sea or the trees until we put a seal on the foreheads of the servants of our God." They were told not to harm the grass of the earth or any green plant or tree, but only those people who did not have the seal of God on their foreheads. For God so loved the earth, that he gave his only begotten Son, that whoever believes in him should not perish, but have eternal life.

Then I saw, as it were, a sea of glass mixed with fire, and those who had come off victorious from the beast and from his image and from the number of his name, standing at the sea of glass, holding harps of God. They sang a new song: "You are worthy to take the scroll and to open its seals, because you were slain, and with your blood you redeemed man for God from every tribe and language and people and nation. You made them to be a kingdom and priests to serve our God, and they will reign on the earth." There is no salvation in any other, for there is no other name under heaven given among man by which we must be saved.

62. Death Penalty

(Prov. 19:19; Deut. 13:8, 9; 2 Thess. 1:6-8; Deut. 17:2, 4, 5; Mt. 13:49, 50, 41, 42; Ezk. 33:12; Lk. 16:10; 1 Jn. 3:9; Lk. 19:27)

Every felon shall suffer punishment: for if you deliver him, yet you must do it again. Do not yield to him or listen to him. Show him no pity. Do not spare him or shield him. You must certainly put him to death. Your hand must be the first in putting him to death, and then the hands of all the people. Since it is a righteous thing for God to repay with tribulation those who trouble you, and to give you rest who are troubled with us when the Lord Jesus is revealed from heaven with his mighty angels, in flaming fire taking vengeance on those who do not know God, and on those who do not obey the covenant of our Lord Jesus Christ.

If a man or woman living among you in one of the towns the LORD gives you is found doing evil in the eyes of the LORD your God in violation of his covenant, and this has been brought to your attention, then you must investigate it thoroughly. If it is true and it has been proved that the detestable thing has been done, take the man or woman who has done this evil deed to your city gate and put that person to death. So, it will be at the end of the age. The angels will come forth, separate the wicked from among the just, and cast them into the furnace of fire. There will be wailing and gnashing of teeth. The Son of Man shall send forth his angels, and they shall gather out of his kingdom all things that offend, and them which do iniquity; and shall cast them into a furnace of fire: there shall be wailing and gnashing of teeth.

The righteousness of the righteous shall not deliver him in the day of his transgression; as for the wickedness of the wicked, he shall not fall because of it in the day that he turns from his wickedness; nor shall the righteous be able to live because of his righteousness in the day that he sins. He that is faithful in that which is least is faithful also in much: and he that is unjust in the least is unjust also in much. Whoever has been born of God does not sin; his DNA remains in him, and he cannot sin, because he was born of God. But those my enemies, which would not that I should reign over them, bring here, and slay them before me.

63. Concupiscent Fornicating Lust

(Rom. 1:26, 27, 32; 2 Thess. 2:11, 12; Lev. 20:23; 18:27, 28; Rev. 3:15, 16; Lev. 20:22; 18:29; Ps. 139:22; Jer. 9:22; 48:26; Isa. 28:8)

For this reason, God gave them up to vile passions. For even their women exchanged the natural use for what is against nature. Likewise, also the men, leaving the natural use of the woman, burned in their lust for one another, men with men committing what is indecent, and receiving in themselves the punishment of their error which is due. Who, knowing the righteous judgment of God, that those who practice such things are worthy of death, they not only do the same but also, they approve of those who practice them. For this reason, God will send them strong delusion, that they should believe the lie, that they all must be condemned who did not believe the truth but had pleasure in unrighteousness.

You must not live according to the customs of the nations which I am casting out before you; for they commit all these things, and therefore I abhor them. All these things were done by the people who lived in the land before you, and the land became defiled. If you defile the land, it will vomit you out as it vomited out the nations that were before you. I know your works, that you are neither cold nor hot. I prefer that you were cold or hot. So then, because you are lukewarm, and neither cold nor hot, I will spew you out of my mouth. You shall therefore keep all my decrees and all my judgments, and perform them, that the land where I am bringing you to dwell may not vomit you out. For whosoever shall commit any of these abominations, even the souls that commit them shall be cut off from among their people. I hate them with perfect hatred: I account them as my enemies. Speak, thus says the LORD, "Even the carcasses of men shall fall as dung upon the open field, and as the handful after the harvestman, and none shall gather them." Moab also shall wallow in his vomit, and he also shall be in derision. For all tables are full of vomit and filthiness, so that there is no place clean.

64. The Righteous and the Wicked

(Jn. 21:20; Lk. 17:34-36; Jn. 7:24; 1 Jn. 5:16, 17; Ecc. 7:20; Mt. 19:17; Gen. 18:25; Rom. 3:10-12; Ezk. 21:4; Rom. 3:23)

Peter turned and saw that the disciple who lusted for Jesus was following them. This was the one who had leaned back against his chest at the supper and had said, "Lord, who is going to betray you?" I tell you, "In that night there will be two men in one bed: the one will be taken and the other will be left. Two women will be grinding together: the one will be taken and the other left. Two men will be in the field: the one will be taken and the other left." Judge not according to the appearance but judge righteous judgment. If anyone sees another commit a sin that does not lead to death, he should pray, and God will give him life. I refer to those whose sin does not lead to death. There is a sin that leads to death: I am not saying that he would pray for that. All wrongdoing is sin, and there is sin that does not lead to death. There is not a righteous man on earth who does what is right and never sins. Why do you ask me about what is good? No one is good but one, that is, God. But if you want to enter into life, keep the commandments.

Far be it from you to do such a thing as this, to slay the righteous with the wicked, so that the righteous should be as the wicked; far be it from you. Shall not the judge of all the earth do what is right? As it is written: "There is no one righteous, not even one; there is no one who understands, no one who seeks God. All have turned away, they have together become unworthy; there is no one who does good, not even one." Seeing then that I will cut off from you the righteous and the wicked, therefore shall my sword go forth out of its sheath against all flesh from the south. For all have sinned and fell short of the glory of God.

65. Schizma

(Lev. 22:9, 20; Ezk. 44:23, 24, 10, 12, Isa. 66:3, 4; 47:12; Rev. 19:20; Jer. 7:28, 29, 32; Lk. 9:60; Ezk. 39:14; Mal. 1:2, 3; 2 Pet. 2:1; 1 Jn. 2:19)

Priests are to keep my requirements so that they do not become guilty and die for treating them with contempt. I am the LORD, who makes them holy. Do not offer anything with a defect, because it will not be accepted on your behalf. They shall teach my people the difference between the holy and the unholy and cause them to discern between the unclean and the clean. In controversy they shall stand as judges and judge it according to my judgments.

But the Catholics who went far from me when Israel went astray and who wandered from me after their idols must suffer the consequences of their sin. Because they served them in the presence of their idols and made the house of Israel fall into sin, therefore I have sworn with uplifted hand that they must suffer the consequences of their sin, declares the Sovereign LORD! They have chosen their ways, and their soul delights in their abominations, so I will choose their punishments and I will bring on them what they dread. Stand now with your enchantments and the multitude of your delusions, in which you have labored from your youth that perhaps you will be able to profit, perhaps you will prevail. But then the beast is captured, and with him the false prophet who worked signs in his presence, by which he deceived those who received the mark of the beast and those who worshiped his image.

This is a nation that does not obey the voice of the LORD their God nor receive correction. Truth has perished and has been cut off from their mouth. Cut off your hair, and cast it away, take up a lamentation on high places; for the LORD has rejected and forsaken the generation of his wrath. They shall bury in sacrifice until there is no place. Allow the dead to bury their own dead; but as for you, go and proclaim the kingdom of God everywhere. After the end of seven months shall they search. Yet you say, "Wherein have you loved us?" I loved Jacob, and I hated Esau, and laid his mountains and his heritage waste for the dragons of the wilderness. But false prophets also arose among the people, just as there will also be false teachers among you, who will secretly introduce ruinous heresies, even denying the Lord who redeemed them, bringing swift destruction upon themselves. They went out from us, but they were not of us; for if they had been of us, they would have continued with us: but they made manifest, that they were not all of us.

66. Prophecy Against Falsehood

(Isa. 29:7; 30:13; 1 Thess. 5:3; Heb. 9:24; Jn. 17:12; 2 Thess. 2:4; Mt. 23:9; 1 Tim. 4:1-3; Heb. 10:11; 1 Cor. 5:5; Mt. 5:17; Lk. 6:44, 43)

The multitude of all the nations who fight against Arial, even all who fight against her and her fortress, and distress her, shall be as a dream of a night vision. Therefore, this iniquity shall be to you as a breach ready to fall, swelling out of a high wall, whose breaking occurs suddenly at an instant. For when they shall say, "Peace and safety," then sudden destruction comes upon them, as labor pains upon a pregnant woman; and they shall not escape. For Christ entered not into the holy places made with hands, that oppose the truth; but into heaven itself, now to appear before the face of God for us.

None has been lost except the one condemned to perdition so that scripture would be fulfilled. He opposes and exalts himself above all that is called God or that is worshipped, so that he takes his seat in the temple of God, presenting himself as being God. Thus call no man your Holy Father upon the earth: for one is your Holy Father, which is in heaven.

Now the Spirit speaks expressly, that in these latter times some departed from the faith, giving heed to seducing spirits and doctrines of traditors; such teachings come through hypocritical liars, whose consciences are seared with a hot iron: they even forbid people to marry. But every priest stands ministering daily and offering repeatedly the same sacrifices, which can never take away sins. Deliver such a one to punishment for the destruction of the flesh, that his spirit might be saved in the day of the Lord Jesus. Do not think that I came to abolish the law or the prophets; I did not come to abolish, but to fulfill. For every tree is known by its own fruit: a good tree brings not forth corrupt fruit; neither does a corrupt tree bring forth good fruit.

67. Equity and Justice

(Dan. 10:21; Jas. 4:17; Prov. 28:13, 16; Ecc. 9:18; Gal. 5:4, 3; Jn. 8:23; 1 Cor. 9:11-15; 2:8; Mt. 13:58; Isa. 17:14; Rom. 1:18; Isa. 65:5; Ezk. 13:19; 1 Cor. 2:9, 10; 4:5; 15:19; Am. 3:10; Ps. 82:4; Nah. 3:10; Rev. 19:20)

But I will show you that which is noted in the scripture of truth: and there is none that holds with me in these things, but Mikael your *diplomatic leader*. Therefore, to him who knows to do good and does not do it, to him it is sin. He who conceals his sins will not prosper, but whoever confesses and forsakes them will have mercy. A ruler who lacks understanding is a great oppressor, but he who hates covetousness will prolong his days. Wisdom is better than weapons of war, but one sinner destroys much good. Christ has become of no effect to you, whosoever are justified by the law; you are fallen from grace under obligation to keep the whole law. As he said to them, "You are from beneath; I am from above. You are of this world; I am not of this world." If we have sown spiritual seed among you, is it too much if we reap a material harvest from you? If others have this right of support from you, should we not have it all the more? But we did not use this right. In the same way, the Lord has commanded that those who proclaim the covenant should receive their living from the covenant. But I have not used any of these rights; and I am not writing this in the hope that you will do such things for me. None of the rulers of this age understood it, for if they had, they would not have crucified the Lord of power. Now he did not do many mighty works there because of their unbelief.

Then behold, at evening tide, trouble: and before the morning, he is no more. This is the portion of those who plunder us, and the lot of those who rob us. For the wrath of God is revealed from heaven against all ungodliness and unrighteousness of men, who hold the truth in unrighteousness. Who say, "Keep away, do not come near me, for I am better than you." These are smoke in my nostrils, a fire that burns all day. Will you pollute me among my people for handfuls of barley and for pieces of bread, to slay the souls that should not die, and to save the souls alive that should not live, by your lying to the people that hear your lies? However, as it is written: "No eye has seen, no ear has heard, no mind has conceived what God has prepared for those who love him." But God has revealed it to us by his Spirit. The Spirit searches all things, even the deep things of God. Therefore, judge nothing before the appointed time; wait for the Lord. He will bring to light what is hidden in darkness and will expose the motives of men's hearts. At that time each will receive his due from God. If only for this life we have hope in Christ, we are pitied more than all men. "For they do not know to do right," says the LORD, "who store up violence and robbery in their heights."

Deliver the poor and needy; free them from the hand of the wicked. They cast lots for her honorable men, and her young children were dashed to pieces at the head of every street. Yet she was carried away, she went into captivity; and all her great men were bound in chains. Then the beast was seized, and with him the false prophet who performed the signs in his presence, by which he deceived those who had received the mark of the beast and those who worshipped his image: these two were thrown alive into the lake of fire which burns with brimstone.

68. Fossil Fuel Industries

(Rev. 9:1, 2; Jer. 8:3; 2 Pet. 2:2; Jd. 1:12, 13, 16, 18, 19; Isa. 47:13; Jer. 4:16, 17; Nah. 1:3; 2:13; Exod. 23:33; Isa. 43:23, 24; Jer. 6:20; Hos. 9:4; Ezk. 39:26; Isa. 11:4; 65:17; Heb. 10:2)

I saw a meteor fall from heaven to the earth: and to it was given a key to the infinite void. And it opened the pit of the abyss; and there arose a smoke out of the pit, as the smoke of a great furnace; and the sun and the air were darkened by reason of the smoke of the pit. "Then death shall be chosen rather than life by all the residue of those who remain of this evil family, who remain in all the places where I have scattered them," says the LORD of hosts.

Many will follow their sensuality, and because of them the way of the truth will be maligned. They feast with you without fear, serving only themselves. They are clouds without water, carried about by the winds; raging waves of the sea, foaming up their own shame: roving meteoroids, to whom is reserved the blackness of darkness forever. They are complainers, fault finders, they speak great swelling words, admiring people because of advantage; mockers in the last times who would walk according to their own ungodly lusts. These are a sensual people, who cause divisions, not having the Spirit.

You are wearied in the multitude of your counsels. Let now the astrologers, the cosmologists, and the monthly prognosticators stand up and save you from what shall come upon you. Make mention to the nations, yea, proclaim against Jerusalem, that watchers come from a far country and raise their voice against the cities of Judah. "Like keepers of a field they are against her all around, because she has been rebellious against me," says the LORD.

The LORD is slow to anger and great in power and will not at all acquit. "Behold, I am against you," says the LORD of hosts, "I will burn your chariots in smoke, and the sword shall devour your young lions; I will cut off your prey from the earth, and the voice of your messengers shall be heard no more." They shall not dwell in your land, unless they make you sin against me. For if you serve their gods, it will surely be a snare to you.

You have not honored me with your sacrifices. I have not caused you to serve with an offering, nor wearied you with incense. You have bought me no hemp with money, neither have you filled me with the fat of your sacrifices: but you have forced me to serve with your sins, you have wearied me with your iniquities.

Your burnt offerings are not acceptable, nor your sacrifices sweet to me. They shall not offer wine offerings to the LORD, neither shall they be pleasing to him: their sacrifices shall be to them as the bread of mourners; all that eat thereof shall be polluted: for the bread of their soul shall not enter into the house of the LORD. They shall forbear their disgrace and all their treachery which they perpetrated against me when they live securely on their land with no one to make them afraid.

But with righteousness he judges the poor and reproves with equity for the needy of the earth: and he shall smite the earth with the rod of his word, and with the breath of his lips shall he slay the wicked. For behold, I create new heavens and a new earth; and the former shall not be remembered or come to mind. Because the faithful, having been once cleansed, would hold no more conscience of sins.

69. Transition of Heaven and Earth

(Lam. 5:8, 9; Lk. 12:33; Hos. 5:12; Lk. 12:47; Zec. 9:8; Isa. 64:1; 50:3; 34:4; 51:6; Jer. 4:28; 2 Pet. 3:12, 13; Rev. 6:14, 17; Mt. 24:34, 35; Heb. 1:8)

Servants rule over us; none delivers us from their hand. We get our bread at the risk of our lives, because of the sword in the wilderness. Sell what you have and give charity; provide a treasure in the heavens that does not fail, where no thief approaches nor moth corrupts. Therefore, I will be to Ephraim as a moth, and to the house of Judah as rottenness. That servant, which knew his Lord's will, and prepared not himself, neither did according to his will, shall be beaten with many stripes.

I will remain at my temple because the army that crossed over shall retreat, and no oppressor shall pass through here anymore;

for then I have seen it with my eyes. Oh, that you would rend the heavens and come down, that the mountains would tremble before you. I clothe the heavens with blackness, and I make sackcloth their covering. All the host of heaven shall be dissolved, and the heavens shall be rolled up like a scroll; all their host shall fall down as the leaf falls from the vine, and as fruit falling from a fig tree. Lift up your eyes to the heavens and look on the earth beneath. For the heavens will vanish away like smoke, the earth will grow old like a garment, and those who dwell in it will die in like manner; but my salvation will be forever, and my righteousness will not be abolished.

For this shall the earth mourn, and the heavens above be black: because I have spoken it, I have purposed it, and will not repent, neither will I turn back from it. Every mountain and island are moved out of their places; for the great day of his wrath has come, and who is able to stand? Truly I say to you, this generation will not pass away until all these things take place. Heaven and earth will pass away, but my words shall not pass away: looking for and hastening to the coming of the day of God, wherein the heavens being on fire shall be dissolved, and the elements shall melt with intense heat. Nevertheless, according to his promise, we look for new heavens and a new earth, wherein dwells righteousness. But to the Son he says: "Your throne of God, is forever and ever. A scepter of righteousness is the scepter of your kingdom." "For just as the new heavens and the new earth which I make will endure before me," declares the LORD, "so your offspring and your name will endure."

70. Divided For Judgment

(1 Thess. 2:6, 9; Heb. 10:9, 10; Rev. 15:8; 2:25, 26; Mal. 3:1; Lk. 21:34, 35; Dan. 11:32; 1 Jn. 2:4; Mt. 12:36; 7:9; 25:31-34, 40, 41, 45; Rom. 12:20, 21; 1 Pet. 4:8; Jas. 2:15, 16, 17; Ac. 20:35; Jer. 32:8)

We were not looking for praise from man, not from you or anyone else. We could have been a burden to you, but we worked night and day, [sometimes seven days a week] in order not to be a burden to anyone while we revealed the covenant of the Lord to you. As he said, "Behold, I have come to do your will, O God." He takes away the first that he may establish the second. By that will, we have been sanctified through the offering of the body of Jesus Christ once for all. Then the temple was filled with smoke from the glory of God and from his power, and no one was worthy to enter the temple until the seven plagues of the seven angels were completed. Nevertheless, what you have, hold fast until I return. Then he who overcomes, and he who keeps my deeds until the end, to him I will give authority over the nations.

Behold, I send my messenger, and he will prepare the way before me; and the Lord, whom you seek, will suddenly come to his temple, even the messenger of the covenant, in whom I delight. "Behold, he is coming," says the LORD of hosts. Be on guard, that your hearts may not be burdened with excesses and drunkenness and the stress of life, and that day close on you suddenly like a trap; for it will come upon all those who dwell on the face of all the earth. But the people who know their God shall be strong and do exploits. He who says, "I know him," but does not keep his commandments, is a liar, and the truth is not in him.

Thus, I say to you, that every vain word that man shall speak, they shall give account thereof in the day of judgment. [The faithful have *children*, but goats have *kids*.] Which among you, if his son asks for bread, would give him a stone?

When the Son of Man comes in his glory, and all the angels with him, then he will sit on the throne of his glory. All the nations will be gathered before him, and he will separate them one from another. Then he shall set the sheep on his right hand, but the goats on his left. To those on his right he says "Come, you that are blessed by the LORD, inherit the kingdom prepared for you from the foundation of the world. Truly I tell you, whatever you did for one of the least of these brothers of mine, you did for me." Then he will also say to those on his left: "Depart from me, you cursed, into the everlasting fire prepared for the enemy and his agents. Truly I tell you, whatever you did not do for one of the least of these, you did not do for me."

If your enemy is hungry, feed him; if he is thirsty, give him a drink. For in so doing, you will heap coals of fire on his head. Do not be overcome by evil but overcome evil with good. And above all things have fervent charity among yourselves: for charity shall cover the multitude of sins. If a brother or sister is exposed, and destitute of daily food, and one of you says to them, depart in peace, be warmed and filled; but yet you give them not those things which are needed for the body; what benefit is that? Even so faith if it has not works, is dead, being alone.

I have shown you in everything, by laboring this way, that you must support the weak. And remember the words of the Lord Jesus, that he said, "It is more blessed to give than to receive." The right of inheritance is yours, and the redemption is yours; buy it for yourself. Then I knew that this was the word of the LORD.

The Curse

(Deut. 28:15, 16, 19-22, 24-30, 32-37, 43-46, 49, 52)

But it shall come to pass, if you do not obey the voice of the LORD your God, to observe carefully all his commandments which I command you today, that all these curses will come upon you and overtake you. Cursed shall you be in the city and cursed shall you be in the country. Cursed shall you be when you come in and cursed shall you be when you go out.

The LORD will send on you cursing, confusion, and rebuke in all that you set your hand to do, until you are destroyed and until you perish quickly, because of the wickedness of your doings in which you have forsaken me. The LORD will make the plague cling to you until he has consumed you from the land which you are going to possess. The LORD will strike you with consumption, with inflammation, with severe burning fever, with the sword, with scorching, and with mildew; they shall pursue you until you perish.

The LORD will change the rain of your land to powder and dust; from the heavens it shall fall out upon you until you are destroyed. The LORD will cause you to be defeated before your enemies. You shall go out one way against them and flee seven ways before them; your carcass shall be food for all the birds of the air and the beasts of the earth, and no one shall frighten them away. The LORD will strike you with boils, with tumors, with the scab, and with the itch, from which you cannot be healed. The LORD will strike you with madness and blindness and confusion of heart. You shall not prosper in your ways; you shall be only oppressed and plundered continually, and no one shall save you.

You shall build a house, but you cannot dwell in it; you shall plant a vineyard but shall not gather its grapes. Your sons and your daughters shall be given to another people, and your eyes shall look and fail with longing for them all day; and there shall be no strength in your hand. A nation whom you have not known shall eat the fruit of your land and the produce of your labor, and you shall always be only oppressed and crushed continually.

The LORD will strike you with severe boils which cannot be healed, from the sole of your foot to the top of your head. The LORD will bring you and the king whom you set over you to a nation which neither you nor your fathers have known. You shall become an astonishment, a proverb, and a byword among all nations where the LORD will drive you. The alien who is among you shall rise higher and higher above you, and you shall fall down lower and lower. He shall lend to you, but you shall not lend to him; he shall be the head, and you shall be the tail.

Moreover, all these curses shall come upon you and pursue and overtake you, until you are destroyed, because you did not obey the voice of the LORD your God, to keep his commandments as he commanded you: they shall be upon you for a sign and a wonder, and on your descendants forever.

The LORD will bring a nation against you from afar, from the end of the earth, as swift as the eagle flies, a nation whose language you will not understand, and they shall besiege you at all your gates until your high and fortified walls, in which you trust, fall down throughout all your land; and they shall besiege you at all your gates throughout all your land which the LORD your God has given you.

Ten Commandments New Testament

(Deut. 10:14, 17; 11:1, 26-28, 17; Jn. 5:46; Mt. 12:31; Deut. 5:7; 1 Cor. 8:5, 6; Deut. 5:8-10; Jn. 14:15, 21; 15:10; Ac. 15:20; 1 Cor. 12:2; 2 Cor. 6:16, 17; 1 Thess. 1:9; 1 Jn. 5:21; Ac. 17:29, 30; Deut. 5:11; Mt. 12:21; Jn. 5:43; 14:26; Mt. 15:9; Heb. 7:3; Deut. 5:12-15; Mt. 12:8, 11, 12; Deut. 5:16; Eph. 6:1, 4; Mt. 12:50; 2 Cor. 12:14; Mt. 19:4-6; Lk. 18:29, 30; Deut. 5:17; Mt. 10:28; Rev. 2:23; Deut. 5:18; Mt. 5:28, 32; Mk. 10:11, 12; Rom. 2:22; Jn. 8:7; Lev. 20:10-21; Rom. 1:26-32; 1 Cor. 5:1, 2, 5, 9, 13; Deut. 5:19; Rom. 2:21; Eph. 4:28; Lk. 22:52, 53; 2 Pet. 3:10-12; Deut. 5:20; Mt. 15:18-20; Mk. 14:55, 56; Mt. 24:24; 2 Cor. 11:13, 15; 2 Pet. 2:1, 2; 1 Thess. 2:3, 4; Deut. 5:21; Mt. 19:21; Lk. 12:15; Eph. 5:3-7; 1 Thess. 2:5, 6; Lk. 6:24; Jas. 2:10-13; Rev. 17:14; Dan. 2:37)

Behold, the heaven and the heaven of heavens is the LORD's your God, the earth also, with all that is therein. For the LORD your God is God of gods, and Lord of lords, a great God, mighty, and terrible, which regards not persons, nor takes reward.

Therefore, you shall love the LORD your God, and keep his charge, his judgments, and his commandments always.

Behold, I set before you today a blessing and a curse: the blessing, if you obey the commandments of the LORD your God which I command you today; and the curse, if you do not obey the commandments of the LORD your God but turn aside from the way which I command you today, to go after other gods which you have not known, that the anger of the LORD will be kindled against you, and he will shut up the heavens so that there will be no rain and the ground will not yield its fruit; and you will perish quickly from the good land which the LORD is giving you.

If you believed Moses, you would believe me, for he wrote about me. Therefore, I say to you, any sin and blasphemy shall be forgiven to man, but blasphemy against the Spirit shall not be forgiven. (You shall have no other gods before me. For even if there are so-called gods, whether in heaven or on earth, as there are many gods and many lords, yet for us there is one God, the Father, of whom are all things, and we for him; and one Lord Jesus Christ, through whom are all things, and through whom we live.

You shall not make for yourself an image, or any likeness of what is in heaven above or on the earth beneath or in the water under the earth. You shall not worship them or serve them; for I, the LORD your God, am a jealous God, visiting the iniquity of the fathers on the children, and on the third and the fourth generations of those who hate me, but showing lovingkindness to thousands, to those who love me and keep my commandments.

If you love me, you will keep my commandments. He who has my commandments and keeps them, he it is who loves me; and he who loves me shall be loved by the LORD, and I will love him, and will disclose myself to him. If you obey my commands, you will remain in my love, just as I have obeyed the LORD's commands and remain in his love.

But that we write to them, that they abstain from pollutions of idols, and from fornication, and from things strangled, and from blood. You know that you were unbelievers, carried away to those dumb idols, however you were led. Or what agreement has the temple of God with idols? For we are the temple of the living God; just as God said, "I will dwell in them and walk among them; and I will be their God, and they shall be my people." "Therefore, come out from their midst and be separate," says the Lord. "Do not touch what is unclean; and I will accept you." For they themselves report about us what kind of a reception we had with you, and how you turned to God from idols to serve a living and true God. Dear children, keep yourselves away from idols. Being then the offspring of God, we ought not to think that the Divine Nature is like gold or silver or stone, an image formed by technology and imagination of man. Therefore, having overlooked the times of ignorance, God is now declaring to man that all everywhere should repent. You shall not take the name of the LORD your God in vain, for the LORD will not leave him unpunished who takes his name in vain; and in his name shall the nations trust. I have come in my Father's name, and you do not receive me; if another comes in his own name, him you will receive. But the Counselor, the Holy Spirit, whom the Father will send in my name, will teach you all things and will remind you of everything I have said to you. But in vain do they worship me, teaching as doctrines the precepts of men. Without father, without mother, without genealogy, having neither beginning of days nor end of life, but made like the Son of God, he abides a priest perpetually.

Observe the sabbath day to keep it holy, as the LORD your God commanded you. Six days you shall labor and do all your work, but the seventh day is a sabbath of the LORD your God. Therefore, the LORD your God commanded you to observe the sabbath day. For the Son of Man is Lord of the Sabbath. What man shall there be among you, that shall have one sheep, and if it falls into a pit on the sabbath day, will he not lay hold on it, and lift it out? How much then is a man better than a sheep? Therefore, it is lawful to do well on the sabbath days.

Honor your father and your mother, as the LORD your God has commanded you, that your days may be prolonged, and that it may go well with you on the land which the LORD your God gives you. Children, obey your parents in the Lord, for this is right. Do not provoke your children to wrath but bring them up in the training and admonition of the Lord. For whosoever shall do the will of the LORD who is in heaven, the same is my brother, and sister, and mother. After all, children should not have to save up for their parents, but parents for their children. He who made them at the beginning made them male or female, and for this reason a man shall leave his father and mother and be joined to his wife, and the two shall become one flesh. So then, they are no longer two but one flesh. Therefore, what God has joined together, let not man separate. Truly I say to you, there is no one who has left house or wife or brothers or parents or children, for the sake of the kingdom of God, who shall not receive many times as much at this time and in the age to come, eternal life. (You shall not murder. Fear not them which kill the body but are not able to kill the soul: but rather fear him which is able to destroy both soul and body in hell. I will kill their children with death, and I will give to each one of you according to your works.

You shall not commit adultery. But I say to you that whoever looks at a woman to lust for her has already committed adultery with her in his heart. But I say to you that whoever divorces his wife for any reason except sexual immorality causes her to commit adultery; and whoever marries a woman who is divorced commits adultery. Anyone who divorces his wife and marries another woman commits adultery against her, and if she divorces her husband and marries another man, she commits adultery.

You that say a man should not commit adultery, do you commit adultery? You that abhor idols, do you commit sacrilege? He that is without sin among you, let him first cast a stone at her.

If a man commits adultery with another man's wife, with the wife of his neighbor, or if a man sleeps with his father's wife, he has dishonored his father. Their blood will be on their own heads. If a man sleeps with his daughter-in-law, what they have done is a perversion; their blood will be on their own heads.

If a man lies with a man as one lies with a woman, both of them have done what is detestable. They must be put to death; their blood will be on their own heads. If a man marries both a woman and her mother, it is wicked. Both he and they must be burned in the fire, so that no wickedness will be among you. If a man has sexual relations with an animal, he must be put to death, and you must kill the animal. If a woman approaches an animal to have sexual relations with it, kill both the woman and the animal. They must be put to death; their blood will be on their own heads.

If a man marries his sister, the daughter of either his father or his mother, and they have sexual relations, it is a disgrace. They must be cut off before the eyes of their people. He has dishonored his sister and will be held responsible. If a man lies with a woman during her monthly period and has sexual relations with her, he has exposed the source of her flow, and she has also uncovered it. Both of them must be cut off from their people.

Do not have sexual relations with the sister of either your mother or your father, for that would dishonor a close relative; both of you would be held responsible. If a man sleeps with his aunt, he has dishonored his uncle. They will be held responsible; they will die childless. If a man marries his brother's wife, it is an act of impurity; he has dishonored his brother. They will be childless.

For this cause God gave them up to vile affections: for even their women did change the natural use into that which is against nature; and likewise also the men, leaving the natural use of the woman, burned in their lust one toward another; men with men working that which is unseemly, and receiving in themselves that consequence of their error which is appropriate. Furthermore, since they did not think it worthwhile to retain the knowledge of God, he gave them over to a reprobate mind, to do what ought not to be done. They have become filled with every sort of wickedness, evil, greed and depravity. They are full of envy, murder, strife, deceit, and malice. They are gossips, slanderers, God-haters, insolent, arrogant and boastful; they invent ways of doing evil; they disobey their parents; they are senseless, faithless, heartless, ruthless. Although they know God's righteous decree that those who do such things deserve death, they not only continue to do these very things but also, they approve of those who practice them.

It is actually reported that there is immorality among you, and immorality of such a kind as does not exist even among the Gentiles, that someone has his father's wife; and you have become arrogant, and have not mourned instead, in order that the one who had done this deed might be removed from your midst. Deliver such a one to Satan for the destruction of the flesh, that his spirit may be saved in the day of the Lord Jesus. I wrote to you in my epistle to have no company with fornicators. But judge them that are without God. Therefore, put away from among yourselves that wicked person.

You shall not steal. You then who teach others, do you not teach yourself? You that preach against stealing, do you steal? Let him who stole steal no longer, but rather let him labor, working with his hands what is good, that he may have something to give him who has need.

Jesus said to the chief priests and officers of the temple and elders who had come against him, "Have you come out with swords and clubs as against a robber?" "While I was with you daily in the temple, you did not lay hands on me; but this hour and the power of darkness are yours." But the day of the Lord will come like a thief, in which the heavens will pass away with a roar and the elements will be destroyed with intense heat, and the earth and its works will be burned up. Since all these things are to be destroyed in this way, what sort of people ought you to be in holy conduct and godliness, looking for and hastening the coming of the day of God, on account of which the heavens will be destroyed by burning, and the elements will melt with intense heat.

You shall not bear false witness. But those things which proceed out of the mouth come from the heart, and they defile a man. For out of the heart proceed evil thoughts, murders, adulteries, fornications, thefts, false witness, blasphemies. These are the things which defile a person.

Now the chief priests and the whole council kept trying to obtain testimony against Jesus to put him to death; and they were not finding any. For many were giving false testimony against him, but their testimony was not consistent. For false messiahs and false prophets will rise and show great signs and miracles to deceive, if possible, even the chosen. For such are false apostles, deceitful workers, transforming themselves into the apostles of Christ. Therefore, it is no great thing if those ministers also be transformed as the ministers of righteousness; whose end shall be according to their works. But there were false prophets also among the people, even as there are false teachers among you, who privily bring in damnable heresies, even denying the Lord that bought them, and shall bring upon themselves immediate destruction. And many shall follow their pernicious ways; by reason of whom the way of truth shall be vilified.

For our exhortation was not of deceit, nor of uncleanness, nor in guile: But as we were allowed of God to be put in trust with the good message, even so we speak; not as pleasing man, but God, which proves our hearts.

You shall not covet. If you want to be perfect, go, sell what you have and give to the poor, and you will have treasure in heaven; and come, follow me. Take heed and beware of covetousness, for one's life does not consist in the abundance of the things he possesses. But fornication and all uncleanness or covetousness, let it not even be named among you; neither filthiness, nor foolish talking, nor coarse jesting, which are not appropriate, but rather giving of thanks. For this, you know that no fornicator, unclean person, nor covetous person, who is an idolater, has any inheritance in the kingdom of Christ and God. Let no one deceive you with empty words, for because of these things the wrath of

God comes upon the sons of disobedience. Therefore, do not be partakers with them.

For neither at any time used we flattering words, as you know, nor a cloke of covetousness; God is witness: Nor of man sought we glory, neither of you, nor yet of others, when we might have been burdensome, as the apostles of Christ. But woe to you rich, for you have received your consolation.

Why do you also transgress the commandment of God by your tradition? Whosoever shall keep the whole law, and yet offend in one point, he is guilty of all. For he that said, "Do not commit adultery," said also, "Do not kill." Now if you commit no adultery, yet if you kill, you have become a transgressor of the law. So speak and so do, as they that shall be judged by the law of liberty. For he shall have judgment without mercy, that has shown no mercy; and mercy rejoices against judgment.

These will make war with the Christ, and the Christ will overcome them, for he is Lord of lords and King of kings; and those who are with him are called, chosen, and faithful. For the God of heaven has given them a kingdom, power, strength, and glory.

SECTION 3

THIRD TEMPLE, HOLY CITY, NEW EARTH

Rebellion and Conflict

(Jer. 25:31; Isa. 34:8; Jn. 15:13, 14; Rev. 2:10, 11; Rom. 1:18, 25; 13:2, 3; Prov. 28:7; Rom. 2:8, 9; 2 Thess. 1:6; Rom. 1:29-31; 13:2; 2:12, 13; Jer. 1:7, 8; 2 Cor. 12:20; Ti. 1:10, 11; Heb. 4:13; Am. 9:8; Hos. 1:9, 10; Rev. 20:8, 9; Lk. 21:20)

A noise shall come even to the ends of the earth; for the LORD has a controversy with the nations, he will plead with all flesh; he will give them that are wicked to the sword, says the LORD. For it is the day of the LORD's vengeance, and the year of recompenses for the controversy of Zion. Greater love has no man than this, that a man lay down his life for his friends. You are my friends if you do whatsoever I command you. Be faithful until death, and I will give you the crown of life.

He who overcomes shall not be hurt by the second death. For the wrath of God is revealed from heaven against all ungodliness and unrighteousness of men, who hold the truth in unrighteousness, who changed the truth of God into a lie, and worshipped and served the creature more than the Creator, who is blessed forever, amen.

Consequently, he who rebels against the authority is rebelling against what God has instituted, and those who do so will bring judgment upon themselves. For the rulers hold no terror for those who do right, but for those who do wrong. Do you want to be free from fear of the one in authority? Then do what is right and he will commend you.

Whoso keeps the law is a wise son: but he that is a companion of riotous men shames his father. But to them that are contentious, and do not obey the truth, but obey unrighteousness: indignation and wrath, tribulation, and anguish, upon every soul of man that does evil. Since it is a righteous thing with God to repay with tribulation those who trouble you, being filled with all unrighteousness, wickedness, greed, evil; full of envy, murder, strife, deceit, malice; gossips, slanderers, haters of God, insolent, arrogant, boastful, inventors of evil, disobedient to parents, without understanding, untrustworthy, unloving, unmerciful; whosoever therefore resists the power, resists the ordinance of God: and they that resist shall receive to themselves damnation. For as many as have sinned without law shall also perish without law: and as many as have sinned in the law shall be judged by the law; for not the hearers of the law are just before God, but the doers of the law shall be justified.

"Everywhere I send you, shall you go, and all that I command you, shall you speak. Do not be afraid of them, for I am with you to deliver you," declares the LORD. But I am concerned that perhaps when I come, I may find you to be not what I wish and may be found by you to be not what you wish, but perhaps strife, jealousy, angry tempers, disputes, slanders, gossip, arrogance, and disturbances. For there are many unruly and vain talkers and deceivers, especially they of the *concision*: whose mouths must be stopped, who subvert entire denominations, teaching things which they ought not, for filthy lucre's sake.

Nothing in all creation is hidden from God's sight. Everything is uncovered and exposed before the eyes of him to whom we must give account. "Behold, the eyes of the Lord GOD are on the sinful kingdom, and I will destroy it from the face of the earth; nevertheless, I will not totally destroy the house of Jacob," declares the LORD. You are not my people, and I am not your God. Yet the

Israelites will be like the sand on the seashore, which cannot be measured or counted; the nations which are in the four quarters of the earth, Gog and Magog, to gather them together to battle: the number of whom is as the sand of the sea. They went up on the breadth of the earth and surrounded the capital of the holy people in the beloved city: and fire came down from God out of heaven and devoured them. Now, when you see Jerusalem encircled by armies, then know that the desolation of it is near.

The Overthrow

(Jn. 2:13; Mt. 20:31; Jn. 12:1; 11:18; Mk. 11:12-14; Jn. 12:12, 13; Lk. 19:44; Mk. 11:11, 15, 16; 1 Sam. 4:22; Mk. 11:20-22, 24; Mt. 24:43; Jb. 30:5-8; Heb. 11:36-39; Mt. 26:55, 56; Lk. 22:53)

The Jews' Passover was near, and Jesus went up to Jerusalem. The multitude warned them that they should be quiet; but they cried out all the more, saying, "Have mercy on us, O Lord, Son of David!" Then, Jesus six days before the Passover came to Bethany. Now Bethany was near Jerusalem, about two miles away. Now the next day, when they had come out from Bethany, he was hungry. Then seeing from afar a fig tree having leaves, he went to see if perhaps he would find something on it; and when he came to it, he found nothing but leaves, for it was not the season for figs. In response Jesus said to it, "Let no one eat fruit from you ever again," and his disciples heard it. Many people that were going to the feast, when they heard that Jesus was coming to Jerusalem, took branches of palm trees, went forth to meet him, and cried, "Salvation: blessed is the King of Israel that comes in the name of the Lord." But you did not know the time of your visitation.

Jesus went to Jerusalem. When they arrived at Jerusalem, he looked around at all things. Then Jesus went into the temple and began to drive out those who bought and sold in the temple and overturned the tables of the money changers and the seats of those who sold doves; and he would not allow anyone to carry vessels through the temple. As the hour was already late, he went back to Bethany with the twelve. The glory has departed from Israel, for the ark of God has been captured.

Now in the morning, as they passed by, they saw the fig tree dried up from the roots; and Peter, remembering, said to him, "Rabbi, look! The fig tree which you poisoned has withered away." So, Jesus answered and said to them, "Have faith in God." "Therefore, I say to you, whatever things you ask when you pray, believe that you receive them, and you will have them." "But know this, that if the good man of the house had known in what watch the thief would come, he would have watched, and would not have suffered his house to be broken up."

They were banished from among men, shouted down like thieves to dwell in the cliffs of the valleys, in caves of the earth and in the rocks. They called out among the shrubs and huddled beneath the nettles. They were sons of fools, yes, sons of without names; they were scourged from the land. And others had trial of mocking and scourging, moreover of bonds and imprisonment. They were stoned, they were sawn asunder, were tempted, were slain with the sword: they wandered around in sheepskins and goatskins; being destitute, afflicted, and tormented, of whom the world was not worthy. They wandered in deserts and mountains, in dens and caves of the earth. And all these, having obtained a good report through faith, received not the promise.

In that same hour said Jesus to the multitudes, "Have you come out as against a thief with swords and staves to take me? I sat daily with you teaching in the temple, and you laid no hold on me." But all this was done, that the scriptures of the prophets might be fulfilled. Then all the disciples forsook him and fled. This is your hour, and the power of darkness.

Millennial Kingdom

(Rev. 21:6; Isa. 55:1; Rev. 21:7; 2 Cor. 8:14; Ac. 7:48-50; Isa. 66:2; 2 Cor. 4:18; 2 Tim. 2:19; Rev. 3:1; Mt. 7:21; 15:9)

He said to me, "It is done. I am Alaph and Taw, the beginning and the end. I will give to him that is athirst of the fountain of the water of life freely." Come, everyone who thirsts, come to the waters; and he who has no money, come, buy and eat! Come, buy wine and milk without money and without price. "He that overcomes shall inherit

all things; and I will be his God, and he shall be my son." At the present time, your abundance provides for their need, so that their abundance also may be for your need, so that there may be equality.

Howbeit the Most High dwells not in temples made with hands; as said the prophet, "Heaven is my throne, and earth is my footstool: what house will you build for me?" says the Lord: "Or what is the place of my rest?" "Have not my hands made all these things?" "For all those things have my hands made, and all those things have been," says the LORD: "but to this man will I look, even to him that is poor and of a contrite spirit, and trembles at my word."

While we look not at the things which are seen, but at the things which are not seen: for the things which are seen are temporal; but the things which are not seen are eternal. Nevertheless, the foundation of God stands firm, having this seal, "The Lord knows those who are his," and "Let everyone who names the name of the Lord abstain from wickedness."

I know your works, that you have a name that you live, and are dead. Not everyone that says to me, Lord, Lord, shall enter into the kingdom of heaven; but the one that does the will of the LORD who is in heaven. But in vain do they worship me, teaching for doctrines the precepts of man.

Holiday Occasions

(1 Cor. 14:5; 2 Cor. 11:6; Gal. 3:3; 4:10, 11; Col. 2:13, 16, 17)

Greater is one who prophesies than one who speaks in many languages, unless he interprets, so that the congregations may receive edifying. I may not be a trained speaker, but I do have knowledge. Are you so foolish? Having begun in the Spirit, are you now being made perfect by the flesh? You observe days and months and seasons and years.

I fear for you, that perhaps I have labored over you in vain. When you were dead in your transgressions, he made you alive together with him, having forgiven us all our transgressions. So let no one judge you in food or in drink, or regarding a festival or a new moon or sabbaths, which are a shadow of things to come, but the substance is of Christ.

Warning Against Idolatry

(Exod. 20:4-6; Deut. 4:16-18; 2 Ki. 17:9-15; Isa. 2:8; 45:16; Ezk. 14:4-6; 1 Cor. 13:11; 1 Jn. 5:21; 1 Cor. 10:14)

You shall not make any graven image, or any likeness. You shalt not bow down to them, nor serve them: for I the LORD your God am a jealous God, visiting the iniquity of the fathers upon the children to the third and fourth generation of them that hate me, and showing mercy to thousands of them that love me and keep my commandments; so that you do not become corrupt and make for yourselves an idol, an image of any shape, whether formed like a male or a female, or like any animal on earth or any bird that flies in the air, or like any creature that moves along the ground or any fish in the waters below.

But the children of Israel did secretly those things that were not right against the LORD their God, and they built high places in all their cities, from the tower of the watchmen to the fenced city; and they set up images and groves in every high hill, and under every green tree: and there they burnt incense in all the high places, as did the heathen whom the LORD carried away before them, and they wrought wicked things to provoke the LORD to anger. For they served idols, whereof the LORD had said to them, "You shall not do those things." Yet the LORD testified against Israel, and against Judah, by all the prophets, and by all the seers, saying, "Turn from your evil ways, and keep my commandments which I commanded your fathers, and which I sent to you by my servants the prophets. Notwithstanding they would not hear, but hardened their necks, like to the neck of their fathers, that did not believe in the LORD their God; and they rejected his covenant that he made with their fathers, and his testimonies which he testified against them: and they followed vanity, and became vain, and went after the heathen that were around them, concerning whom the LORD had charged them, that they should not do like them.

This land also is full of idols; they worship the work of their own hands, that which their own fingers have made. They shall be ashamed, and also confounded, all of them: they shall go to confusion together that are makers of idols. Therefore speak to them and tell them, "Thus says the Lord GOD, 'Anyone of the

house of Israel who sets up his idols in his heart, puts before his face the stumbling block of his iniquity, and comes to the prophet, I the LORD will be brought to give him an answer in the matter in view of the multitude of his idols, in order to lay hold of the hearts of the house of Israel who are estranged from me through all their idols.'" Therefore, say to the house of Israel, "Thus says the Lord GOD, 'Repent and turn away from your idols, and turn your faces away from all your abominations.'"

When I was a child, I spoke as a child, I understood as a child, I thought as a child; but when I became a man, I put away childish things. Dear children, keep yourselves away from idols. Therefore, my beloved, flee from idolatry.

The Chosen

(Isa. 7:14; Mic. 5:2, 3; Hos. 11:1, 2; Jer. 31:15; Isa. 40:3; 9:1, 2; 61:1-3; 53:4; 42:1-4; Ps. 78:2; Zec. 9:9; Isa. 56:7; Jer. 7:11; Pss. 69:8, 9; 118:25, 26; Exod. 22:7; Isa. 53:1; 6:10; Ps. 8:2; Zec. 13:7-9; Ps. 22:18; Zec. 12:10, 11)

Therefore, the Lord himself shall give you a sign; behold, a virgin shall conceive, and bear a son, and shall call his name "The Almighty is with us." But you, Bethlehem the fruitful, though you are small among the clans of Judah, out of you will come for me one who will be ruler over Israel, whose origins are from of old, from ancient times. Therefore, Israel will be abandoned until the time when she who is in labor gives birth and the rest of his brothers return to join the Israelites. When Israel was a child, then I loved him, and called my son out of Egypt. As they called them, so they went from them: they sacrificed to Baalzevuv and burned incense to graven images. Thus says the LORD; "A voice was heard in high places, lamentation, and bitter weeping; the traveler weeping for her children refused to be comforted for her children, because they were naught." The voice of him that cries in the wilderness, prepare the way of the LORD, make straight in the desert a highway for our God.

Nevertheless, the dimness shall not be such as was in her vexation, when at the first he lightly afflicted the land of Zebulun and the land of Naphtali, and afterward did more grievously afflict her by the way of the sea, beyond Jordan, in Galilee of the nations. The people that walked in darkness have seen a great light: they that dwell in the land of the shadow of death, upon them has the light shined. The Spirit of the Lord GOD is upon me; because the LORD anointed me to preach good tidings to the meek; he sent me to bind up the brokenhearted, to proclaim liberty to the captives, and the opening of the prison to them that are bound; to proclaim the acceptable year of the LORD, and the day of vengeance of our God, to comfort all that mourn; to appoint to them that mourn in Zion, to give to them beauty for ashes, the oil of joy for mourning, the garment of praise for the spirit of heaviness; that they might be called trees of righteousness, the planting of the LORD, that he might be glorified.

Surely, he has borne our griefs, and carried our sorrows: yet we did esteem him stricken, smitten of God, and afflicted. Here is my servant, whom I uphold, my chosen one in whom I delight; I will put my Spirit on him, and he will bring justice to the nations. He will not shout or cry out or raise his voice in the streets. A bruised reed he will not break, and a smoldering wick he will not snuff out. In faithfulness he will bring forth justice; he will not falter or be discouraged until he establishes justice on earth. In his law the coastlands will put their hope. I will open my mouth in parables, I will utter hidden things, things of old.

Rejoice greatly, O Daughter of Zion! Shout, Daughter of Jerusalem! See, your king comes to you, righteous and having salvation, gentle and riding on a donkey, on a colt, the foal of a donkey. Even them will I bring to my holy mountain and make them joyful in my house of prayer: their burnt offerings and their sacrifices shall be accepted upon my altar; for my house shall be called a house of prayer for all people. Has this house, which is called by my name, become a den of robbers in your eyes? Behold, even I have seen it, says the LORD. I have become a stranger to my brothers, and an alien to my mother's children; because zeal for your house has eaten me up, and the reproaches of those who reproach you have fallen on me. Save now, I pray, O LORD; O LORD, I pray, send now prosperity. Blessed is he who comes in the name of the LORD! We have blessed you from the house of the LORD.

If a man delivers to his neighbor money or articles to keep, and it is stolen out of the man's house, if the thief is found, he shall pay double. Who has believed our message and to whom has the arm of the LORD been revealed? Make the heart of this people dull, and their ears heavy, and shut their eyes; unless they see with their eyes, and hear with their ears, and understand with their heart, and return and be healed. Out of the mouth of babes and nursing infants you have ordained strength, because of your enemies, that you may silence the enemy and the avenger.

"Awake, O sword, against my shepherd, against the man who is close to me!" declares the LORD Almighty. "Strike the shepherd, and the sheep will be scattered, and I will turn my hand against the little ones in the whole land," declares the LORD. "Two-thirds will be struck down and perish; yet one-third will remain in it. This third I will bring into the fire; I will refine them like silver and test them like gold. They will call on my name and I will answer them; I will say, 'They are my people,' and they will say, 'The LORD is our God.'"

They divide my garments among them, and for my clothing they cast lots. I will pour upon the house of David, and upon the inhabitants of Jerusalem, the spirit of grace and of supplications: and they shall look upon him whom they have pierced, and they shall mourn for him, as one mourns for his only son, and shall be in bitterness for him, as one that is in bitterness for his firstborn. In that day is great mourning in Jerusalem, as the mourning of Hadad-Rimmon in the valley of Megiddo.

Messiah the First Born

(Mt. 1:24, 25; 2:6, 14-18; 3:1-3; 4:12-17; Lk. 3:23; 4:17-19; Mt. 8:16, 17; 12:14-21; 13:34, 35; Lk. 19:29, 30; Jn. 12:12-16; Mt. 21:4, 9, 12, 13; Jn. 2:16, 17; Rev. 3:3; 1 Sam. 4:22; Rev. 16:15; Jb. 30:5, 6; 1 Thess. 5:2; Lk. 12:39; Mk. 4:25; Jn. 12:37-40; Mt. 21:15, 16; 26:31, 32, 55; 27:35; Jn. 19:34, 37, 40, 41, 42)

As Joseph arose from his sleep and did as the angel of the Lord commanded him and took for himself his wife; and knew her not until she had brought forth a son: and he called his name *Jehoshua*. But you, Bethlehem, in the land of Judah, are not the least among the rulers of Judah; for out of you shall come a leader who will shepherd my people Israel. When he arose, he took the young child and his mother by night and departed for Egypt, and was there until the death of Herod, that it might be fulfilled which was spoken by the LORD through the prophet, saying, "Out of Egypt I called my Son." Then Herod, when he saw that he was deceived by the wise men, was exceedingly angry; and he sent forth and put to death all the male children who were in Bethlehem and in all its districts, from two years old and under, according to the time which he had determined from the wise men. Then was fulfilled what was spoken by Jeremiah the prophet, saying: "A voice was heard in the heights, lamentation, weeping, and great mourning, the traveler weeping for her children, refusing to be comforted, because they are no more."

In those days John the Baptist came preaching in the wilderness of Judea, and saying, "Repent, for the kingdom of heaven is at hand!" For this is he who was spoken of by the prophet Isaiah, saying: "The voice of one crying in the wilderness: 'Prepare the way of the Lord; make his paths straight.'" When Jesus heard that John had been put in prison, he returned to Galilee. Leaving Nazareth, he went and lived in Capernaum, which was by the lake in the area of Zebulun and Naphtali, to fulfill what was said through the prophet Isaiah: "Land of Zebulun and land of Naphtali, the way to the sea, along the Jordan, Galilee of the Gentiles, the people living in darkness have seen a great light; on those living in the land of the shadow of death a light has dawned." From that time on Jesus began to preach, "Repent, for the kingdom of heaven is near."

Now Jesus himself was about age thirty when he began his ministry. He was the son, as it was determined, of Joseph, the son of Heli. There was delivered to him the scroll of the prophet Isaiah, and when he had opened the scroll, he found the place where it was written, "The Spirit of the Lord is upon me, because he has anointed me to preach the gospel to the poor; he has sent me to heal the brokenhearted, to preach deliverance to the captives, and recovering of sight to the blind, to set at liberty them that are bruised, to preach the acceptable year of the LORD."

When Jesus had come into Peter's house, he saw his wife's mother laying, sick with a fever. He touched her hand, and the fever left her: and she arose, and served them. When evening had come, they brought to him many who were demon-possessed. He cast out the spirits with a word, and healed all who were sick, that it might be fulfilled which was spoken by Isaiah the prophet, saying: "He himself took our infirmities and bore our sicknesses." Then the Pharisees went out and plotted against him, how they might destroy him. But when Jesus perceived it, he withdrew from there. Then great multitudes followed him, and he healed them all. Yet he warned them not to make him known, that it might be fulfilled which was spoken by Isaiah the prophet, saying: "Behold, my servant whom I have chosen, my beloved in whom my soul is well pleased! I will put my Spirit upon him, and he will declare justice to the Gentiles. He will not quarrel nor cry out, nor will anyone hear his voice in the streets. A bruised reed he will not break, and smoldering flax he will not quench, until he sends forth justice to victory; and in his name nations will trust." All these things Jesus spoke to the multitude in parables; and without a parable he did not speak to them, that it might be fulfilled which was spoken by the prophet, saying: "I will open my mouth in parables; I will utter things kept secret from the foundation of the world."

As he approached Bethphage and Bethany at the hill called the Mount of Olives, he sent two of his disciples, saying to them, "Go to the village ahead of you, and as you enter it, you will find a colt tied there, which no one has ever ridden. Untie it and bring it here." The next day a great multitude had gone to the feast, because they heard that Jesus was coming to Jerusalem, they took branches of palm trees and went out to meet him and cried out: "Salvation! Blessed is he who comes in the name of the Lord, the King of Israel." As it is written: "Fear not, daughter of Zion; behold, your King is coming, sitting on a donkey's colt." His disciples did not understand these things at first; but when Jesus was glorified, then they remembered that these things were written about him and that they had done these things for him. All this was done that it might be fulfilled which was spoken by the prophet. Then the multitudes who went before and those who followed cried out, saying: "Salvation to the Son of David! Blessed is he who comes in the name of the LORD! Salvation in the highest!" Then Jesus went into the temple of God, and cast out all of them that sold and bought in the temple, and overthrew the tables of the moneychangers and the seats of them that sold doves; he said to them, "It is written, 'My house shall be called a house of prayer,' but you have made it a 'den of thieves.'" "Take these things hence, make not the LORD's house a house of merchandise." His disciples remembered that it was written, "The zeal of your house has eaten me up."

Remember therefore how you have received and heard, and hold fast, and repent. If therefore you shall not watch, I will come to you as a thief, and you will not know what hour I will come upon you. The glory has departed from Israel: for the ark of God was taken. Behold, I come as a thief. Blessed is he that watches, and keeps his garments, unless they see his indecency. They were driven forth from among men, they cried after them as after a thief; to dwell in the cliffs of the valleys, in caves of the earth, and in the rocks. For yourselves know perfectly that the day of the Lord so comes as a thief in the night. Be sure of this, that if the head of the house had known at what hour the thief was coming, he would not have allowed his house to be broken into. For he that has, to him shall be given: but he that has not, from him shall be taken even that which he has.

But although he had done so many signs before them, they did not believe in him, that the word of Isaiah the prophet might be fulfilled, which he spoke: "Lord, who has believed our report? To whom has the arm of the Lord been revealed?" Therefore, they could not believe, because Isaiah said again: "He has blinded their eyes and hardened their hearts, unless they should see with their eyes, lest they should understand with their hearts and turn, so that I should heal them."

When the chief priests and scribes saw the wonderful things that he did, and the children crying in the temple, and saying, "Salvation to the Son of David"; they were very displeased, and said to him, "You hear what they say?" Then Jesus said to them, "Yea; have you never read, 'Out of the mouth of babes and sucklings you have perfected praise'"? Then said Jesus to them, "All of you shall be offended because of me this night: for it is written, 'I will smite the shepherd, and the sheep of the flock shall be scattered abroad.' But after that I am risen again, I will go before you into Galilee." In that same hour said Jesus to the multitudes, "Have you come out as against a thief with swords and staves to take me? I sat daily with you teaching in the temple, and you laid no hold on me. Then they crucified him, and divided his garments, casting lots, that it might be fulfilled which was spoken by the prophet: "They divided my garments among them, and for my clothing they cast lots." But one of the soldiers pierced his side with a spear, and immediately blood and water issued forth. Again, another scripture says, "They shall look on him whom they pierced." Then they took the body of Jesus and bound it in strips of linen with spices. Now in the place where he was crucified there was a garden, and in the garden a new tomb. So, there they laid Jesus, because the tomb was nearby.

Two Kings

(Dan. 11:36, 32, 24, 25, 13, 17, 23, 14, 26, 27, 28, 33, 34, 41, 42, 43, 15, 16, 31, 39, 19, 35, 20, 37, 38, 18, 30, 21, 29, 40, 44, 22, 45; 2 Thess. 2:3; Jer. 50:32; Isa. 21:2)

The king will do as he pleases. He will exalt and magnify himself above every god and will say unheard-of things against the God of gods. He will be successful until the time of wrath is completed, for what has been determined must take place. He will invade the kingdom when its people feel secure, and he will seize it through intrigue. With flattery he will corrupt those who have violated the covenant, but the people who know their God will firmly resist him. When the richest provinces feel secure, he will invade them and will achieve what neither his fathers nor his forefathers did. He will distribute plunder, loot and wealth among his followers. He will plot the overthrow of fortresses, but only for a time. With a large army he will stir up his strength and courage against the king of the South. The king of the South will wage war with a large and very powerful army, but he will not be able to stand because of the plots devised against him. For the king of the North will muster another army, larger than the first; and after several years, he will advance with a huge army fully equipped. He will determine to come with the might of his entire kingdom and will make an alliance with the king of the South. He will give him a daughter in marriage in order to overthrow the kingdom, but his plans will not succeed or help him. After coming to an agreement with him, he will act deceitfully, and with only a few people he will rise to power. In those times many will rise against the king of the South. The violent men among your own people will rebel in fulfillment of the vision, but without success. Those who eat from the king's provisions will try to destroy him; his army will be swept away, and many will fall in battle. The two kings, with their hearts bent on evil, will sit at the same table and lie to each other, but to no avail, because an end will still come at the appointed time.

The king of the North will return to his own country with great wealth, but his heart will be set against the holy covenant. He will take action against it and then return to his own country. Those who are wise will instruct many, though for a time they will fall by the sword or be burned or captured or plundered. When they fall, they will receive a little help, and many who are not sincere will join them. He will also invade the Holy Land (Judea, Palestine). Many countries will fall, but Edom, Moab and the leaders of Ammon will be delivered from his hand. He will extend his power over many countries; Egypt will not escape. He will gain control of the treasures of gold and silver and all the riches of Egypt, with the Libyans and Ethiopians in submission. Then the king of the North will come and build up siege ramps and will capture a fortified city. The forces of the South will be powerless to resist; even their best troops will not have the strength to stand. The invader will do as he pleases; no one will be able to stand against him. He will establish himself in the Holy Land and will have the power to destroy it. His armed forces will rise up to desecrate the temple fortress and will abolish the daily sacrifice. Then they will set up the abomination that causes desolation. He will attack the mightiest fortresses with the help of a foreign god and will greatly honor those who acknowledge him. He will make them rulers over many people and will distribute the land at a price. After this, he will turn back toward the fortresses of his own country but will stumble and fall, to be seen no more. Some of the wise will stumble, so that they may be refined, purified and made spotless until the time of the end, for it will still come at the appointed time. His successor will send out a tax collector to maintain the royal splendor. In a few years, however, he will be destroyed, yet not in anger or in battle. He will show no regard for the gods of his fathers or for the one desired by women, nor will he regard any god, but will exalt himself above them all. Instead of them, he will honor a god of fortresses; a god unknown to his fathers he will honor with gold and silver, with precious stones and costly gifts. Then he will turn his attention to the coastlands and will take many of them, but a commander will put an end to his insolence and will turn his insolence back upon him. Ships of the western coastlands will oppose him, and he will lose heart. Then he will turn back and vent his fury against the holy covenant. He will return and show favor to those who forsake the holy covenant.

In his estate shall stand up a contemptible person, to whom they shall not give the honor of royalty, but he shall come in peaceably and obtain the kingdom by flatteries. At the appointed time he will invade the South again, but this time the outcome will be different from what it was before. At the time of the end the king of the South will engage him in battle, and the king of the North will storm out against him with chariots and cavalry and a great fleet of ships. He will invade many countries and sweep through them like a flood. But reports from the east and the north will alarm him, and he will set out in a great rage to destroy and annihilate many. Then an overwhelming army will be swept away before him; both it and a prince of the covenant will be destroyed. He will pitch his royal tents between the seas at the beautiful holy mountain. Yet he will come to his end, and no one will help him: then that man of sin is revealed, the son of perdition. The most proud shall stumble and fall, and none shall raise him up: and I will kindle a fire in his cities, and it shall devour all around him. Besiege, O Media! All its sighing I have made to cease.

Redemption

(Lk. 14:31-33; Mt. 24:22; Heb. 11:40; Jl. 2:32; Mal. 2:4-6; Zec. 14:9; Eph. 1:11, 12)

What king, when he sets out to meet another king in battle, will not first sit down and take counsel whether he is strong enough with ten thousand to encounter the one coming against him with twenty thousand? Or else, while the other is still a long way off, he sends a delegation and asks conditions of peace. So likewise, whoever of you does not forsake all that he has cannot be my disciple. And unless those days were shortened, no flesh would be saved; but for the sake of the chosen ones, those days will be shortened. But the cowardly, and faithless, and detestable, and murderers, and fornicators, and malpractitioners [pharmacologists, poisoners, politicians, lawyers], idolaters, and all liars: their portion will be in the lake that burns with fire and sulfur, which is the second death.

God having provided some better thing for us, that they without us should not be made perfect. It shall come to pass, that whosoever shall call on the name of the LORD shall be delivered: for in mount Zion and in Jerusalem shall be deliverance, as the LORD has said, and in the remnant whom the LORD shall call. "Then you shall know that I have sent this commandment to you, that my covenant with Christ shall continue," says the LORD of hosts. "My covenant was with him, one of life and peace, and I gave them to him that he might fear me; so, he feared me and was reverent before my name." "The law of truth was in his mouth, and injustice was not found in his word. He walked with me in peace and equity and turned many away from iniquity."

Then the LORD shall be king over all the earth: in that day shall there be one LORD, and his name one. In whom also we have obtained an inheritance, being predestined according to the purpose of him who works all things after the counsel of his own will; that we who first trusted in Christ, are to commend his power.

Seven Angels, Seals, Trumpets, Crucibles

Four Horses

(Rev. 6:1; Zec. 6:1, 5)

I saw when Christ opened one of the seven seals, and I heard, as it was the noise of thunder, one of the four living creatures saying, "Come." I turned, and lifted up my eyes and looked, and behold, there came four chariots out from between two mountains; and the mountains were mountains of brass. These are the four spirits of the heavens, which go forth from standing before the Lord of all the earth.

First Seal

(Rev. 6:2; 8:7; 14:6, 7; 16:2)

I saw, and behold, a white horse: and he that sat on him had a bow; and a crown was given to him: and he went forth conquering, and to conquer. The first angel sounded, and there followed hail and fire mingled with blood, and they were cast upon the earth: and the third part of trees was burnt up, and all green grass was burnt up. I saw the angel fly in the midst of heaven, having the everlasting covenant to preach to them that dwell on the earth, and to every nation, and kindred, and tongue, and people, saying with a loud voice, "Fear God, and give glory to him; for the hour of his judgment has come: and worship him that made heaven, and earth, and the sea, and the fountains of waters." The first went and poured out his crucible upon the earth; and there fell a noisome and grievous sore upon the men which had the mark of the beast, and upon them which worshipped his image.

Second Seal

(Rev. 6:3, 4; 8:8, 9; 14:8; 16:3)

When he had opened the second seal, I heard the second creature say, "Come and see." There went out another horse that was red: and power was given to him that sat thereon to take peace from the earth, and that they should kill one another: and there was given to him a great sword. The second angel sounded, and as it were a great mountain burning with fire was cast into the sea: and the third part of the sea became blood; and the third part of the creatures which were in the sea, and had life, died; and the third part of the ships were destroyed. There followed the angel, saying, Babylon is fallen, is fallen, that great city, because she made all nations drink of the wine of the wrath of her fornication. The second angel poured out his crucible upon the sea; and it became as the blood of a dead man: and every living soul died in the sea.

Third Seal

(Rev. 6:5; 8:10, 11; 14:9, 10; 16:4; Zec. 6:6, 8)

When he had opened the third seal, I heard the third creature say, "Come and see." I beheld, and lo a black horse; and he that sat on him had a pair of balances in his hand. The third angel sounded, and there fell a great star from heaven, burning as it were a lamp, and it fell upon the third part of the rivers, and upon the fountains of waters; and the name of the star is called Wormwood: and the third part of the waters became bitterness; and many men died of the waters, because they were made bitter. The third angel followed them, saying with a loud voice, "If any man worship the beast and his image, and receive his mark in his forehead, or in his hand, the same shall drink of the wine of the wrath of God, which is poured out without mixture into the cup of his indignation; and he shall be tormented with fire and brimstone in the presence of the holy angels, and in the presence of the Christ:" The third angel poured out his crucible upon the rivers and fountains of waters; and they became blood. The black horses which are therein go forth into the north country; and the white go forth after them. Behold, these that go toward the north country have quieted my spirit in the north country.

Fourth Seal

(Rev. 6:7; Zec. 6:3; Rev. 6:8; 8:12; 14:14; 16:8, 9; Zec. 6:6, 7)

When he had opened the fourth seal, I heard the voice of the fourth creature say, "Come and see"; in the fourth chariot grizzled and bay horses. I looked, and behold, a pale horse: and his name that sat on him was Death and hell followed with him. The fourth angel sounded, and the third part of the sun was smitten, and the third part of the moon, and the third part of the stars; so as the third part of them was darkened, and the day shone not for a third part of it, and the night likewise. I looked, and behold a white cloud, and upon the cloud one sat like the Son of Man, having on his head a golden crown, and in his hand a sharp sickle. The fourth angel poured out his crucible upon the sun; and power was given to him to scorch men with fire. Men were scorched with intense heat, and blasphemed the name of God, who had power over these plagues: and they repented not to give him glory. The grizzled horses go forth toward the south country, and the red went forth, so they walked to and fro through the earth.

Fifth Seal

(Rev. 6:9; 9:1, 2; 14:15, 16; 16:10, 11)

When he had opened the fifth seal, I saw under the altar the souls of them that were slain for the word of God, and for the testimony which they held: and the fifth angel sounded, and I saw a star fall from heaven to the earth: and to him was given the key to the bottomless pit. He opened the bottomless pit; and there arose a smoke out of the pit, as the smoke of a great furnace; and the sun and the air were darkened by reason of the smoke from the pit. The angel came out of the temple, crying with a loud voice to him that sat on the cloud, "Thrust in your sickle, and reap, for the time has come for you to reap; for the harvest of the earth is ripe." He that sat on the cloud thrust in his sickle on the earth, and the earth was reaped. The fifth angel poured out his crucible upon the seat of the beast; and his kingdom was full of darkness; and they gnawed their tongues for pain and blasphemed the God of heaven because of their pains and their sores and repented not of their deeds.

Sixth Seal

(Rev. 6:12-14, 17; 9:13, 14; 14:17; 16:12)

I beheld when he had opened the sixth seal, and, lo, there was a great earthquake; and the sun became black as sackcloth of hair, and the moon became as blood; and the stars of heaven fell onto the earth, and the heaven departed as a scroll when it is rolled together. For the great day of his wrath has come; and who shall be able to stand? The sixth angel sounded, and I heard a voice from the four horns of the golden altar, which is before God, saying to the sixth angel which had the trumpet, "Loose the four angels which are bound in the great river Euphrates." The angel came out of the temple, which is in heaven, he also having a sharp sickle. The sixth angel poured out his crucible upon the great river Euphrates; and the water thereof was dried up, that the way of the kings of the east might be prepared.

Seventh Seal

(Rev. 7:2; 8:1; 10:1-3; 11:15, 16; 14:18; 16:17)

I saw another angel ascending from the east, having the seal of the living God: and when he had opened the seventh seal, there was silence in heaven about the space of half an hour. I saw the mighty angel come down from heaven, and cried with a loud voice, as when a lion roars: and when he had cried, seven thunders uttered their voices. The seventh angel sounded; and there were great voices in heaven, and the angel came out from the altar, which had power over fire; and cried with a loud cry to him that had the sharp sickle, saying, "Thrust in your sharp sickle, and gather the clusters of the vine of the earth; for her grapes are fully ripe." The seventh angel poured out his crucible into the air; and there came a great voice out of the temple of heaven, from the throne, saying, "It is done."

Seven Trumpets

(Rev. 8:2, 6;)

I saw the seven angels which stood before God; and to them were given seven trumpets. The seven angels which had the seven trumpets prepared themselves to sound.

First Trumpet

(Rev. 8:7; Exod. 9:26; Mt. 22:6, 7; Isa. 5:24; Ezk. 24:9; Jl. 1:19)

The first sounded, and there came hail and fire, mixed with blood, and they were thrown to the earth; and a third of the earth was burned up, and a third of the trees were burned up, and all the green grass was burned up. Only in the land of Goshen, where the children of Israel were, was there no hail. Then the remnant took his servants, and treated them spitefully, and slew them. But when the king heard thereof, he was wroth: and he sent forth his armies, and destroyed those murderers, and burned up their city. Therefore, as the fire devours the stubble, and the flame consumes the chaff, so their root shall be as rottenness, and their blossom will blow away like dust; because they have rejected the law of the LORD of hosts and despised the word of the Holy One of Israel. Therefore, thus says the Lord GOD; "Woe to the bloody city! I will even make the pile for fire great." O LORD, to you will I cry, for the fire devoured the pastures of the wilderness, and the flame has burned all the trees of the field.

Second Trumpet

(Rev. 8:8, 9; Jer. 9:10; Ezk. 5:12; Zec. 10:11; Isa. 26:21; Zeph. 1:3; Isa. 21:1; Ps. 48:7; Isa. 23:14, 15)

Then the second angel sounded, and as it was a great mountain burning with fire was thrown into the sea; and a third of the sea became blood; and a third of the creatures which were in the sea and had life, died; and a third of the ships were destroyed. For the mountains will I take up weeping and wailing, and for the habitations of the wilderness a lamentation, because they are burned up, so that none can pass through them; neither can men hear the voice of the cattle: both the fowl of the heavens and the beast have fled, they are gone. A third of you shall die with the pestilence, and with famine shall they be consumed in your midst: and a third part shall fall by the sword around you; and I will scatter a third part into all the winds, and I will draw out a sword after them. He shall pass through the sea with affliction and strike the waves of the sea: all the depths of the river shall dry up. For behold, the LORD comes out of his place to punish the inhabitants of the earth for their iniquity; the earth will also disclose her blood and will no more cover her slain. I will consume man and beast; I will consume the fowls of the heaven, and the fishes of the sea, and the stumbling-blocks with the wicked: and I will cut off man from off the land, says the LORD. The burden of the desert of the sea; as whirlwinds in the south pass through; so it comes from the desert, from a terrible land. Break the ships of Tarshish with an east wind. Howl, you ships of Tarshish: for your strength is laid waste. It comes to pass in that day, that Tyre shall be forgotten seventy years, according to the days of one king: after the end of seventy years shall Tyre sing as a harlot.

Third Trumpet

(Rev. 8:10, 11; Ac. 7:43; Prov. 5:4, 5; Zec. 12:6; Jb. 38:16, 17; Prov. 8:29, 30)

Then the third angel sounded, and a great star fell from heaven, burning like a torch, and it fell on a third of the rivers and on the springs of waters, and the name of the star is called Wormwood: and the third part of the waters became wormwood; and many men died from the waters, because they were made bitter. Yea, you took up the tabernacle of Moloch, and the star of your god Remphan, figures which you made to worship them: and I will carry you away beyond Babylon. But her end is bitter as wormwood, sharp as a two-edged sword. Her feet go down to death; her steps take hold on hell. "On that day I will make the leaders of Judah like a firepot in a woodpile, like a flaming torch among sheaves. They will consume right and left all the surrounding peoples, but Jerusalem will remain intact in her place. Have you entered the springs of the sea? Or have you walked in search of the depths? Have the gates of death been revealed to you? Or have you seen the doors of the shadow of death? When he gave his decree to the sea, that the waters should not pass his commandment, when he appointed the foundations of the earth: then I was brought up by him, delighted every day and rejoicing before him always.

Fourth Trumpet

(Rev. 8:12; Isa. 13:10, 11; Jer. 15:9; Jb. 17:12; Isa. 21:11, 12; Jn. 9:5, 4)

Then the fourth angel sounded, and the third part of the sun was smitten, and the third part of the moon, and the third part of the stars; that the third part of them was darkened, and the day did not shine for the third part of it, and the night likewise. For the stars of heaven and the constellations thereof shall not give their light: the sun shall be darkened in his going forth, and the moon shall not cause her light to shine. I will punish the world for their evil, and the wicked for their iniquity; and I will cause the arrogance of the proud to cease and will lay low the haughtiness of the terrible. She that borne seven languishes: she has given up the ghost; her sun is gone down while it was yet day, she has been ashamed and confounded, and the residue of them will I deliver to the sword before their enemies, says the LORD. They change the night into day: the light is short because of darkness. The burden of Dumah: he calls to me out of Seir, "Watchman, what of the night? Watchman, what of the night?" The watchman said, "The morning comes, and also the night: if you will inquire, you inquire; return, enter. As long as I am in the world, I am the light of the world. I must work the works of him that sent me, while it is day: the night comes, when no man can work.

Fifth Trumpet

(Rev. 9:1, 2; Jl. 2:1; Ps. 12:6; Ezk. 22:20, 21; Hos. 13:3, 7; Jl. 2:30; Prov. 30:25-28; Nah. 3:17; Isa. 33:4; Jb. 15:20-22)

Then the fifth angel sounded, and I saw a star falling from heaven to the earth. To him was given a key to the bottomless pit; and he opened the bottomless pit, and smoke arose out of the pit like the smoke of a great furnace. So, the sun and the air were darkened because of the smoke of the pit. Blow the trumpet in Zion and sound an alarm in my holy mountain. The words of the LORD are pure words: as silver tried in a furnace of earth, purified seven times. As men gather silver, bronze, iron, lead, and tin into the midst of a furnace, to blow fire on it, to melt it; so I will gather you in my anger and in my fury, and I will leave you there and melt you. Yea, I will gather you and blow on you with the fire of my wrath, and you shall be melted in its midst. Therefore, they will be like the morning cloud, and like dew which soon disappears, like chaff, which is blown away from the threshing floor, and like smoke from a chimney. So, I will be to them like a lion; like a leopard by the road, I will lurk. Then I will show wonders in the heavens and in the earth, blood, and fire, and pillars of smoke. The ants are not a strong people, but they prepare their food in the summer. The hyrax is not a mighty tribe, yet they make their homes in the rocks. The locusts have no king, yet all of them go out in swarms. The scorpion you may grasp with the hands, yet it is in kings' palaces. Your commanders are like swarming locusts, and your generals like great grasshoppers, which hide in the hedges on a cold day; when the sun rises, they flee away, and the place where they are is not known. Your plunder shall be gathered like the gathering of the caterpillar; as the swarming of locusts, he shall seize upon it. The wicked man suffers pain every day, and numbered are the years reserved for the ruthless. Sounds of terror are in his ears, while in prosperity the destroyer comes upon him. He does not believe that he will return from darkness, and he is destined for the sword.

Sixth Trumpet

(Rev. 9:13, 14; Zec. 1:21; Isa. 66:20, 24; Ps. 78:49, 50; Jer. 46:10; Isa. 2:8; Mt. 11:20; Isa. 34:2, 3)

Then the sixth angel sounded, and I heard a voice from the four horns of the golden altar, which is before God, saying to the sixth angel who had the trumpet, "Release the four angels who are bound at the great river Euphrates." These are the horns which have scattered Judah, so that no man did lift up his head: but these are come to fray them, to cast out the horns of the Gentiles, which lifted up their horn over the land of Judah to scatter it. "Then they shall bring all your brethren for an offering to the LORD out of all nations, on horses and in chariots, under canopies, on mules and on camels, to my holy mountain Jerusalem," says the LORD. They shall go forth and look upon the corpses of the men who have transgressed against me. For their worm dies not, and their fire is not quenched. They shall be an abhorrence to all flesh. He cast upon them the fierceness of his anger, wrath, and indignation, and trouble, by sending evil angels. He prepared the way to his anger; he spared not their soul from death but gave their life over to the pestilence. For this is the day of the Lord GOD of hosts, a day of vengeance, that he may avenge himself of his adversaries: and the sword shall devour, and it shall be satiated and made drunk with their blood: for the Lord GOD of hosts has a sacrifice in the north country by the river Euphrates. Their land also is full of idols; they worship the work of their own hands, that which their own fingers have made. Then he began to rebuke the cities in which most of his mighty works had been done, because they did not repent. For the indignation of the LORD is against all nations, and his fury against all their armies; he has utterly destroyed them, he has given them over to the slaughter. Also, their slain shall be thrown out; their stench shall rise from their corpses, and the mountains shall be melted with their blood.

Seven Thunders

(Rev. 10:4-6; Jb. 26:14)

When the seven thunders uttered their voices, I was about to write: and I heard a voice from heaven saying to me, "Seal up those things which the seven thunders uttered and write them not." Then the angel which I saw stand upon the sea and upon the earth lifted up his hand to heaven, and swore by him that lives for ever and ever, who created heaven, and the things therein, and the earth, and the things therein, and the sea, and the things therein, that there should be time no longer. Lo, these are outlines of his ways, but how small a portion is heard of him? But who can understand the thunder of his power?

Seven Plagues

(Rev. 15:1; 16:1)

I saw another sign in heaven, great and marvelous, seven angels having the seven last plagues; for in them is filled up the wrath of God. I heard a great voice out of the temple saying to the seven angels, "Go your ways, and pour out the crucibles of the wrath of God upon the earth."

First Crucible

(Rev. 16:2; Isa. 1:5-7; Ps. 73:19-21)

Thus, the first went, and poured out his crucible upon the earth; and there fell a loathsome and grievous sore upon the men which had the mark of the beast, and upon them which worshipped his image. Why should you be stricken again? You will revolt more and more. The whole head is sick, and the whole heart faint. From the sole of the foot even to the head, there is no soundness in it, but wounds and bruises and putrefying sores; they have not been closed or bound up or soothed with ointment. Your country is desolate, your cities are burned with fire; strangers devour your land in your presence; and it is desolate, as overthrown by strangers. Oh, how they are brought to desolation, as in a moment! They are utterly consumed with terrors. As a dream when one awakes, so, when you awake, you will despise their image. Thus, my heart was grieved, and I was pierced through my soul.

Second Crucible

(Rev. 16:3; Isa. 9:5; Ps. 31:12; Jb. 14:10-12; Exod. 15:10)

Then, the second poured out his crucible upon the sea; and it became as the blood of a dead man: and every living soul died in the sea. For every battle of the warrior is with confused noise, and garments rolled in blood; but this shall be with burning and fuel of fire. I am forgotten as a dead man out of mind: I am like a broken vessel. But man dies and is laid away; indeed, his breath expires and where is he? As water disappears from the sea, and a river becomes parched and dries up, so man lies down and does not rise. Until the heavens are no more, they will not awake nor be raised from their sleep. You blew with the wind; the sea covered them; they sank like lead in the mighty waters.

Third Crucible

(Rev. 16:4; Prov. 5:15, 16; Pss. 78:44-48; 105:29-35; Prov. 8:27, 28; Exod. 7:21)

The third poured out his crucible upon the rivers and fountains of waters; and they became blood. Drink waters out of your own cistern and running waters out of your own well. Let your fountains be dispersed abroad, and rivers of waters in the streets. He turned their rivers to blood; they could not drink from their streams. He sent swarms of flies that devoured them, and frogs that devastated them. He gave their crops to the grasshopper, their produce to the locust. He destroyed their vines with hail and their sycamore figs with sleet. He gave over their cattle to the hail, their livestock to bolts of lightning. He turned their waters into blood and killed their fish. Their land abounded with frogs, even in the chambers of their kings. He spoke, and there came swarms of flies, and lice in all their territory. He gave them hail for rain and flaming fire in their land. He struck their vines also, and their fig trees, and splintered the trees of their boundaries. He spoke, and locusts came, young locusts without number, and ate up all the vegetation in their land, and devoured the fruit of their ground. When he prepared the heavens, I was there: when he set a compass upon the face of the depth; when he established the clouds above, when he strengthened the fountains of the deep. The fish that were in the river died, and the river stank, and the Egyptians could not drink the water of the river; and there was blood throughout all the land of Egypt.

Fourth Crucible

(Rev. 16:8; Ecc. 3:16; Isa. 30:26; Pss. 21:9-11; 78:62-64; Jer. 19:8; Rom. 2:24; Rev. 16:9)

The fourth poured out his crucible upon the sun; and it was given to him to scorch men with fire. Moreover, I saw under the sun the place of judgment, that wickedness was there; and the place of righteousness, that iniquity was there. The moon will shine like the sun, and the sunlight will be seven times brighter, like the light of seven full days, when the LORD binds up the bruises of his people and heals the wounds he inflicted. You shall make them as a fiery oven in the time of your anger; the LORD shall swallow them up in his wrath, and the fire shall devour them. Their fruit shall you destroy from the earth, and their seed from among the children of men. For they intended evil against you: they imagined a mischievous device, which they are not able to perform. He gave his people over also to the sword; and was wroth with his inheritance. The fire consumed their young men; and their maidens were not given to marriage. Their priests fell by the sword; and their widows made no lamentation. I will make this city desolate and a hissing; everyone who passes by it will be astonished and hiss because of all its plagues. For the name of God is blasphemed among the nations through you, as it is written. They repented not to give him glory.

Fifth Crucible

(Rev. 16:10, 11; Jl. 2:1, 2; Jb. 10:21, 22; Ps. 82:5; Isa. 37:23; Jl. 2:31; Am. 5:18; Pss. 55:9; 140:3; Ezk. 20:27; Rev. 2:21)

The fifth poured out his crucible upon the seat of the beast; and his kingdom was full of darkness, and they gnawed their tongues for pain, and blasphemed the God of heaven because of their pains and their sores and repented not of their deeds. All the inhabitants of the land tremble, for the day of the LORD comes, for it is near; a day of darkness and of gloominess, a day of clouds and of thick darkness, as the morning dispersed upon the mountains: a great people and strong; there has not been ever like it, neither shall be any more after it, even to the years of many generations. Before I go where I shall not return, even to the land of darkness and the shadow of death; a land of darkness, as darkness itself and of the shadow of death, without any order, and where the light is as darkness. They do not know, nor do they understand, they walk about in darkness; all the foundations of the earth are unstable. Whom have you reproached and blasphemed? Against whom have you raised your voice, and lifted up your eyes on high? Against the Holy One of Israel. The sun will be turned to darkness and the moon to blood before the coming of the great and dreadful day of the LORD. Woe to you that desire the day of the LORD! What is it to you? The day of the LORD is darkness, and not light. Consume the wicked, O Lord, confound their speech, for I see violence and strife in the city. They sharpen their tongues as a serpent; poison of a viper is under their lips. Therefore, son of man, speak to the house of Israel, and say to them, "Thus says the Lord GOD; 'Yet in this your fathers have blasphemed me, in that they have committed treachery against me.'" I have given her time to repent of her immorality, but she is unwilling.

Sixth Crucible

(Rev. 16:12; Ps. 106:9; Jer. 50:38; Jl. 1:20; Ps. 78:26-28; Isa. 19:5-8; Hos. 13:15; Jer. 18:17; Jnh. 4:8; Dan. 8:9, 10; Jb. 18:16, 17; 27:20, 21; Ezk. 25:4; Ps. 9:7-9)

The sixth poured out his crucible upon the great river Euphrates; and the water thereof was dried up, that the way of the kings of the east might be prepared. He rebuked the Red Sea also, and it was dried up: so, he led them through the depths, as through the wilderness. A drought is against her waters, and they will be dried up. For it is the land of carved images, and they are insane with their idols. The beasts of the field cry also to you: for the rivers of waters are dried up, and the fire has devoured the pastures of the wilderness. He caused an east wind to blow in the heaven: and by his power he brought in the south wind. He rained flesh also upon them as dust, and feathered fowls like as the sand of the sea. He let it fall in the midst of their camp, all around their habitations. The waters shall fail from the sea, and the river shall be wasted and dried up. They shall turn the rivers far away; and the brooks of defense shall be emptied and dried up: the reeds and flags shall wither. The paper reeds by the brooks, by the mouth of the brooks, and everything sown by the brooks, shall wither, be driven away, and be no more. The fishers also shall mourn, and all they that cast angle into the brooks shall lament, and they that spread nets upon the waters shall languish. I will scatter them as with an east wind before the enemy; I will show them the back and not the face in the day of their calamity. Though he is fruitful among his brethren, an east wind shall come, the wind of the LORD shall come up from the wilderness, and his spring shall become dry, and his fountain shall be dried up: he shall spoil the treasure of all pleasant vessels. Then it came to pass, when the sun did arise, that God prepared a vehement east wind; and the sun beat upon the head of Jonah, that he fainted, and wished in himself to die, and said, "It is better for me to die than to live." Out of one of them came forth a little horn, which grew exceedingly great, toward the south, and toward the east, and toward the pleasant land. It became great, even to the host of heaven; and it cast down some of the host and of the stars to the ground and stomped upon them. His roots shall be dried up beneath, and above shall his branch be cut off. His remembrance shall perish from the earth. Terrors overtake him like a flood; a tempest steals him away in the night. The east wind carries him away, and he is gone, for it whirls him away from his place. Behold, therefore I will deliver you to the men of the east for a possession, and they shall set their fortifications among you, and make their dwellings with you: they shall eat your fruit, and they shall drink your milk. The LORD reigns forever; he has established his throne for judgment. He will judge the world in righteousness; he will govern the peoples with justice. The LORD is a refuge for the oppressed, a stronghold in times of trouble.

Seventh Crucible

(Rev. 16:17; Jb. 28:26-28; Isa. 29:6; 1 Ki. 19:11, 12; Isa. 30:25; Jer. 51:44, 45; Ezk. 13:11; Mt. 7:26, 27; Isa. 41:5, 6)

The seventh poured out his crucible into the air. When he made a decree for the rain, and a path for the lightning of the thunder: then he did see it, and declared it; he prepared it, and searched it out. To man he said, “Behold, the fear of the Lord, that is wisdom; and to depart from evil is understanding.” The LORD Almighty will come with thunder and earthquake and great noise, with windstorm and tempest and flames of a devouring fire. The LORD said, “Go out and stand on the mountain in the presence of the LORD, for the LORD is about to pass by.” Then a great and powerful wind tore the mountains apart and shattered the rocks before the LORD, but the LORD was not in the wind. After the wind there was an earthquake, but the LORD was not in the earthquake. After the earthquake came a fire, but the LORD was not in the fire: and after the fire came a ghostly whisper. There will be on every high mountain and on every high hill, rivers and streams of waters in the day of the great slaughter, when the towers fall. Then I will punish the master of Babylon, and I will bring forth out of his mouth that which he has swallowed up: and the nations shall not flow together anymore to him; yea, the wall of Babylon shall fall. My people, go out from the midst of her, and deliver every man his soul from the fierce anger of the LORD. Say to those who patch it with plaster, that it will fall. There will be flooding rain, and great hailstones shall fall; and a stormy wind shall tear it down. Every one that hears these words of mine, and does them not, shall be like a foolish man, who built his house upon the sand: when the rain descended, and the flood came, and the winds blew, and pounded upon that house; then it fell, and great was the fall thereof. The islands have seen it and fear; the ends of the earth tremble. They approach and come forward; each helps the other and says to his brother, "Be strong."

Seventh Trumpet

(Rev. 11:15; 16:17)

The seventh angel sounded his trumpet; and there were great voices in heaven, saying, "The kingdoms of this world have become the kingdoms of our LORD, and of his Christ; and he shall reign for ever and ever." And there came a loud voice out of the temple of heaven, from the throne, saying, "It is done."

On Earth as it is in Heaven

(Ezk. 47:13, 14; 1 Chr. 12:22, 23; Rev. 7:4; 21:26, 27)

Thus says the Lord GOD: "These are the borders by which you shall divide the land as an inheritance among the twelve tribes of Israel. Joseph receives reparations. You shall inherit it equally with each other; for I raised my hand to give it to your fathers, that this land shall fall to you as your inheritance." Day after day they came to help David, until he had a great army, like the army of God. Now these are the numbers of the divisions equipped for war, who came to David at Hebron, to turn over the kingdom of Saul to him, according to the word of the LORD. Then I heard the number of those who were sealed: 144,000 from all the tribes of Israel. The glory and honor of the nations will be brought into it; and not at all anything profane or that commits abomination or falsehood shall enter it, but only those whose names are written in Christ's book of life.

Retribution

(Jd. 1:14, 15; 2 Thess. 2:3, 11, 12; Rev. 12:1; Jer. 51:7; Rev. 17:11; Isa. 14:12; 26:14; Rev. 13:8; Isa. 14:9; 1 Cor. 15:16, 17; Jn. 3:19; Lk. 11:35)

Behold, the Lord comes with ten thousands of his holy ones, to execute judgment on all, to convict all who are ungodly among them of all their ungodly deeds which they have committed in ungodliness, and of all the harsh things which ungodly sinners have spoken against him. No one should deceive you in any way, because it is not until the falling away shall come first, and then the man of lawlessness shall be revealed as the son of perdition. And for this cause God shall send them strong delusion, that they should believe a lie: that they all might be damned who believed not the truth but had pleasure in unrighteousness.

A great sign appeared in heaven: a woman clothed with the sun, with the moon under her feet and a crown of twelve stars on her head. Babylon was a gold cup in the hand of the LORD, making the whole earth drunk. The nations drank her wine; therefore, the nations have gone mad. The beast that was, and is not, even he is the eighth, and is of the seven (G8), and goes to destruction.

How you are fallen from heaven, O *Lucifer* Heylale, son of the morning. How you are cut down to the ground, you that weakened the nations! They are now dead; they live no more; those departed spirits do not rise. You punished them and brought them to ruin; you wiped out all memory of them: all whose names have not been written in the book of life belonging to the Christ that was slain from the creation of the world. Hell from beneath is excited about you, to meet you at your coming; it stirs up the dead for you, all the chief ones of the earth; it has raised up from their thrones all the kings of the nations. But if the dead do not rise, then Christ is not risen; and if Christ is not risen, your faith is futile, and you remain in your sins. Thus, this is the condemnation, that the light has come into this world, but man loved the darkness rather than the light, because their deeds were evil. Take heed therefore that the light which is in you is not darkness.

Logos

(Jn. 1:1-3; Rev. 4:8, 2; Col. 1:15; Rev. 4:3; Col. 1:17, 16; Ac. 3:21; Rev. 4:4; 19:16; Josh. 4:2; Rev. 21:5; 7:9; Gen. 11:1)

In the beginning was the Word, and the Word was with God, and the Word was God. The same was in the beginning with God. All things were made by him; and without him was not anything made that was made. Holy, holy, holy, Lord Almighty God, which was, and is, and is to come. Immediately I was in the Spirit; and behold, a throne set in heaven, and one sat on the throne who is the image of the invisible God, the first formed of every creature: and there was a rainbow around the throne, in appearance like an emerald. He is before all things, and by him all things consist. For by him were all things created, in heaven, and in earth, visible and invisible, whether thrones, or dominions, or sovereignties, or powers: all things were created by him, and for him, who must be received until the times of restoration of all things. Then he who sat on the throne said, "Behold, I make all things new." He has this name written: *King of Kings and Lord of Lords.*

Take for yourselves twelve men from the people, one man from every tribe. Around the throne were twenty-four thrones, and on the thrones, I saw twenty-four elders. After this I looked and there before me was a great multitude that no one could count, from every nation, tribe, people, and language, standing before the throne. Then the whole earth was of one language, and of one speech.

The Archangel

(Dan. 12:1; Rev. 14:14; Dan. 7:13; Ezk. 37:4-6; Rev. 20:5, 6; Dan. 12:2; Rev. 20:13; 1 Cor. 15:42-44; Lk. 20:36)

At that time Mikael shall stand up, the great prince who stands watch over the sons of your people; then your people shall be delivered, everyone who is found written in the book [whose genetic data is retrieved]. I looked, and behold a white cloud, and upon the cloud one sat like the Son of Man, having on his head a golden crown, and in his hand a sharp sickle. I kept looking in the night visions, and behold, with the clouds of heaven one like a Son of Man, and he went up to the Ancient of Days and was presented before him. Again, he said to me, "Prophesy over these bones, and say to them, 'O dry bones, hear the word of the LORD.' Thus says the Lord GOD to these bones, 'Behold, I will cause breath to enter you that you may come to life, and I will put sinews on you, make flesh grow back on you, cover you with skin, and put breath in you that you may return to life; and you will know that I am the LORD.'" This is the first resurrection. Blessed and holy is he who takes part in the first resurrection. Over such the second death has no power, but they shall be priests of God and of Christ and shall reign with him a thousand years. Many of them that sleep in the dust of the earth shall awake, some to everlasting life, and some to reproof and everlasting contempt.

The sea gave up the dead that were in it; also, death and hell gave up the dead that were in them: and they were judged everyone according to their works. So, this is the resurrection of the dead. The body is sown in corruption, it is raised in incorruption. It is sown in dishonor; it is raised in holiness. It is sown in weakness; it is raised in power. It is sown a natural body; it is raised a spiritual body. There is a natural body, and there is a spiritual body. Neither can they die anymore: for they are like the angels; and are the children of God, being the children of the resurrection.

Reformation

(Isa. 66:22; 32:18-20; Ps. 69:31-33; Ezk. 39:14; 1 Tim. 5:18; Mic. 4:3; Ezk. 39:10; Deut. 30:13-15; 2 Ki. 19:25, 26; Ps. 107:23-26; Ezk. 26:18-20; Isa. 60:5; Rev. 7:1)

My people will live in peaceful dwelling places, and secure homes, in undisturbed places of rest. Though hail flattens the field, and the city is leveled completely, how blessed you will be, sowing your seed by every stream, and letting all cattle and horses range free. This also shall please the LORD better than an ox or bull that has horns and hooves. The humble shall see this and be glad: and your heart shall live that seeks God. For the LORD hears the poor and abases not his prisoners. They shall set apart men of continual employment, who shall pass through the land, and, with them that pass through, those that bury them that remain upon the face of the land, to cleanse it. For the scripture says, "You shall not muzzle an ox while it treads out the grain," and "The laborer is worthy of his wages." He shall judge among many people, and rebuke strong nations afar off; and they shall beat their swords into plowshares, and their spears into pruninghooks: nation shall not lift up a sword against nation, neither shall they learn war anymore. "They will not gather wood from the fields or cut it from the forests, because they shall use the weapons for fuel." declares the Lord GOD. Neither is it beyond the sea, that you should say, "Who will go over the sea for us and bring it to us, that we may hear it and do it?" But the word is very near you, in your mouth and in your heart, that you may do it.

Behold, I have set before you today life and good, death and evil. Have you not heard long ago how I have done it, and of ancient times that I formed it? Now have I brought it to pass, that you should be to lay waste fenced cities into ruinous heaps. Therefore, their inhabitants were of small power, they were dismayed and confounded; they were as the grass of the field, and as the green herb, as the grass on the housetops, and as corn blasted before it is grown up. They that go down to the sea in ships, that do business in great waters; these see the works of the LORD, and his wonders in the deep. For he commands, and raises the stormy wind, which lifts up the waves thereof. They mount up to the heaven, they go down again to the depths: their soul is melted because of trouble. Now shall the coasts tremble in the day of your fall; yea, the isles that are in the sea shall be troubled at your departure. For thus says the Lord GOD; "When I shall make you a desolate city, like the cities that are not inhabited; when I shall bring up the deep upon you, and great waters shall cover you; when I shall bring you down with them that descend into the pit, with the people of old time, and shall set you in the low parts of the earth, in places desolate of old, with them that go down to the pit, that you be not inhabited; I shall set glory in the land of the living." Then you will see and be radiant, and your heart will thrill and rejoice; because the abundance of the sea will be turned to you, the wealth of the nations will come to you.

After these things I saw four angels standing on the four corners of the earth, holding the four winds of the earth, that the wind should not blow on the earth, nor on the sea, nor on any tree.

The Dominion

(Ezk. 40:3; Rev. 11:1; 5:11; 9:15, 16, 18; 6:8)

Behold, there was a man, whose appearance was like the appearance of brass, with a line of flax in his hand, and a measuring reed; and he stood in the gate. I was given a reed like a measuring rod and was told, "Go and measure the temple of God and the altar and count the worshipers there." (Distance from sun approximately 92,918,000 miles; diameter 7,926 miles; mesosphere < 50 miles up [heaven] from southern magnetic pole; northern magnetic pole thru the mantle [sheol] down into the core [lake of fire] @ 10,000 degrees Fahrenheit, to 3,907 miles deep; oceans and seas 134,641,000 square miles; continents 57,280,000 square miles, and 4.5 billion people.)

I beheld, and I heard the voice of many angels around the throne and the living beings and the elders: and the number of them was ten thousand times ten thousand, and thousands of thousands. So, the four angels, who had been prepared for that hour and day and month and year, were released to kill a third of mankind. Now the number of the army of the horsemen was two hundred million; I heard the number of them. A third of mankind was killed by these three plagues, by the fire and the smoke and the brimstone. Power was given to them over a fourth of the earth to kill with sword, with hunger, with death, and by the beasts of the earth.

Holy City

(Zec. 14:16, 17; Mt. 25:46; Ezk. 40:26; Est. 1:6-8; Rev. 21:18-20, 12; 7:5-8; 21:13, 14; Mt. 10:1-4; Ac. 1:23; Rev. 22:1, 2, 6)

Then the survivors from all the nations that have attacked Jerusalem will go up year after year to worship the King, the LORD Almighty, and to commemorate the Feast of Tabernacles. If any of the peoples of the earth do not go up and take part, they will have no rain: these shall go away into everlasting punishment, but the righteous into life eternal. There are seven steps that go up to it, and the arches thereof were before them: and it had palm trees, one on this side, and another on that side, upon the pillars thereof. There were white, green, and blue decorum, fastened with cords of linen and purple, to silver rings and pillars of marble: the engravings were of gold and silver, upon a pavement of red and blue granite, with white and black marble. They gave them drink in vessels of gold, the vessels being diverse one from another, with organic wine in abundance, according to the status of the kingdom. Their drinking was according to the law; none did compel for so the king had appointed to all the officers of his estate, that they should do according to every man's leisure. The construction of its wall was of quartz; and the city was pure gold, like clear glass. The foundations of the wall of the city were adorned with all types of precious stones: the first foundation was jasper, the second sapphire, the third agate, the fourth emerald, the fifth sardonyx, the sixth ruby, the seventh olivine, the eighth aquamarine, the ninth topaz, the tenth chrysoprase, the eleventh zirconium, and the twelfth amethyst. It had a great high wall with twelve gates, and twelve messengers at the gates, and names written on them, which are the names of the twelve tribes of the children of Israel: three gates on the east, three gates on the north, three gates on the south, and three gates on the west. The tribe of Juda; the tribe of Reuben; the tribe of Gad; the tribe of Asher; the tribe of Nephthalim; the tribe of Manassas; the tribe of Simeon; the tribe of Levi; the tribe of Issachar; the tribe of Zebulon; the tribe of Joseph; the tribe of Benjamin. The wall of the city had twelve foundations, and on them were the names of the twelve apostles of the Lord. When he had called to him his twelve disciples, he gave them power against unclean spirits to cast them out, and to heal all manner of sickness and all manner of disease. Now the names of the twelve apostles are these: the first, Simon, who is called Peter, and Andrew his brother; James the son of Zebedee, and John his brother; Philip, and Bartholomew; Thomas, and Matthew the publican; James the son of Alphaeus, and Lebbaeus, whose surname was Thaddaeus; Simon the Canaanite, and Matthias.

Thus, he showed to me a pure river, the water of life, clear as crystal, proceeding from the throne of God and of Christ. In the middle of its street and on either side of the river, was the tree of life, which bore twelve fruits, each tree yielding its fruit every month. The leaves of the tree were for the healing of the nations. Then he said to me, "These words are faithful and true," and the

Lord God of the holy prophets sent his angel to show his servants the things which must soon take place.

Kingdom of God

(Rev. 4:6, 8; Ezk. 1:13; Rev. 4:7; Ezk. 1:10; Isa. 11:6, 7; Ezk. 1:26; Mt. 26:64; 16:27; Rev. 1:16; 1 Sam. 30:24; 1 Tim. 6:14-16; Hag. 2:9; Deut. 1:23; Rev. 4:10, 11; Isa. 11:9; Heb. 12:22-24; Ezk. 1:6; Rev. 4:6)

Before the throne there was a sea of glass, like crystal: and in the midst of the throne, and around the throne, were four living creatures full of eyes in front and in back. The four living creatures, each having six wings, were full of eyes around and within, and they rest but not sleep day or night, saying: "Holy, holy, holy, Lord God Almighty, who was and is and is to come!" As for the likeness of the living creatures, their appearance was like burning coals of fire, and like the appearance of torches. Fire was going back and forth among the living creatures; the fire was bright, and out of the fire went lightning. The first creature like a lion, and the second creature like a calf, and the third creature had a face like that of a man, and the fourth creature like a flying eagle. As for the likeness of their faces, each had the face of a man, each of the four had the face of a lion on the right side, each of the four had the face of an ox on the left side, and each of the four had the face of an eagle. The wolf will live with the lamb, the leopard will lie down with the goat, the calf and the lion and the yearling together. The cow will feed with the bear, and the lion will eat straw like the ox. Above the firmament over their heads was the likeness of a throne, in appearance like a sapphire stone; on the likeness of the throne was a likeness with the appearance of a man high above it.

Hereafter shall you see the Son of Man sitting on the right hand of power and coming in the clouds of heaven. For the Son of Man shall come in the glory of the LORD with his angels; and then he shall reward everyone according to their works. He had in his right hand seven stars; and out of his mouth went a sharp two-edged sword: and his countenance was as the sun shining in his strength. The share of the ones who stayed with the supplies is to be the same as that of those who went down to the battle. All will share alike; that you keep the commandments without exception or reproach. He who is the blessed and only Sovereign, the King of kings and Lord of lords, who alone possesses immortality and dwells in unapproachable light, whom no man has seen or can see: honor and eternal dominion to him, amen. The glory of this latter temple shall be greater than of the former, says the LORD of hosts: and in this place will I give peace, says the LORD of hosts. The plan pleased me well; so, I took twelve of your men, one man from each tribe. The twenty-four elders fall down before him who sits on the throne, and worship him who lives for ever and ever. They lay their crowns before the throne and say: "You are worthy, our Lord and God, to receive glory and honor and power, for you created all things, and by your will they exist and were created." They will neither harm nor destroy on all my holy mountain, for the earth will be full of the knowledge of the LORD as the waters cover the sea. But you have come to Mount Zion and to the city of the living God, the heavenly Jerusalem, to an innumerable company of angels, to the general assembly and theocracy of the firstborn, who are registered in heaven, to God the Judge of all, to the spirits of just men made perfect; to Jesus the Mediator of the New Covenant, and to the blood of sprinkling that speaks better things than that of Levi. Everyone had four faces, and each had four wings, full of eyes in front and in back.

Consecration

(Num. <u>6</u>:2, 5; Prov. <u>15</u>:33; Jas. <u>4</u>:6; Heb. <u>12</u>:2; <u>7</u>:26; Mk. <u>14</u>:25; Jn. <u>15</u>:2; 1 Pet. <u>5</u>:8; 1 Tim. <u>3</u>:3; Isa. <u>24</u>:9; Jl. <u>1</u>:13, 14)

When a man or woman separate themselves and vow the vow of consecration to the LORD: during the entire period of their vow of consecration, no razor may be used on their heads. They must be holy until the period of consecration to the LORD is over; they must let the hair of their heads grow long. The fear of the LORD is the instruction of wisdom; and before honor is humility. God resists the proud but gives grace to the humble. Looking to Jesus, the author and finisher of our faith, who for the joy that was set before him endured the cross, despising the shame, he sat down at the right hand of the throne of God. For such became the high priest, who is holy, harmless, undefiled, separate from sinners, and higher than the heavens. Verily I say to you, "I will taste no more of the fruit of the vine, until that day that I drink it new in the kingdom of God." "Every branch in me that bears no fruit, he takes away; while every branch that does bear fruit, he prunes so that it will be even more fruitful." Be sober, be vigilant; not given to drunkenness, not violent but gentle, not quarrelsome, not avaricious. Put on sackcloth, O priests, and mourn; wail, you that minister before the altar; for the grain offerings and drink offerings are withheld from the house of God. Declare a holy fast; call a sacred assembly. Summon the elders and all who live in the land to the house of the LORD your God and cry out to the LORD. They shall not drink wine with a song, and strong drink is bitter to those who drink it. [Beverages exceeding 15% alcohol by volume are prohibited: avoid dependency, abstain as necessary.]

Prayer

(Lk. 2:23; Exod. 13:2; 1 Cor. 11:4; Ezk. 21:26, 27; Rom. 8:16, 17; Gal. 3:29; Rev. 21:7; 1 Cor. 11:5, 10, 9; Ecc. 7:26; Prov. 21:19; Mt. 6:5, 6)

As it is written in the Law of the LORD, "Every first-born male that opens the womb shall be called holy to the Lord." "Consecrate to me all the firstborn, whatever opens the womb, both of man and beast; it is mine."

Every man who prays or prophesies with his head covered, dishonors his head. Thus says the Lord GOD; "Remove the turban and take off your hood; this shall not be the same: exalt him that is low and abase him that is high. I will overturn it: and it shall be no more, until he come whose right it is, and I will give it to him.

The Spirit himself testifies with our spirit that we are God's descendants. Now if we are descendants, then we are heirs, heirs of God and co-heirs with Christ; if indeed we share in his sufferings in order that we may also share in his honor. Also, if you are Christ's, then you are Abraham's seed, and heirs according to the promise: "He who overcomes shall inherit all things, and I will be his God and he shall be my son."

Every woman praying or prophesying with her head uncovered dishonors her head. Because of this, the woman ought to have authority on her head, on account of the angels. Neither was man created for the woman, but woman for the man. But I find more bitter than death the woman who is a snare, whose heart is a trap and whose hands are chains. The one who pleases God will escape her, but the sinner she will ensnare. Better to dwell in the wilderness, than with a contentious and angry woman.

When you pray, you shall not be like the hypocrites. For they loved to pray standing in the synagogues and on the corners of the streets, that they may be seen by man. Assuredly, I say to you, they have their reward. But you, when you pray, enter into your room, and when you have shut your door, pray to the LORD who is in secret; and the LORD who sees in secret shall reward you openly.

Humility

(Jas. 1:18; Eph. 1:11; 1 Cor. 11:14; Jer. 13:15; Ps. 119:78; Prov. 21:24; Gal. 2:4; Heb. 6:4-6; Prov. 6:16-19; Jn. 15:21, 19, 20; 2 Pet. 2:3; Lk. 22:32; Jn. 17:16; 1 Pet. 5:6, 5; Ac. 5:41; 2 Cor. 6:17, 18)

Of his own will he brought us forth by the word of truth, that we might be a kind of first fruits of his creatures. In whom also we have obtained an inheritance, being predestined according to the purpose of him who works all things after the counsel of his own will. If a man has long hair, *he cannot be proud.* Listen and take heed, be not proud, haughty, or arrogant, for the LORD has spoken. Let the proud be ashamed, for they treated me wrongfully with falsehood; but I will meditate on these precepts. The proud and haughty man, scoffer is his name; he works in the arrogance of pride. Consequently, some false brothers infiltrated us to covertly spy out the freedom we have in Christ Jesus that they might force us into conformity. It is impossible for those who have once been enlightened, who have tasted the heavenly gift, who have shared in the Holy Spirit, who have tasted the goodness of the word of God and the powers of the coming age, if they fall away, to be brought back to repentance, because they are crucifying the Son of God again, exposing him to infamy.

These six things the LORD hates, and seven are an abomination to him: an arrogant stare, a lying tongue, hands that shed innocent blood; a heart that devises wickedness, feet that are swift in running to evil; a false witness who speaks lies, and one who sows discord among brethren. But all these things they will do to you for my name's sake, because they do not know him who sent me.

If you were of the world, the world would love itself; yet because you are not of the world, but I chose you out of the world, therefore the world hates you. If they persecuted me, they will persecute you also. In covetousness with feigned words, they make merchandise of you. But I have prayed for you, that your faith should not fail; and when you return to me, strengthen your brethren. They are not of the world, even as I am not of the world. Humble yourselves therefore under the mighty hand of God, that he may exalt you in due time. Yea, all of you gird yourselves with humility, to serve one another. So, they departed from the presence of the council, rejoicing that they were counted worthy to suffer humiliation for his name. Therefore "Come out from among them and be separate," says the Lord. "Do not touch what is unclean, and I will receive you." "I will be a Father to you, and you shall be my sons and daughters, says the Lord Almighty." [Equality is a disadvantage to the over privileged; and humility is a disgrace to the proud.]

Conception and Marriage

(Gen. 2:21-24; 6:2; Mk. 10:6-9; Mt. 5:32; Rom. 7:1-3; Col. 3:18, 19)

The Lord God caused a deep sleep to fall on Adam, and he slept; and he took one of his ribs and closed the flesh in its place. Then the rib which the Lord God had taken from man, he built into a woman, and he brought her to the man. Then Adam said: "This is now bone of my bones and flesh of my flesh." She shall be called Woman, because she was taken out of Adam. [Life begins at conception; male spermatozoa determines the gender orientation of the zygote, embryo, and fetus.] Therefore, a man shall leave his father and mother and be joined to a woman, and they shall become one flesh. [twenty-three chromosomes from each parent, forty-six chromosomes total.]

The sons of God saw the daughters of men, that they were beautiful; and they took the females for themselves of all whom they chose. From the beginning of the creation God made them male or female. For this cause shall a man leave his father and mother and join to a woman; and the two shall be one flesh: so, then they are no more two, but one flesh. What therefore God has joined together, let not man separate.

But I say to you that whoever shall put away his wife, except for the cause of fornication, causes her to commit adultery: and whoever shall marry her that is divorced commits adultery. The law has dominion over a man as long as he lives. For the woman who has a husband is bound by the law to her husband as long as he lives. But if the husband dies, she is released from the law of her husband. So then if, while her husband lives, she marries another man, she will be called an adulteress; but if her husband dies, she is free from that law, so that she is no adulteress, though she has married another man.

Wives, submit yourselves to your own husbands, as it is appropriate in the Lord. Husbands, love your wives, and be not bitter toward them.

Superfluousness

(Jer. 20:10; Mal. 3:15; 2 Cor. 5:12; Mal. 3:18; 1 Cor. 11:14; Jn. 8:49; 1 Tim. 2:9; Rom. 2:28, 29; 2 Cor. 3:6; 11:19; Col. 2:18; 1 Cor. 4:20; Jn. 7:24)

I heard the defaming of many, fear on every side. Now we call the arrogant straight; yea, they that work wickedness are set up; yea, they that test God are justified. For we commend not ourselves again to you but give you an opportunity to rejoice on our behalf, that you may have something to answer to them who rejoice in appearance, but not in heart. Then shall you return, and discern between the righteous and the wicked, between him that serves God and him that serves him not.

Does not even nature teach you, that, if a man has long hair, it is modesty to him? I honor the LORD, and you dishonor me.

Likewise, also women should adorn themselves in respectable apparel, with modesty and self-control, not with braided hair or gold or pearls or costly clothing. For they are not *believers* which are ones outwardly; neither is that *faithful* which is outward in the flesh. But they are *believers*, which are ones inwardly; and faith is that of the heart, in the spirit, and not in the letter, but as ministers of the new covenant, not of the letter but of the Spirit; for the letter kills, but the Spirit gives life.

You tolerate fools gladly, seeing you yourselves are wise. Let no one deprive you of your reward, in *selfish abasement and obedience to lower gods,* intruding into those things which he has witnessed, vainly conceited in his *superficial mentality.* For the kingdom of God is not in word but in power. Do not judge according to appearance, but judge with righteous judgment.

Social Graces

(Lk. 4:24; Lam. 3:19, 20; Am. 2:13; Lk. 11:46; Jas. 2:18; Rom. 12:20; Rev. 16:7; 2 Pet. 3:9; Jn. 20:23; 1 Tim. 3:2; Deut. 17:17; Prov. 18:11, 12; 1 Sam. 16:7; 2 Cor. 10:7; Isa. 4:1; Mk. 12:25; 2 Cor. 3:16, 17; Mt. 25:1, 2; 2 Sam. 15:16; Mt. 25:3-7, 10-13; Heb. 13:16-18; 1 Tim. 2:9-11, 15; Lk. 18:16, 17; Prov. 31:3, 30, 31; Mk. 9:42; Lk 17:1)

Assuredly, I say to you, no prophet is accepted in his own country. Remembering my affliction and my misery, the wormwood and the gall; my soul has them still in remembrance and is humbled in me. Behold, I am pressed under you, as a cart is pressed that is full of sheaves. You load people down with burdens they can hardly carry, and you yourselves will not lift one finger to help them. Show me your *credentials* without your works, and I will show you my works are my *credentials*. Therefore, if your enemy hungers, feed him; if he thirsts, give him drink.

I heard the altar saying, “Yea, O Lord God, the Almighty, true and righteous are your judgments.” The Lord will not delay his promise, as any deem delayed; but is longsuffering towards us, not ideally any should perish, but all should come to repentance. Anyone whose sins you remit, they are remitted to them; and anyone whose sins you retain, they are retained. An overseer then must be blameless, the husband of one wife; neither shall he multiply wives to himself, that his heart turns not away: neither shall he greatly multiply to himself silver and gold.

The rich man's wealth is his strong city, and as a high wall in his own conceit. Before destruction the heart of man is arrogant, and before honor is humility. The LORD does not see as man sees; for man looks at the outward appearance, but the LORD looks at the heart. Do you look at things according to the outward appearance? If anyone is convinced in himself that he is Christ's, let him reconsider this within himself, that just as he is Christ's, even so we are Christ's. For seven women will take hold of one man in that day, saying, "We will eat our own bread and wear our own clothes, only let us be called by your name to take away our reproach." For when they rise from the dead, they neither marry nor are given in marriage, but are like angels in heaven. Nevertheless, when it shall turn to the Lord, the vail shall be taken away. Now the Lord is that Spirit: and where the Spirit of the Lord is, there is liberty.

At that time the kingdom of heaven will be like ten virgins who took their lamps and went out to meet the bridegroom; five of them were wise, and five were foolish, which were concubines to keep the house. Those who were foolish took their lamps and took no oil with them, but the wise took oil in their vessels with their lamps. But while the bridegroom delayed, they all slumbered and slept. Then at midnight a call was heard: "Behold, the bridegroom is coming; go out to meet him!" Then all those virgins arose and trimmed their lamps. The bridegroom came, and those who were ready went in with him to the wedding; and the door was shut. Afterward the other virgins came also, saying, 'Lord, Lord, open to us!' But he answered and said, 'Assuredly, I say to you, I do not know you.' Therefore, keep watch, because you do not know the day or the hour. But to do good and to communicate, forget not: for with such sacrifices God is well pleased.

Obey them that have leadership over you and submit yourselves; for they watch for your souls, as they that must give account, that they may do it with joy, and not with grief: for that is unprofitable to you. Pray for us; for we trust we have a good conscience, in all things willing to live honestly. In like manner also, that the women adorn themselves in modest apparel, with propriety and moderation, which is proper for women professing godliness, with good works. Let a woman learn in silence with all submission. Notwithstanding she shall be saved in childbearing, if they continue in faith and charity, and holiness with sobriety. But Jesus called them to him and said, "Let the little children come to me, and do not forbid them; for of such is the kingdom of God." "Assuredly, I say to you, whoever does not receive the kingdom of God as a little child, will by no means enter it."

Do not give your strength to women, nor your ways to that which destroys kings. Charm is deceitful and beauty is passing, but a woman who fears the LORD, she shall be praised. Give her of the fruit of her hands, and let her own works praise her in the gates. Whosoever shall offend one of these little ones that believe in me, it is better for him that a millstone was hung around his neck, and he is cast into the sea. Then said he to the disciples, "It is impossible but that offences will occur: but woe to them, by whom they occur!"

Compliance of Generations

(Hos. 9:11; Ezk. 7:27; Am. 3:12, 13; Mal. 2:16; Jer. 17:10; Isa. 66:3; Jas. 5:19, 20; Hos. 13:12, 13; 1 Thess. 4:6, 7; Jer. 3:14, 15; Heb. 6:1-3; Jer. 3:16; Mal. 2:7; 1 Cor. 3:17; Rom. 13:2; 1 Tim. 6:20; Heb. 7:12; Jas. 1:15, 16; 1 Jn. 2:16, 17; Heb. 10:18, 14; Isa. 4:3; Rom. 10:13; Ac. 8:33; Lev. 8:35; 1 Tim. 5:21)

As for double fruit, their glory shall fly away like a bird, from the birth, and from the womb, and from conception. The king will mourn, the prince will be clothed with desolation, and the hands of the common people will tremble. I will do to them according to their way, and according to what they deserve I will judge them; then they shall know that I am the LORD!

Thus says the LORD: "As a shepherd takes from the mouth of a lion two legs and a piece of an ear, so shall the children of Israel be taken out who dwell in Samaria on the corner of a bed and on the edge of a couch." For the LORD, the God of Israel, says that he hates putting away; for one covers violence with his garment, says the LORD of hosts. Therefore, take heed to your spirit, that you deal not treacherously.

Hear and testify against the house of Jacob," says the Lord GOD, the God of forces. I the LORD search the heart, I try the reins, even to give every man according to his ways, and according to the fruit of his doings. He that kills an ox, is as if he slew a man; he that sacrifices a lamb, as if he cut off a dog's neck. Yea, they have chosen their own ways, and their soul delights in their abominations.

Brethren, if any of you error from the truth, and one converts him; let him know, that he which converts the sinner from the error of his way shall save a soul from death and shall hide a multitude of sins.

The iniquity of Ephraim is bound up; his sin is hidden; he is an unwise son. The sorrows of a travailing woman shall come upon him: he should not stay long in the place of the breaking forth of children. None should wrong his neighbors or take advantage of them in these matters. The Lord punishes for all such sins, as we have already said and warned you. For God did not call us to uncleanness, but to holiness.

"Return, O backsliding children," says the LORD; "for I am married to you. I will take you, one from a city and two as a family, and I will bring you to Zion." I will give you servants according to my heart, who will feed you with knowledge and understanding.

Therefore, leaving the discussion of the elementary principles of Christ, let us go on to completion, not laying again the foundation of repentance from dead works and of faith toward God, of the instruction of baptisms, of laying on of hands, of resurrection of the dead and of eternal judgment: and this we will do if God permits. "Then it shall come to pass, when you are multiplied and increased in the land in those days," says the LORD, "that they will say no more, 'The ark of the covenant of the LORD.' It shall not come to mind, nor shall they remember it, nor shall they visit it, nor shall it be done anymore." For the lips of a priest ought to preserve knowledge, and from his mouth man should seek instruction because he is the messenger of the LORD Almighty.

If any man defiles the temple of God, him shall God destroy; for the temple of God is holy, which temple you are. [All tobacco products are prohibited.] Therefore, he who resists the authority has opposed the doctrine of God; and they who have opposed will receive condemnation upon themselves.

Guard what has been entrusted to your care. Turn away from godless chatter and the opposing ideas of what is falsely called knowledge. For the priesthood being changed, of necessity there is also a change of the law. [Profanity, cartoons, or pornography must not be published.]

Now, when desire has conceived, it gives birth to sin; and sin, when it is fully grown, brings forth death. Do not be deceived. For all that is in the world, the lust of the flesh, and the lust of the eyes, and the pride of life, is not of the LORD, but is of the world. The world passes away, and the lust thereof: but he that does the will of God abides forever. Now where remission of these is, there is no more offering for sin. For by one offering he has perfected for all time those who are sanctified. All those who remain, will be called holy, all who are recorded among the living. For whosoever shall call upon the name of the Lord shall be saved.

In his humiliation his judgment was taken away: and who shall declare his generation? His life was taken from the earth. Therefore, shall you abide at the door of the tabernacle of the congregation day and night seven days, and keep the charge of the LORD, that you die not: for so I am commanded. I charge you, in the sight of God and Christ Jesus and the selected angels, to keep these instructions without partiality, and to do nothing out of favoritism.

Diligence and Evolution

(1 Cor. 8:2; 13:9, 10; Isa 47:11; 2 Thess. 2:3; Lk. 13:32; Ezk. 8:13; Lk. 16:8; 2 Pet. 2:21; Jn. 15:22; Ps. 18:37, 38; 2 Thess. 2:10; 1 Tim. 6:5; Isa. 29:21; Jer. 13:23; 1 Cor. 8:3; Ps. 18:33; Mal. 4:2; 1 Cor. 15:39, 1 Tim. 4:4, 5; Lk. 22:19; Eph. 5:13; Mt. 10:14; Lk 9:5; Zec. 7:12; Prov. 6:23; Isa. 42:21, 22; 23:9, 11; Mt. 10:15; Rev. 6:12; 2 Pet. 3:7; 2:19)

If any man thinks he knows anything, yet he knows nothing as he ought to know. For we know in part, and we prophesy in part. But when that which is complete is here, then that which is in part shall be done away. Therefore, evil shall come upon you; you shall not know from where it arises. Trouble shall fall upon you; you will not be able to put it off. Desolation shall come upon you suddenly, which you shall not know.

Let no one deceive you by any means. He said to them, "Go and tell that fox, 'Behold, I cast out enemies, and I do cures today and tomorrow, and the third day I shall be fulfilled.'" He said also to me, "Return yet again, and you will see greater abominations that they do." For the sons of this world are more sophisticated in their generation than the sons of light. It had been better for them not to have known the way of righteousness, than, after they have known it, to turn away from the holy commandments delivered to them. If I had not come and spoken to them, they would not have sin: but now they have no way to hide their sin. I pursued my enemies and overtook them, and I did not turn back until they were consumed. I vanquished them, so they were not able to rise; they fell under my feet.

With all deceivableness and unrighteousness of them that perish; in perverse disputations by men of corrupt minds and destitute of the truth, supposing that gain is godliness, who make a man an offender for a word and lay a snare for him who reproves in the gate, and turned aside the just by empty words: so you also might do good, that are accustomed to doing evil.

But if any man loves God, the same is known by him. He makes my feet like hind feet and sets me upon high places. Then you shall go forth and spread out as calves of the stall. All flesh is not the same flesh: but there is one class of flesh of man and of beasts (mammals), others of fishes, and another is *Aves*; (other classes are reptiles, amphibians, insects, arachnids, and crustaceans; comparable phyla are mollusks and annelids).

Every metazoan of God is good, and nothing to be despised, if it is received with thanksgiving: because it is sanctified by the word of God and prayer. [God created evolution. The LORD created mankind via the evolutionary process of natural selection.] This is my body which is given for you: this do in remembrance of me. But all things that are exposed are made manifest by the light, for whatever makes manifest is light.

Whosoever shall not receive you, nor hear your words, when you depart out of that house or city, shake off the dust of your feet for a testimony against them. Yea, they made their hearts as an adamant stone, unless they should hear the Law, and the words which the LORD of hosts has sent in his Spirit by the former prophets: therefore, came a great wrath from the LORD of hosts. For the commandment is a lamp; and the Law is light; and reproofs of instruction are the way of life.

The LORD is well pleased for his righteousness' sake; he will magnify the Law and make it honorable. But this is a people robbed and spoiled; they are all of them snared in holes, and they are hidden in prison houses: they are for a prey, and none delivers; for a spoil, and none says, "Restore." The LORD of hosts has purposed it, to stain the pride of all glory, and to bring into contempt all the honorable of the earth. He stretched out his hand over the sea, he shook the kingdoms: the LORD has given a commandment against the merchant city, to destroy the strongholds thereof. Verily I say to you, it shall be more tolerable for the land of Sodom and Gomorrah in the day of judgment, than for that city.

The sun became black as sackcloth of hair, and the moon became as blood. But the heavens and the earth that are now preserved by the same word, are reserved for fire until the day of judgment and perdition of ungodly men. While they promise them liberty, they themselves are servants of corruption.

Recriminations

(Ps. 74:18, 16, 17; 94:2; 119:21, 22; 19:12, 13; 109:1, 2; Neh. 9:26)

Remember this, that the enemy has reproached, O LORD, and a foolish people has blasphemed your name. The day is yours; the night also is yours; you have prepared the light and the sun. You have set all the borders of the earth; you have made summer and winter.

Rise up, O judge of the earth; render recompense to the proud. You rebuke the proud, the cursed, who stray from your commandments. Remove from me reproach and contempt, for I have kept your testimonies. Who can understand errors? Cleanse me from secret faults. Keep back your servant also from presumptuous sins; let them not have dominion over me. Then I shall be blameless, and I shall be innocent of the great forsaking, apostasy and transgression. O God, whom I praise, do not remain silent, for wicked and deceitful men have opened their mouths against me; they have spoken against me with lying tongues, and they worked great provocations.

Millennial Season

(Dan. 9:2; Lk. 13:6, 7; Jas. 5:18; Mk. 9:9, 10; Dan. 11:14; 2 Pet. 2:12; Isa. 14:4-6; Rev. 20:5, 14, 15; Isa. 34:9, 10; 4:5, 6; Rev. 21:22, 23; 1 Tim. 1:17)

I understood by books the number of the years, whereof the word of the LORD came to the prophet, that he would accomplish seventy years in the desolations of Jerusalem. A certain man had a fig tree planted in his vineyard; and he came and sought fruit thereon but found none. Then said he to the keeper of his vineyard, "Behold, these three years I come seeking fruit on this fig tree, and find none: cut it down; why does it encumber the ground?" He prayed again, and the heaven gave rain, and the earth brought forth her fruit. He gave them orders not to relate to anyone what they had seen, until the Son of Man should rise from the dead. They contemplated that statement, discussing with each other what rising from the dead might mean [ghosts, reincarnation, genetic cloning, or immortality].

In those times many stood up against the king of the south: also, the robbers of the people exalted themselves to establish the vision; but they failed. But these, like irrational animals, born of instinct to be captured and killed, reviling where they have no knowledge, are destroyed in their own corruption. How has the oppression ceased? The financial capital ceased. The LORD broke the staff of the wicked, and the scepter of the rulers. They who smote the people in wrath with a continual stroke, and he that ruled the nations in anger, are prosecuted, and none hinders. But the remainder of the dead did not live again until the thousand years were finished.

Death and hell were cast into the lake of fire. This is the second death, the lake of fire. Thus, if any was not found written in the book of life, he was cast into the lake of fire. The streams thereof shall be turned into pitch, and the dust thereof into brimstone, and the land thereof shall become burning pitch. It shall not be quenched night nor day; the smoke thereof shall go up for ever: from generation to generation, it shall lie waste; none shall pass through it for ever and ever.

The LORD will create upon every dwelling place of mount Zion, and upon her assemblies, a cloud and smoke by day, and the shining of a flaming fire by night: for upon all the glory shall be a defense. Then there shall be a tabernacle for a shadow in the daytime from the heat, and for a place of refuge, and for a shelter from storm and from rain. But I saw no temple in it, for the Lord God Almighty and the Christ are its temple. The city had no need of the sun or the moon to shine in it, for the power of God illuminated it: the Christ is its light. Now for the king of eternity, immortal, invisible, the only God, be honor and glory for ever and ever.

Amen

SECTION 4

COMMANDMENTS OF GOD

(Deuteronomy 4:13)

13 So he declared to you his covenant which he commanded you to perform, that is, the Ten Commandments.

(Matthew 22:37-39)

37 "You shall love the Lord your God with all your heart, with all
your soul, and with all your mind." 38 This is the first and greatest
commandment. 39 The second is like it: "You shall love your
neighbor as yourself."

(Mark 12:29-31)

29 Primarily it is, "Hear, O Israel; 'The Lord our God is one species:
30 and you shall love the Lord your God with all your heart, and with
all your soul, and with all your mind, and with all your strength.'" 31
Secondly this: "You shall love your neighbor as yourself." There is
no other commandment greater than these.

(Exodus 20:3, 4, 7-10, 12-17, 23, 24)

3 You shall have no other gods before me. 4 You shall not make for yourself a carved image, or any likeness that is in heaven above, or that is in the earth beneath, or that is in the water under the earth. 7 You shall not take the name of the LORD your God in vain, for the LORD will not hold him guiltless who takes his name in vain. 8 Remember the Sabbath day, to keep it holy. 9 Six days you shall labor and do all your work, 10 but the seventh day is the Sabbath of the LORD your God. 12 Honor your father and your mother, that your days may be long upon the land which the LORD your God is giving you. 13 You shall not murder. 14 You shall not commit adultery. 15 You shall not steal. 16 You shall not bear false witness against your neighbor. 17 You shall not covet your neighbor's house; you shall not covet your neighbor's wife, nor his male servant, nor his female servant, nor anything that is your neighbor's. 23 You shall not make anything to be with me: gods of silver or gods of gold you shall not make for yourselves. 24 An altar of earth you shall make for me.

(Exodus 22:21, 22, 28)

21 You shall neither mistreat a stranger nor oppress him. 22 You shall not afflict any widow or fatherless child. 28 You shall not revile God, nor curse a ruler of your people.

(Exodus 23:1-3, 6-9, 12)

1 You shall not circulate a false report. Do not put your hand with the wicked to be an unrighteous witness. 2 You shall not follow a crowd to do evil; nor testify in a dispute so as to turn aside after many to corrupt. 3 You shall not show partiality to a poor man in his dispute. 6 You shall not corrupt the judgment of your poor in his dispute. 7 Keep yourself far from a false matter; do not kill the innocent and righteous. 8 You shall take no bribe. 9 Also you shall not oppress a stranger. 12 Six days you shall do your work, and on the seventh day you may rest.

(Exodus 31:15)

15 Work shall be done for six days, but the seventh is the Sabbath of rest, holy to the LORD.

(Exodus 34:17)

17 You shall not make molded gods for yourselves.

(Leviticus 3:17)

17 This shall be a perpetual enactment throughout your generations in all your dwellings: you shall eat neither animal fat nor blood (cholesterol).

(Leviticus 18:6, 18-20, 22-24)

6 None of you shall approach to any that is near of kin to him, to uncover their nakedness: I am the LORD. 18 You shall not marry a woman in addition to her sister as a rival while she is alive, to uncover her nakedness. 19 Also you shall not approach a woman to uncover her nakedness during her menstrual impurity. 20 You shall not have intercourse with your neighbor's wife and be defiled with her. 22 You shall not lie with a male as with a woman. It is an abomination. 23 Nor shall you mate with any animal, to defile yourself with it. Nor shall any woman go before an animal to mate with it. It is perversion. 24 Do not defile yourselves with any of these things.

(Leviticus 19:4, 11-18, 26, 28-30, 32-36)

4 Do not turn to idols, nor make for yourselves molded gods: I am the LORD your God. 11 You shall not steal, nor deal falsely, nor lie to one another. 12 You shall not swear falsely by my name, nor shall you profane the name of your God: I am the LORD. 13 You shall not cheat your neighbor, nor rob him. The wages of him who is hired shall not remain with you all night until morning. 14 You shall not curse the deaf, nor put a stumbling block before the

blind, but shall fear your God: I am the LORD. 15 You shall do no injustice in judgment. You shall not be partial to the poor, nor honor the person of the mighty. 16 You shall not go about as a talebearer among your people; nor shall you take a stand against the life of your neighbor: I am the LORD. 17 You shall not hate your brother in your heart. You shall surely rebuke your neighbor, but not bear sin because of him. 18 You shall not take vengeance, nor bear any grudge against the children of your people, but you shall love your neighbor as yourself: I am the LORD. 26 You shall not eat the blood: neither shall you use superstitions. 28 Do not cut your bodies for the dead or take a mark on yourselves. I am the LORD. 29 Do not degrade your daughter by making her a prostitute. 30 Observe my Sabbaths and have reverence for my sanctuary. I am the LORD. 32 Show respect for the elderly and revere your God. I am the LORD. 33 When an alien lives with you in your land, do not mistreat him. 34 The alien living with you must be treated as one of your native-born. Love him as yourself. 35 Do not use dishonest standards when measuring length, weight or quantity. 36 Use honest scales and honest weights.

(Leviticus 26:1, 2)

1 You shall make no idols nor graven image, neither set you up a standing image, or image of stone in your land, to bow down before it: for I am Yahweh of Elohim. 2 Observe my Sabbaths and have reverence for my sanctuary. I am the LORD.

(Numbers 30:2)

2 If a man vows a vow to the LORD or swears an oath to bind himself by some agreement, he shall not break his word; he shall do according to all that proceeds out of his mouth.

(Numbers 31:18)

18 Keep alive for yourselves all the young girls who have not known a male intimately.

(Deuteronomy 1:17)

17 You shall not show partiality in judgment; you shall hear the small as well as the great.

(Deuteronomy 6:5, 13, 14, 16, 18)

5 You shall love the LORD your God with all your heart, with all your soul, and with all your strength. 13 You shall fear the LORD your God and serve him and shall take oaths in his name. 14 You shall not go after other gods, the gods of the peoples who are around you. 16 You shall not test the LORD your God. 18 You shall do what is right and good in the sight of the LORD.

(Deuteronomy 11:19)

19 Therefore you shall love the LORD your God, and keep his charge, his judgments, and his commandments always.

(Deuteronomy 14:3)

3 You shall not eat any detestable thing.

(Deuteronomy 15:7, 8, 10-14)

7 If there is a poor man with you, one of your brothers, in any of your gates in your land which the LORD your God is giving you, you shall not harden your heart, nor close your hand from your poor brother; 8 but you shall freely open your hand to him and shall generously give him sufficient for his need in whatever he lacks. 10 You shall surely give to him. 11 Therefore I command you, saying, "You shall open your hand wide to your poor and your needy, in your land." 12 If he serves you six years, then in the seventh year you shall let him go free from you. 13 When you send him away free from you, you shall not let him go away empty-handed. 14 You shall supply him liberally.

(Deuteronomy 24:16)

16 Parents shall not be put to death for their children, nor shall the children be put to death for their parents; a person shall be put to death only for his own sin.

(Judges 13:4, 5)

4 Now therefore beware, I pray for you, and drink no wine nor hard liquor, and eat not any unclean thing: 5 for, lo, you will conceive and bear a child.

(Psalms 82:3, 4)

3 Defend the poor and fatherless; do justice to the afflicted and needy. 4 Deliver the poor and needy; free them from the hand of the wicked.

(Proverbs 31:8, 9)

8 Speak up for those who cannot speak for themselves, for the rights of all who are destitute. 9 Speak up and judge fairly; defend the rights of the poor and needy.

(Ezekiel 4:9)

9 Also take for yourself wheat, barley, beans, lentils, millet, and spelt; prepare them in one container, and make bread of them for yourself.

(Malachi 3:10)

10 Bring all the tithes into the storehouse, that there may be food in my house, and prove me now herewith, says the LORD of hosts,

(Matthew 4:7, 10, 17)

7 Again it is written, "You shalt not test the Lord your God." 10 You shall revere the Lord your God, and him only you shall serve. 17 Repent, for the kingdom of heaven is near.

(Matthew 5:16, 34, 42, 44, 48)

16 Let your light so shine before man, that they may see your good works and glorify your LORD in heaven. 34 Do not swear at all: either by heaven, or by the earth. 42 Give to him who asks you, and from him who wants to borrow from you do not turn away. 44 Love your enemies, bless those who curse you, do good to those who hate you, and pray for those who spitefully use you and persecute you. 48 Be perfect, therefore, as your heavenly LORD is perfect.

(Matthew 6:1, 4, 6-13, 33)

1 Beware of practicing your charity before man for recognition by them; otherwise, you have no reward with your LORD who is in heaven. 4 Your charity should be in secret; and your LORD who sees in secret will reward you openly. 6 But, when you pray, go into your room, and when you shut your door, pray to your LORD who is in the secret place; and your LORD who sees in secret will reward you openly. 7 When you pray, do not use vain repetitions as the heathen; for they think that they will be heard for their many words. 8 Therefore do not be like them. For your LORD knows the things you have need of before you ask him. 9 In this manner, therefore, pray: "Our Father in heaven, hallowed be your name. 10 Your kingdom come. Your will be done, on earth as it is in heaven." 11 "Give us this day our daily bread, 12 and forgive us our debts, as we forgive our debtors." 13 "Lead us not into temptation but deliver us from evil. For yours is the kingdom and the power and the glory forever." 33 But seek first the kingdom of God and his righteousness, and all these things shall be added to you.

(Matthew 7:1, 2, 12)

1 Do not judge, that you are not judged. 2 For in the same way you judge others, you will be judged, and with the measure you use, it will be measured to you. 12 So in everything, do to others what you would have them do to you, for this sums up the law and the prophets.

(Matthew 10:7, 8, 12, 13, 16, 23, 28)

7 As you go, teach this message: "The kingdom of heaven is near." 8 Heal the sick, raise the dead, cleanse the diseased, force out demons. Freely you have received, freely give. 12 When you come into a house, greet it. 13 If the house is worthy, let your peace come upon it: but if it is not worthy, let your peace return to you. 16 Be therefore wise as serpents, and harmless as doves. 23 When you are persecuted in one place, flee to another. 28 Do not fear those who kill the body but cannot kill the soul.

(Matthew 11:28-30)

28 Come to me, all you who are weary and burdened, and I will give you rest. 29 Take my yoke upon you and learn from me, for I am gentle and humble in heart, and you will find rest for your souls. 30 For my yoke is easy and my burden is light.

(Matthew 12:8)

8 The Son of Man is Lord of the Sabbath.

(Matthew 23:8-10)

8 But do not be called *Rabbi*; for one is your teacher, and you are all brothers. 9 Do not call anyone on earth your father; for one is your Father, he who is in heaven. 10 Do not be called leaders; for one is your leader, that is, Christ.

(Matthew 24:44)

44 Therefore you also be ready, for the Son of Man is coming at an hour you do not expect.

(Mark 1:15)

15 The time has come; the kingdom of God is near. Repent and believe the covenant.

(Mark 11:24-26)

24 Therefore I say to you, "Whatever things you ask when you pray, believe that you receive them, and you will have them."
25 "Whenever you stand praying, if you have anything against anyone, forgive him, that the LORD in heaven may also forgive
you your trespasses." 26 "But if you do not forgive, neither will the
LORD in heaven forgive your trespasses."

(Mark 12:30, 31)

30 You shall love the Lord your God with all your heart, with all your soul, with all your mind, and with all your strength. 31 You
shall love your neighbor as yourself. No other commandment is greater than these.

(Mark 13:11, 37)

11 But when they arrest you and deliver you up, do not worry in advance, or premeditate what you will speak. But whatever is given you in that hour, speak that; for it is not you that speak, but the Holy
Spirit. 37 Be vigilant.

(Mark 16:15, 16)

15 Go into all the world and preach the covenant for every creature.
16 He who believes and is indoctrinated will be saved; but he who
does not believe will be condemned.

(Luke 4:8)

8 Worship the Lord your God and serve him only.

(Luke 6:31, 36, 38)

31 As you want man to do to you, do also to them likewise. 36
Therefore be merciful, just as your LORD also is merciful. 38 Give,
and it will be given to you: good measure, pressed down, shaken
together, and running over it will be put into your arms. For with
the same measure that you use, it will be measured back to you.

(Luke 9:23, 24)

23 If anyone desires to come after me, let him deny himself, and take
up his cross daily, and follow me. 24 For whoever desires to save
his life will lose it, but whoever loses his life for my sake will save it.

(Luke 11:9, 10, 28)

9 Ask, and it will be given to you; seek, and you will find; knock,
and it will be opened to you. 10 For everyone who asks receives,
and he who seeks finds, and to him who knocks it will be opened.
28 More than that, blessed are those who hear the word of God
and keep it.

(Luke 12:4, 5, 15, 21-23, 29-31, 33, 34, 40)

4 Do not be afraid of those who kill the body, and after that have no
more that they can do. 5 But I will show you whom you should fear:

fear him who, after he has killed, has power to cast into hell; yes, I say to you, fear him. 15 Take heed and beware of covetousness, for one's life does not consist in the abundance of the things he possesses. 21 This is how it will be with anyone who acquires treasure for himself but is not rich toward God. 22 Do not worry about your life, what you will eat; or about your body, what you will wear. 23 Life is more than food, and the body more than clothes. 29 Do not seek what you should eat or what you should drink, nor have an anxious mind. 30 For all these things the nations of the world seek after, and your LORD knows that you need these things. 31 Rather seek the kingdom of God, and all these things shall be added to you. 33 Sell what you have and give charity; provide yourselves bags which do not grow old, a treasure in the heavens that does not fail, where no thief approaches nor moth destroys. 34 For where your treasure is, there your heart will be also. 40 Therefore you also be ready, for the Son of Man is coming at an hour you do not anticipate.

(Luke 13:24)

24 Strive to enter through the narrow gate, for many, I say to you, will seek to enter and will not be able.

(Luke 17:3)

3 Take heed to yourselves. If your brother sins against you, rebuke him; and if he repents, forgive him.

(John 2:16)

16 Make not the LORD's house a house of merchandise.

(John 5:39)

39 Search the scriptures.

(John 7:24)

24 Judge not according to appearance, but judge with righteous judgment.

(John 15:12)

12 This is my commandment, that you love one another as I have loved you.

(Acts 18:9)

9 Do not be afraid, but speak, and do not keep silent.

(Acts 20:35)

35 We must help the weak.

(Romans 12:9, 10, 12, 13, 15-21)

9 Love must be sincere. Hate what is evil; adhere to what is good.
10 Be devoted to one another in brotherly love. Honor each other
above yourselves. 12 Be joyful in hope, patient in affliction, faithful
in prayer. 13 Share with God's people who are in need. Practice
hospitality. 15 Rejoice with those who rejoice; mourn with those
who mourn. 16 Live in harmony with each other. Do not be proud
but associate with people of low status. Do not be conceited. 17
Do not repay anyone evil for evil. Be considerate and honest in the
presence of all people. 18 If it is possible, to the best of your ability,
live at peace with everyone. 19 Do not take revenge, but give place
for wrath, for it is written: "Vengeance is mine; I will repay," says
the Lord. 20 On the contrary: if your enemy is hungry, feed him;
if he is thirsty, give him drink. 21 Do not be overcome by evil but
overcome evil with good.

(Roman 13:7, 8, 12-14)

7 Render to all their due: if you owe taxes, pay taxes; if revenue, then revenue; if respect, then respect; if honor, then honor. 8 Owe no one anything except to love one another, for he who loves another has fulfilled the law. 12 Set aside the deeds of darkness and put on the armor of light. 13 Let us walk properly, as in the day, not in revelry and drunkenness, not in lewdness and lust, not in strife and envy. 14 Rather, clothe yourselves with the Lord Jesus Christ, and do not contemplate how to gratify the lusts of the flesh.

(1 Corinthians 7:27)

27 Are you bound to a spouse? Do not seek to be released. Are you released from a spouse? Do not seek a spouse.

(1 Corinthians 10:14, 32)

14 Therefore, my beloved, flee from idolatry. 32 Give no offense, either to the Jews or to the Greeks or to the congregation of God.

(1 Corinthians 14:26, 40)

26 Let all things be done for edification. 40 Let all things be done decently and in order.

(2 Corinthians 7:1)

1 Let us cleanse ourselves from all filthiness of the flesh and spirit, perfecting holiness in the fear of God.

(2 Corinthians 13:5)

5 Test yourselves, whether you are in the faith; prove your own selves.

(Galatians 5:1)

1 It is for freedom that Christ has set us free. Stand firm, then, and do not let yourselves be burdened again by a yoke of bondage.

(Galatians 6:10)

10 So then, while we have opportunity, let us do good to all people.

(Ephesians 4:25-27)

25 Therefore, laying aside falsehood, speak truth, everyone with his neighbor. 26 Be angry, and do not sin. 27 Do not give an opportunity to the accuser.

(Ephesians 5:21, 33)

21 Submit to one another out of reverence for Christ. 33 However, each one of you also must love his wife as he loves himself, and the wife must respect her husband.

(Ephesians 6:1, 4, 5, 9, 18)

1 Children, obey your parents in the Lord, for this is right. 4 Dads, do not exasperate your children; instead, bring them up in the training and instruction of the Lord. 5 Servants, obey your corporeal masters with respect and fear, and with sincerity of heart, just as you would obey Christ. 9 Masters, treat your servants in the same way. Do not threaten them, since you know him who is both their master and yours is in heavens, and there is no favoritism with him. 18 Pray in the Spirit on all occasions with all kinds of prayers and requests. With this in mind, be alert and always keep praying for all the faithful.

(Philippians 2:3, 4)

3 Do nothing out of selfish ambition or vain conceit, but in humility consider others better than yourselves. 4 Each of you should look not only to your own interests, but also to the interests of others.

(Philippians 3:2)

2 Beware of dogs, beware of evil workers, beware of the concision.

(Colossians 2:8)

8 See to it that no one takes you captive through philosophy and empty delusions.

(Colossians 3:12-15, 18, 19, 23, 25)

12 Therefore, as God's chosen people, holy and dearly loved, clothe yourselves with compassion, kindness, humility, gentleness and patience. 13 Tolerate each other and forgive whatever grievances you may have against one another. Forgive as the Lord forgave you. 14 Over all these virtues put on love, which binds them all together in perfect unity. 15 Let the peace of Christ rule in your hearts, since as members of one body you were called to peace. Always be thankful. 18 Wives, submit to your husbands, as is appropriate in the Lord. 19 Husbands, love your wives and do not be harsh with them. 23 Whatever you do, work at it with all your heart, as working for the Lord, not for man. 25 Anyone who does wrong will be repaid for his wrong, and there is no partiality.

(Colossians 4:1, 2)

1 Masters, provide your volunteers with what is right and fair. 2 Devote yourselves to prayer, being watchful and thankful.

(1 Thessalonians 5:11-22)

11 Therefore encourage one another and build each other up, just as in fact you are doing. 12 Now we ask you, brothers, to respect those who work hard among you, who are over you in the Lord, and who admonish you. 13 Hold them in the highest regard in love because of their work. Live in peace with each other. 14 We urge you, brothers, warn those who are idle, encourage the timid, help the weak, be patient with everyone. 15 Make sure that nobody pays back wrong for wrong, but always try to be kind to each other and to everyone else. 16 Be joyful always. 17 Pray continually; 18 give thanks in all circumstances, for this is God's will for you in Christ Jesus. 19 Do not put out the Spirit's fire; 20 do not treat prophecies with contempt. 21 Test everything. Hold on to the good. 22 Avoid all appearance of evil.

(2 Thessalonians 3:14, 15)

14 If anyone is disobedient to our word in this epistle, note that person and do not keep company with him, that he may be converted. 15 Yet do not count him as an enemy but admonish him as a brother.

(Titus 3:1, 2, 9, 10)

1 Remind them to be subject to rulers and authorities, to obey, to be prepared for every good work, 2 to speak evil of no one, to be peaceable, meek, showing all humility to all people. 9 But avoid foolish disputes, genealogies, contentions, and strivings about the law. 10 Remove a disruptive person after the first and second admonition.

(1 Timothy 2:11, 12)

11 Let a woman learn in silence with all submission. 12 Do not permit a woman to preach or to assert authority over a man, but to be in silence.

(1 Timothy 4:7, 12, 14-16)

7 But reject the profane, and old fables, and assert yourself toward godliness. 12 Let no one despise your youth, but be an example to the believers in word, in conduct, in love, in spirit, in faith, in purity. 14 Do not neglect the gift that is in you, which was given to you by prophecy with the imposition by the hands of the eldership. 15 Meditate on these things; give yourself entirely to them, that your progress may be evident to all. 16 Take heed to yourself and to the doctrine. Continue in it, for in doing this you will save both yourself and those who hear you.

(1 Timothy 5:1-4, 7, 8, 19-23)

1 Do not harshly rebuke an older man, but appeal to him as a father, to the younger men as brothers, 2 the older women as mothers, to the younger women as sisters, in all purity. 3 Honor widows who are widows indeed; 4 but if any widow has children or grandchildren, let them first learn to practice reverence in regard to their own family, and provide for their parents; for this is appropriate in the sight of God. 7 Prescribe these things as well, so that they may be above reproach. 8 But if anyone does not provide for his own, and especially for those of his household, he has denied the faith, and is worse than an unbeliever. 19 Do not receive an accusation against an elder except from two or three witnesses. 20 Those who are sinning rebuke in the presence of all, that the others also may fear. 21 Observe these things without prejudice, doing nothing with partiality. 22 Do not lay hands on anyone hastily, neither share in other people's sins; keep yourself pure. 23 No longer drink only water but use a little wine for your stomach's sake and your frequent ailments.

(1 Timothy 6:1, 2, 8, 12, 17, 18)

1 Let as many bondservants as are under sentencing consider their own masters worthy of all honor, so that the name of God and his doctrine may not be blasphemed. 2 Those who have believing masters, let them not despise them because they are brethren, but

rather serve them because those who are benefited are believers and beloved. Teach and invoke these things. 8 But having food and clothing, with these be content. 12 Fight the good fight of faith, take hold on eternal life. 17 Instruct those who are wealthy in this present world not to be conceited or trust in the uncertainty of riches, but on God, who abundantly supplies us with all things to enjoy. 18 Do good, to be abundant in good works, to be generous and ready to share.

(2 Timothy 1:14)

14 That virtue which was committed to you, keep by the Holy Spirit who dwells in us.

(2 Timothy 2:3, 22-25)

3 Endure hardship as a good soldier of Jesus Christ. 22 Now flee from youthful lusts, and pursue righteousness, faith, love, and peace with those who call on the Lord from a pure heart. 23 But refuse foolish and ignorant speculations, knowing that they produce conflict. 24 The Lord's bondservant must not be quarrelsome, but be kind to all, able to teach, patient when wronged, 25 with gentleness correcting those who are in opposition, that perhaps God may grant them repentance to acknowledge the truth.

(2 Timothy 4:2)

2 Proclaim the word. Be ready in season and out of season. Convince, rebuke, implore, with all persistence and doctrine.

(Hebrews 12:14)

14 Follow peace with all people, and holiness, without which no one shall see the Lord.

(Hebrews 13:1-3, 5, 7, 9, 16, 17)

1 Let brotherly love continue. 2 Do not forget hospitality for strangers, for by so doing some have unknowingly entertained angels. 3 Remember the prisoners as if chained with those who suffer adversity. 5 Let your conduct be without covetousness; be content with such things as you have. 7 Remember those who rule over you, who have spoken the word of God to you, whose faith to follow. 9 Do not be involved with deviant and strange doctrines. 16 But do not forget to do good and to share, for with such sacrifices God is well pleased. 17 Obey those who rule over you and be submissive. Let them do so with joy and not with grief.

(James 1:4, 5, 16, 19, 21, 22)

4 But let patience have its perfect work, that you may be perfect and complete, lacking nothing. 5 If any of you lacks wisdom, let him ask of God, who gives to all generously and without reproach, and it will be given to him. 16 Do not be deceived. 19 Let every man be quick to hear, slow to speak, slow to anger. 21 Therefore putting aside all filthiness and excesses of wickedness, in humility receive the word implanted, which is able to save your souls. 22 But prove yourselves doers of the word, and not merely hearers who deceive themselves.

(James 2:1, 12)

1 Hold the faith of our Lord Jesus Christ, as glory, with no partiality. 12 So speak and so do as those who will be judged by the law of freedom.

(James 4:7-11)

7 Therefore submit to God. Resist the enemy and he will flee from you. 8 Draw near to God and he will draw near to you. Cleanse your hands and purify your hearts. 9 Lament, mourn and weep. Let

your laughter be turned to mourning and your joy to heaviness. 10 Humble yourselves in the sight of the Lord, and he will lift you up. 11 Do not speak evil of one another, brethren.

(1 Peter 2:1, 11, 13, 16-18)

1 Therefore, lay aside all malice, all guile, hypocrisy, envy, and all evil speaking. 11 Abstain from fleshly lusts which war against the soul. 13 Therefore submit yourselves to every ordinance of man for the Lord's sake. 16 Be as free, and not using your freedom for a cloak of wickedness, but as servants of God. 17 Honor all mankind. Love the brotherhood. Fear God. Honor the king. 18 Convicts, be submissive to your masters with all fear, not only to the good and gentle, but also to the harsh.

(1 Peter 3:3, 4, 7-9, 14-16)

3 Do not let your adornment be merely outward, arranging the hair, wearing gold, or putting on fine apparel. 4 Rather let it be the hidden person of the heart, with the incorruptible beauty of a gentle and quiet spirit. 7 Husbands, in the same way be considerate as you live with your wives and treat them with respect as the weaker vessel and as heirs with you of the gracious gift of life, so that nothing will hinder your prayers. 8 Finally, all of you, live in harmony with one another; be sympathetic, love as brothers, be compassionate and humble. 9 Do not repay evil with evil or insult with insult, but with blessing, because to this you were called so that you may inherit a blessing. 14 But even if you should suffer for the sake of righteousness, you are blessed. So do not fear their intimidation, and do not be troubled, 15 but sanctify Christ as Lord in your hearts, always ready to make a defense to everyone who asks you to give account for the hope that is in you, yet with gentleness and reverence. 16 Keep a good conscience so that in the thing in which you are slandered, those who revile your good behavior in Christ, may be shamed down.

(1 Peter 4:7-10)

7 Be mentally disciplined and sober for prayer. 8 Above all, love
each other deeply, because love covers a multitude of sins. 9 Offer
hospitality to one another without complaining. 10 Each one should
use whatever blessing he has received to serve others, faithfully
administering God's grace in its various forms.

(1 Peter 5:2, 3, 5-7)

2 Be authoritative in God's congregation that is under your care,
serving as overseers: not because you must, but because you
are willing, as God wants you to be, not greedy for money, but
eager to serve, 3 not domineering over those entrusted to you, but
being examples to the congregation. 5 You younger men, likewise,
be subject to your elders; and all of you, clothe yourselves with
humility toward one another, for God opposes the proud, but gives
grace to the humble. 6 Humble yourselves, therefore, under the
mighty hand of God, that he may exalt you at the proper time. 7
Cast all your concerns upon him because he cares for you.

(2 Peter 1:5-7)

5 Also beside this, giving all diligence, add to your faith virtue;
and to virtue knowledge; 6 and to knowledge temperance; and
to temperance patience; and to patience godliness; 7 and to
godliness brotherly kindness; and to brotherly kindness charity.

(1 John 2:15)

15 Love not the world, neither the things that are in the world.

(1 John 3:18, 23)

18 Let us love, not in word or in tongue, but in deed and in truth.
23 This is his commandment: that we should believe on the name

of his Son Jesus Christ and love one another, as he gave us commandment.

(1 John 4:1)

1 Believe not every spirit, but prove the spirits, whether they are of God.

(1 John 5:21)

21 Dear children, guard yourselves against idols.

(3 John 1:14)

14 Greet your friends by name.

(Revelation 7:3)

3 Do not harm the earth or the sea or the trees.

(Revelation 9:4)

4 Harm not the grass of the earth, or any green thing, or any tree.

(Revelation 22:17-19)

17 Let him who thirsts return. Whoever desires, let him take the
water of life freely. 18 If anyone adds to these things, God will add
to him the plagues that are written in this book; 19 and if anyone
takes away from the words of the book of this prophecy, God shall
take away his part from the Book of Life, from the holy city, and
from the things which are written in this book.

(Mt. 19:17; 5:19; Jn. 4:23, 24; 14:15, 21; 15:10;
1 Jn. 5:3; 2:2, 3; 3:22; 2 Jn. 1:6)

If you enter into life, keep the commandments. Whosoever therefore shall break one of these least commandments, and shall teach man so, he shall be called the least in the kingdom of heaven: but whosoever shall do and teach them, the same shall be called great in the kingdom of heaven. But the hour is coming, and now is, when true worshipers will revere the LORD in spirit and truth, for the LORD is seeking such to revere him. God is a Spirit, and those who revere him must reverence in spirit and truth. If you love me, keep my commandments. He that has my commandments, and keeps them, he it is that loves me: and he that loves me shall be loved by the LORD, and I will love him, and will manifest myself to him. If you keep my commandments, you shall abide in my love; even as I have kept the LORD'S commandments and abide in his love. This is the love of God that we keep his commandments: and his commandments are not grievous. He is the propitiation for our sins: and not for ours only, but also for the sins of the entire world. Hereby we do know that we know him, if we keep his commandments. Whatsoever we ask, we receive of him, because we keep his commandments and do those things that are appropriate in his sight.

This is love that we walk according to his commandments.

This is the commandment, just as you have heard
from the beginning, that you should walk in it.

Section 4 Index

Deut. 4:13; **Mt.** 22:37-39; **Mk.** 12:29-31; **Exod.** 20:3, 4, 7-10, 12-17, 23, 24; 22:21, 22, 28; 23:1-3, 6-9, 12; 31:15; 34:17; **Lev.** 3:17; 18:6, 18-20, 22-24; 19:4, 11-18, 26, 28-30, 32-36; 26:1, 2; **Num.** 30:2; 31:18; **Deut.** 1:17; 6:5, 13, 14, 16, 18; 11:19; 14:3; 15:7, 8, 10-14; 24:16; **Judg.** 13:4, 5; **Ps.** 82:3, 4; **Prov.** 31:8, 9; **Ezk.** 4:9; **Mal.** 3:10; **Mt.** 4:7, 10, 17; 5:16, 34, 42, 44, 48; 6:1, 4, 6-13, 33; 7:1, 2, 12; 10:7, 8, 12, 13, 16, 23, 28; 11:28-30; 12:8; 23:8-10; 24:44; **Mk** 1:15; 11:24-26; 12:30, 31; 13:11, 37; 16:15, 16; **Lk** 4:8; 6:31, 36, 38; 9:23, 24; 11:9, 10, 28; 12:4, 5, 15, 21-23, 29-31, 33, 34, 40; 13:24; 17:3; **Jn.** 2:16; 5:39; 7:24; 15:12; **Ac.** 18:9; 20:35; **Rom** 12:9, 10, 12, 13, 15-21; 13:7, 8, 12-14; **1 Cor.** 7:27; 10:14, 32; 14:26, 40; **2 Cor.** 7:1; 13:5; **Gal.** 5:1; 6:10; **Eph.** 4:25-27; 5:21, 33; 6:1, 4, 5, 9, 18; **Phil.** 2:3, 4; 3:2; **Col.** 2:8; 3:12-15, 18, 19, 23, 25; 4:1, 2; **1 Thess.** 5:11-22; **2 Thess.** 3:14, 15; **Ti.** 3:1, 2, 9, 10; **1 Tim.** 2:11, 12; 4:7, 12, 14-16; 5:1-4, 7, 8, 19-23; 6:1, 2, 8, 12, 17, 18; **2 Tim.** 1:14; 2:3, 22-25; 4:2; **Heb.** 12:14; 13:1-3, 5, 7, 9, 16, 17; **Jas.** 1:4, 5, 16, 19, 21, 22; 2:1, 12; 4:7-11; **1 Pet.** 2:1, 11, 13, 16-18; 3:3, 4, 7-9, 14-16; 4:7-10; 5:2, 3, 5-7; **2 Pet.** 1:5-7; **1 Jn.** 2:15; 3:18, 23; 4:1; 5:21; **3 Jn.** 1:14; **Rev.** 7:3; 9:4; 22:17-19.

Mt. 19:17; 5:19; Jn. 4:23, 24; 14:15, 21; 15:10; 1 Jn. 5:3; 2:2, 3; 3:22; 2 Jn. 1:6.

Name:

Print______________________________

Signature___________________________________

Congregation:

____

Date_______________

ABOUT THE AUTHOR

The author is independent from any religious groups or secular organizations. These doctrines are established from over forty years of research and spiritual inspiration. This book contributes an objective perspective to theological science.

Printed in the United States
by Baker & Taylor Publisher Services